Literary Criticism and Cultural Theory
Outstanding Dissertations

edited by
William E. Cain
Wellesley College

A Rout

Other Books in This Series:

THE LIFE WRITING OF OTHERNESS
Woolf, Baldwin, Kingston, and Winterson
Lauren Rusk

FROM WITHIN THE FRAME
Storytelling in African American Fiction
Bertram D. Ashe

THE SELF WIRED
Technology and Subjectivity in Contemporary Narrative
Lisa Yaszek

THE SPACE AND PLACE OF MODERNISM
The Little Magazine in New York
Adam McKible

THE FIGURE OF CONSCIOUSNESS
William James, Henry James, and Edith Wharton
Jill M. Kress

WORD OF MOUTH
Food and Fiction after Freud
Susanne Skubal

THE WASTE FIX
Seizures of the Sacred from Upton Sinclair to The Sopranos
William G. Little

WILL THE CIRCLE BE UNBROKEN?
Family and Sectionalism in the Virginia Novels of Kennedy, caruthers, and Tucker, 1830–1845
John L. Hare

POETIC GESTURE
Myth, Wallace Stevens,, and the Motions of Poetic Language
Kristine S. Santilli

BORDER MODERNISM
Intercultural Readings in American Literary Modernism
Christopher Schedler

THE MERCHANT OF MODERNISM
The Economic Jew in Anglo-American Literature, 1864–1939
Gary Martin Levine

THE MAKING OF THE VICTORIAN NOVELIST
Anxieties and Authorship in the Mass Market
Bradley Deane

OUT OF TOUCH
Skin Tropes and Identities in Woolf, Ellison, Pynchon, and Acker
Maureen F. Curtin

WRITING THE CITY
Urban Visions and Literary Modernism
Desmond Harding

FIGURES OF FINANCE CAPITALISM
Writing, Class, and Capital in the Age of Dickens
Borislav Knezevic

BALANCING THE BOOKS
Faulkner, Morrison, and the Economies of Slavery
Erik Dussere

BEYOND THE SOUND BARRIER
The Jazz Controversy in Twentieth-Century American Fiction
Kristen K. Henson

SEGREGATED MISCEGENATION
On the Treatment of Racial Hybridity in the U.S. and Latin American Literary Traditions
Carlos Hiraldo

DEATH, MEN, AND MODERNISM
Trauma and Narrative in British Fiction from Hardy to Woolf
Ariela Freedman

THE SELF IN THE CELL
Narrating the Victorian Prisoner
Sean Grass

REGENERATING THE NOVEL
Gender and Genre in Woolf, Forster, Sinclair, and Lawrence

James J. Miracky

NEW YORK AND LONDON

Published in 2003 by
Routledge
711 Third Ave,
New York NY 10017
www.routledge-ny.com

Published in Great Britain by
Routledge
2 Park Square, Milton Park,
Abingdon, Oxon, OX14 4RN
www.routledge.co.uk

Copyright © 2003 by Taylor & Francis Books, Inc.

Routledge is an imprint of the Taylor & Francis Group.

Transferred to Digital Printing 2010

First issued in paperback 2013

All rights reserved. No part of this book may be reprinted or reproduced or utilized in any form or by any electronic, mechanical, or other means, now known or hereafter invented, including photocopying and recording, or in any information storage or retrieval system, without written permission from the publishers.

Excerpts from *Collected Essays* by Virginia Woolf © 1967 by Leonard Woolf. Reprinted by permission of Harcourt, Inc.

Excerpts fom *Orlando* by Virginia Woolf © 1928 by Virginia Woolf and renewed 1956 by Leonard Woolf. Reprinted by permission of Harcourt, Inc.

Excerpts from *A Passage to India* by E. M. Forster © 1924 by Harcourt, Inc., and renewed 1954 by E. M. Forster, reprinted by permission of the publisher.

Excerpts from *Aspects of the Novel* by E. M. Forster © 1927 by Harcourt, Inc., and renewed 1954 by E. M. Forster. Reprinted by permission of the publisher.

Excerpts from *Lady Chatterley's Lover, Study of Thomas Hardy, The Letters of D. H. Lawrence, Vol. I-VI, Phoenix: The Posthumous Papers of D. H. Lawrence*, and *Phoenix II: Uncollected Writings* by D. H. Lawrence, reprinted by permission of Pollinger Limited and the Estate of Frieda Lawrence Ravagli.

Portions of chapters one and four previously appeared in the article "Regen(d)erating the Modernist Novel: Literary Realism vs. the Language of the Body in D. H. Lawrence and Virginia Woolf," *D. H. Lawrence Review*, Volume 31, Number 1 (2002).

Portions of chapter two previously appeared in two articles: "Filming a Fantasy: Cinematic Renditions of E. M. Forster's Queered Realism," *Interfaces: Image Texte Language*, Volume 18 (2001); and "Pursuing (a) Fantasy: E. M. Forster's Queering of Realism in *The Longest Journey*," *Journal of Modern Literature*, Volume XXVI, Number 1 (Fall 2002).

Excerpts from *Maurice* by E.M. Forster. Copyright © 1971 by the trustees of the late E.M. Forser. Used by permission of W.W. Norton & Company, Inc.

Library of Congress Cataloging-in-Publication Data

Miracky, James J., 1959–
    Regenerating the novel : gender and genre in Woolf, Forster, Sinclair and Lawrence / by James J. Miracky.
       p. cm. — (Literary criticism and cultural theory)
    Includes bibliographical references (p.) and index.
    ISBN 0-415-94205-5 (alk. paper)
    1. English fiction—20th century—History and criticism. 2. Gender identity in literature. 3. Lawrence, D. H. (David Herbert), 1885–1930—Criticism and interpretation. 4. Forster, E. M. (Edward Morgan), 1879–1970—Criticism and interpretation. 5. Woolf, Virginia, 1882–1941—Criticism and interpretation. 6. Sinclair, May—Criticism and interpretation. 7. Modernism (Literature)—Great Britain. 8. Sex role in literature. 9. Literary form. I. Title. II. Series.
    PR888.G35M57 2003
    823'.91209353—dc21

2002155375

ISBN 13: 978-0-415-94205-8 (hbk)
ISBN 13: 978-0-415-86709-2 (pbk)

For my mother, Barbara Foster Miracky,
and my late father, Robert Miracky,
whose love and intellectual gifts
led me to the world of ideas and literature

Contents

Acknowledgments	ix
Preface	xi
CHAPTER ONE: Gender and Genre Matters: *Virginia Woolf as Pioneer and Paradigm*	1
Introduction	1
Gendering Literary History and the Novel	5
Woolf's Take on the Male Novel Tradition: Realism as Erection	9
Constructing a Women's Literary History	12
Writing a Woman's Sentence . . . and Novel	15
Considering Woolf's Peers: Gendering the Novel as Well?	18
CHAPTER TWO: Pursuing (a) Fantasy: *E. M. Forster's Doubled-up Fiction*	25
Introduction	25
Aspects of Fantasy	29
Where Homosexuality Fears to Tread: The Italian Novels	35
Fantasy in Conflict: *The Longest Journey*	41
Fantasy Rerouted: *Howards End*	50
From Phobia to Fulfillment: *Maurice*	55
From Fantasy to the "Not Yet" of Reality: *A Passage to India*	61
CHAPTER THREE: The Sexing of Genius: *May Sinclair's Experimental Novels*	67
Introduction	67
Tales of Idealism and Realism: Sinclair's Early Novels	70
Transitions in Theory and Technique: *The Three Sisters*	76

Entering the "Stream": *Mary Olivier* and *Harriet Frean* 85
The "Stream" Dries Up: *Arnold Waterlow* and *Anthony Waring* 96

CHAPTER FOUR: From Consummation to "Remasculation":
D. H. Lawrence's Quest for the Phallic Novel 103
   Introduction 103
   Consummation of Male and Female: Early Views on the Novel 106
   Man-Loving and Woman-Hating: Postwar Views of the Novel 117
   Quickening the Novel: Lawrence's Later Theory 129
   The Feminization of Fiction and Its Antidote 136

Notes 147

Bibliography 159

Index 171

Preface

D. H. Lawrence calls the novel "the one bright book of life" and "the highest example of subtle inter-relatedness that man has discovered. . . . If you try to nail anything down, in the novel, either it kills the novel, or the novel gets up and walks away with the nail" (*Phoenix* 528 & 535). For his part, E. M. Forster calls the novel, "a formidable mass, that is so amorphous," and "that spongy tract, those fictions in prose of a certain extent which extend so indeterminately" (*Aspects* 5 & 23). These writers were, by no means, the first novelists to conceive of their medium in such admirable and flexible or such frustrating and indistinct terms. The novel has been celebrated by many throughout its history as the most expansive and adaptable of genres, drawing numerous artists to take its name seriously in their attempts to represent new experiences in the novel's renewable shape. In a way, because of its malleability, the novel seems the most historical of genres, its form both reflecting and being produced by the shifting concerns and cultural material of each of its developmental phases. As Michael McKeon puts it, in his dialectical theorizing about the novel inspired by Georg Lukács, "the [novel's] search for form is . . . thematized—on the level of content, which reflects, and reflects upon, its own formal problem" (180).

One of the ways in which the novel performs what McKeon calls "the matching of matter and form" (180) is in terms of gender. This is not surprising if one agrees with Judith Butler in seeing the category of gender as a "performative" discourse itself, consisting of "words, acts, gestures, and desire [that] produce the effect of an internal core or substance" (Butler 136). From the period of its rise in the eighteenth century, the novel has been strongly linked to gender, particularly the feminine in its early days. Critics such as Ian Watt, Nancy Armstrong and Tony Tanner have highlighted the novel's gendered connections, such as its early ties to romance, the domestic sphere, and a largely female audience. The connections between gender and genre continued to develop in the nineteenth century as the novel settled into its realist period. However, in this era, explored by critics like George Levine, Gillian Brown, and others, the novel's gendering became more complicated, as realism was diversely constructed in both masculine and feminine matter and forms.

Given the interrelatedness of gender and genre in the history and theory of the novel, it is no wonder that the early twentieth century, considered a time of "gender crisis" and instability, ushered in a period of contestation over the form of the novel that was often articulated in gendered terms. For modernist novelists, the era's artistic drive to "make it new" pointed toward the novel as the most promising medium for innovation. Since a major arena for exploring modern identity was the world of gender roles and sexual identities, this world was bound to be engaged in the matter and form of the modernist novel. Of course, Virginia Woolf was a pioneering figure in this period, providing a voice that both proclaimed the indeterminacy of gender roles and articulated the ways the novel could reform itself and thus reformulate attitudes about sex and gender in the modern era.

My interest in this project emerged from a study of Woolf's theory of the novel in comparison with that of D. H. Lawrence, who initially appeared to stand as her theoretical nemesis in many ways, particularly in their exploration of gender roles. While feminist and gender studies had much to offer in terms of the links between gender and genre in Woolf's work, I found little on the matter in Lawrence scholarship, although his theoretical writings seemed to lend themselves to a similar study. This led me to pose the question of whether and how the novel was gendered in the theory and practice of some of Woolf's contemporaries, and thus my project was born. After reviewing the work of several key British modernist novelists, I found that E. M. Forster and May Sinclair, along with Lawrence, produced ample theoretical and fictional works steeped in sex-gender discourse through which to pursue the relation of gender categories to the genre of the novel in this period.

As is laid out much more thoroughly in my Introduction, this book presents four extremely diverse yet, in some ways, startlingly similar figures whose literary work cannot seem to escape the gender negotiations and contestations that were so ripe in the early twentieth century. Woolf's fluctuation between her seemingly essentialist project of calling for a space and a form for writing women's experience and her constructionist call to defy gender categories becomes the jumping off point for my exploration of the other three writers. What I find is that, in their theory and practice of the novel, Forster, Sinclair, and Lawrence all struggle to represent gender identities and sexual desires that are often painfully in conflict, yet these tensions yield innovations in their fiction that take shape, sometimes consciously and sometimes unconsciously, in gendered terms. First, for Forster, this gender tension takes shape in his use of the submode of fantasy to express forbidden homosexual desire. In Sinclair's case, her project to represent her characters' struggles with their conversely gendered experience of genius ultimately produces a version of the stream of consciousness novel that seems best suited to her conception of female experience. Finally, Lawrence's sometimes violent reaction to what he perceives as the feminized state of the realist novel leads to his pursuit of a kind of literary "gender redressing" through a novel of "phallic consciousness." In their quest to create novels that represent modern experience in a time of gender crisis, all of these novelists, while not always achieving success from an aesthetic point of view, both regenerate and "regenderate" the form of the novel to suit their particular aims.

This revised version of my original project includes an updating of the literary scholarship of the last five years concerning these writers, which is understandably varied. Forster criticism has blossomed as a result of developments in queer theory, most notably in Martin and Piggford's collection, *Queer Forster*. During the same time, Lawrence scholarship in the area of gender studies has been engaged in a largely recuperative effort, moving the discourse from a reductive criticism of Lawrence's anti-feminism to a broader recognition of his often inconsistent yet sometimes surprisingly feminist stances. May Sinclair's literary standing seems to be undergoing an ebb since her last recovery by feminist scholars in the 1970's, and thus recent work on May Sinclair has been minimal. Where appropriate, these developments have been incorporated into the body of the text or through extended endnotes.

CHAPTER ONE

Gender and Genre Matters
Virginia Woolf as Pioneer and Paradigm

INTRODUCTION

> ... before a woman can write exactly as she wishes to write, she has many difficulties to face. To begin with, there is the technical difficulty ... that the very form of the sentence does not fit her. It is a sentence made by men; it is too loose, too heavy, too pompous for a woman's use. Yet in a novel, which covers so wide a stretch of ground, an ordinary and usual type of sentence has to be found to carry the reader on easily and naturally from one end of the book to the other. And this a woman must make for herself, altering and adapting the current sentence until she writes one that takes the natural shape of her thought without crushing or distorting it. (*Essays 2*: 145)

Virginia Woolf has been a major inspiration in the reassessment of literary modernism that has taken place over the past three decades. The only female English writer of her generation to achieve canonical status, Woolf consistently drew attention to gender issues and inequities in her critical writing and fiction, as in the above quotation, which identifies the challenges modern women encounter when writing within what Woolf perceives as the male-dominated novel tradition. Despite Woolf's innovative contributions in this area, considerations of gender remained curiously absent from accounts of modernism until the emergence of feminist literary criticism in the 1970s, which made Woolf a central figure and gender a central factor in its reconsideration of the modernist era.

A primary reason for the previous neglect of gender issues in relation to modernism is that, Woolf's presence in the canon notwithstanding, until recently modernism "was unconsciously gendered masculine" (Scott 2) and critical attention was largely paid to male modernists like Joyce and Proust, while women writers of the period were generally forgotten or considered poor imitators of their male progenitors' more "complex" experimental texts. Only through recovery efforts like those of Bonnie Kime Scott, Rachel Blau DuPlessis, Elaine Showalter, Sandra M. Gilbert and Susan Gubar, and Ellen G. Friedman and Miriam Fuchs, has the "neglect of woman innovators" (Friedman and Fuchs 5) in the modernist period been remedied and a tradition of women's experimental writing been gathered. The emergence of this "new" female literary tradition has revealed how modern women authors and their more contemporary successors, "[i]n exploding dominant forms, . . . not only assail the social structure, but also produce an alternate fictional space, a space in which the feminine, marginalized in traditional fiction and patriarchal culture, can be expressed" (4).

The exclusion of groundbreaking women writers from the modernist literary canon is evidence of Scott's contention that the "politics and aesthetics of gender may lie at the heart of a comprehensive understanding of early twentieth-century literature" (16). Marianne DeKoven suggests that the connection between gender and modern literary practice is a consequence of the "the advent of twentieth-century modernity," which she configures as a "sea-change" carrying tremendous political and cultural implications of late nineteenth- and early twentieth-century feminism and socialism and generating in modernist texts an "irresolvable ambivalence toward the possibility of radical social change" that was "differently inflected for male and female modernists" (3–4). Gilbert and Gubar also stress the importance of gender issues in the appreciation of modernist texts, characterizing the period in which they were written as a "war of words" in which "both men and women engendered words and works which continually sought to come to terms with, and find terms for, an ongoing battle of the sexes that was set in motion by the late nineteenth-century rise of feminism and the fall of Victorian concepts of 'femininity'" (xii).

Besides the feminist movement, numerous other factors linked to matters of sex and gender are identified by critics as influential forces during this turbulent yet artistically fertile literary period, and many of them hold a central place in the novels of Woolf and her peers. In his study of "the regulation of sexuality within the period of industrial capitalism" in England, Jeffrey Weeks writes of how, in the Victorian and modern periods, sexuality assumes "major symbolic importance as a target of social intervention and organisation" and eventually becomes "the supreme secret . . . and the general substratum of our existence" (11–12). Among other things, Weeks cites: the politics of birth control and eugenics; the theorization of sex and the construction of homosexuality by the legal and medical establishment; and the substantial intellectual, political and material gains for women achieved through the feminist or New Woman movement as key elements of the early twentieth-century social and cultural matrix which is tied to the literary productions of modernism. Other political forces which had repercussions for gender relations and literary change in the modern era include the increased influence of socialist ideas and programs and the militarization and devastation wrought by the "Great War."

One other cultural element which achieved tremendous power during the modernist period and had an immeasurable impact on its literature is the dissemination of psychoanalytic theory and practice in England, which occurred gradually at first, through the efforts of Freudians like Havelock Ellis and Ernest Jones, but then more rapidly because of the "psychological disorders, and the disturbance of traditional liberal views on human nature that the war produced" (Weeks 155). In her essay "Modern Fiction," Virginia Woolf herself acknowledges the unique connection between psychology and modern literary practice: "For the moderns . . . the point of interest, lies very likely in the dark places of psychology. At once, therefore, the accent falls a little differently; the emphasis is upon something hitherto ignored; at once a different outline of form becomes necessary" (*Essays 2* 108). However, like many of her literary peers, Woolf engages the concerns of psychology indirectly. According to Elizabeth Abel, "Woolf . . . was familiar with the debates unfolding within British psychoanalysis, but rather than addressing them specifically, she engages in her novels the set of terms that generated the debates." In doing so, Woolf's narratives both reflect and participate in the "gender discourse" constituted by "Freud's construction of the Oedipal narrative, Klein's excavation of the early mother-infant bond, and the rival anthropological claims for an originary matriarchy or patriarchy" (xvi–xvii).

All of the aforementioned social and political forces are linked to what Lyn Pykett calls the "gender crisis" that dominated late nineteenth- and early twentieth-century discourse and was both "a crisis in social experience" and "a crisis in representation . . . in both the representation of gender and the gender of representation" (*Engendering* 15). Pykett argues that not only modernist but all forms of early twentieth-century fiction in England were "constructed . . . on the terrain of gender" and are best understood in terms of the "anxieties about gender, discourses on gender, and gendered discourses of various kinds" (13) of the period. An overview of these discourses yields a fascinating if confusing picture: the turn-of-the-century discussion and valuation of gender categories were usually connected to contradictory representations of the New Woman and the homosexual "as either symptoms of cultural degeneration and decadence, or as forms of resistance to cultural crisis and as points of cultural renewal and regeneration" (25). It is on this "shifting ground" of gender and sexuality, in which the terms of masculinity and femininity were "contradictory, unstable, and fiercely contested," that "the novel of the early twentieth century was produced" (20).

Although the categories of gender and sexuality are often separated theoretically as being produced by different forces (e.g., cultural construction, in the case of gender, and biological or psychological conditioning, in the case of sexuality), this distinction has been problematized in recent years by the contention of Foucault and others that the entire sex-gender system is a cultural formation. In speaking of early twentieth-century theoretical and literary discourse, the gender/sexuality distinction is difficult to maintain since the debates over masculinity and femininity were often fueled by anxieties over unconventional sexual behavior, especially as seen in the figures of the New Woman and the homosexual who were disrupters "of conventional gender boundaries and the natural, moral, and social order which those boundaries supported" (Pykett, *Engendering* 18). As we shall see, the gendering of the novel and certain of its techniques often goes hand-in-hand with the representation of homo- or bisexual desire.

In many ways, Virginia Woolf was a pioneer in articulating and representing the matters of gender and sexuality that are so central to modernist culture and discourse, and there have been many contemporary studies on how gender and genre are related in Woolf's fiction and criticism. Without detracting from the uniqueness of Woolf's work, however, I think that it can serve as a paradigm of the interconnection between gender issues and formal developments that is a hallmark of early twentieth-century English literature, especially the modernist novel. In this study, I will investigate how this relationship, which has been so thoroughly and brilliantly articulated in Woolf scholarship, is reflected in the novels and critical work of three of her literary peers, E. M. Forster, May Sinclair, and D. H. Lawrence. Although the level of conscious engagement with gender issues varies tremendously among these authors, all of them were influenced by and participated in the "gender crisis" of this period, and in each case the cultural forces and discourses of gender and sexual identity clearly bear upon innovations in the form and content of their novels. As I hope to show, for all four authors, the regeneration of the novel in the modernist period involved its "regenderation" (Pykett, *Engendering* 133) as well.

Given the well-traversed nature of gender scholarship on Woolf, in this introductory chapter I will provide a brief account of several key issues that Woolf raises in her essays and novels about the connection between gender issues and formal choices, issues which will be applied to the theory and novels of Forster, Sinclair, and Lawrence in succeeding chapters. As a way of illustrating some of the ways in which Woolf theorizes and fictionalizes the relationship between gender and genre, I will draw textual examples from two related iconoclastic works that were written at the center of her literary career, *Orlando* (1928) and *A Room of One's Own* (1929). I will conclude this chapter with a sketch of the web of personal and professional relations among all four authors and the gender-related questions they share with Woolf, all of which, I hope, suggests how my comparative project is both warranted and potentially fruitful.

GENDERING LITERARY HISTORY AND THE NOVEL

One of the most provocative and telling statements Woolf makes in *A Room of One's Own* is that "it is fatal for any one who writes to think of their sex" (104). Although her frustrations with sex and gender roles may have contributed to the depression that led to her untimely death, it seems that Virginia Woolf continually thought of her sex in the process of her writing. Over a course of more than twenty-five years and a series of essays and reviews, novels and stories, Woolf repeatedly explored the relationship between the vocation of the artist and his or her sex, and she frequently demonstrated the fact that, in matters of literary creation, gender matters, especially for women. From her debut novel, *The Voyage Out* (1915), "a female bildungsroman in which the young protagonist cannot pass alive the obstacle of marriage in a patriarchal culture" and "[g]ender is an overt preoccupation" (DeKoven 85), to her last novel, *Between the Acts* (1941), a final attempt to document "[t]he artist's struggle against masculine values" (Gillespie, "Virginia" 45) through Miss LaTrobe's conflict-laden pageant of English literary and social history, Woolf demonstrates the intimate connection between gender and literary production and reshapes the language and form of the novel in order to move away from the patriarchal confinement of the "sentence made by men" toward a freer style that more truthfully and effectively represents female consciousness and experience.

For the purposes of this study, I wish to draw attention to three important aspects of Woolf's treatment of the connection between gender and genre, which I will illustrate with examples from *Orlando* and *A Room of One's Own*. Although her ideas are applicable to other literary forms (and I will be briefly referring to Woolf's consideration of poetry in this light), the primary focus here is how, in both theory and practice, Woolf relates the category of gender to the form of the novel. In doing so, she clearly participates in the discourse of degeneration and renovation that is characteristic of her age. First of all, Woolf's version of literary history is represented in gendered terms. For the most part, this is done in a critical vein as Woolf employs the language of degeneration to characterize English culture, especially that of the Victorian age, in patriarchal terms and indict its restrictions on women and its male-determined literary forms (most specifically those of realism) for the absence and/or lack of recognition of women writers up to the modern age.

A second aspect of how Woolf relates gender and genre is found on the constructive side of her literary project, which employs the language of renovation to call for a revolution in literary style and form that will better represent life (which Woolf sometimes codes as feminine) and embody female experience. The chapter's opening quote gives an excellent example of how Woolf directly ties gender identity to novelistic form and technique in her description of the need for a woman's "altering and adapting the current sentence until she writes one that takes the natural shape of her thought." There is a suggestion of essentialism here as Woolf represents female thought processes in "natural" terms. Woolf does not simply theorize about gender and novel form, however; the first half of her novel writing career can be read as an attempt to create a specifically female form of the novel by moving away from novels of realism like *The Voyage Out* (1915) and *Night and Day* (1919) to novels of feminine consciousness like *Mrs. Dalloway* (1925) and *To The Lighthouse* (1927).[1]

The constructive element of Woolf's literary project is complicated, however, by her seemingly contradictory wishes in articulating how women should write. While she often speaks of the need to develop specifically female forms of literature, and thereby "seems to be polarizing and possibly reinforcing gender categories," at other times she "appears to argue for a transgressing or erosion of tradition gender categories" (Pykett, *Engendering* 107) by calling for an androgynous ideal of thought and literary practice (or a "post-gendered mind" (110)). Woolf describes this ideal as a "marriage of opposites" that is "consummated" in the artist's mind "between the woman and the man" through which the writer can communicate "his experience with perfect fulness" (*Room* 104). Woolf's metaphor is clearly influenced by Edward Carpenter's ideas on the homosexual or "sexual invert," who is represented "as a 'gender bender,' in whom masculine and feminine characteristics combine to form a third, or intermediate sex" (Pykett, *Engendering* 18). In her representation in *A Room of One's Own* and *Orlando* of this more utopian goal of androgynous or "post-gendered" writing, Woolf recognizes the artificiality of gender roles and hopes for a day when gender will no longer be an issue in creating art.

In a way, Woolf's two literary aims may not be so much contradictory as consecutive. Although Gilbert and Gubar believe that Woolf's idea of the "woman's sentence" is "essentially a *fantasy* about a utopian linguistic structure" (Gilbert and Gubar 230), Woolf's efforts to envision in theory and embody in practice a "woman's sentence" are grounded in the literary realities of her day. In fact, her project is enacted primarily in terms of the critique and creation of the novel, the literary form by which women have gotten their foot in the door of the literary world and which Woolf offers as the best present hope for the advancement of women's literature. In contrast, Woolf's ideal of creative androgyny seems directed toward a future age, a time when women will have achieved more material and artistic equity, thereby giving them the necessary freedom and experience to pursue more sophisticated genres like that of poetry.

The tensions inherent in Woolf's approach to the relation between gender and the novel are perhaps most evident in the two genre-challenging books she wrote in the middle of her literary career, *Orlando* (1928) and *A Room of One's Own* (1929). A fantasy *Bildungsroman* with a transsexual protagonist, *Orlando* is a work that defies categorization: what started out (in Woolf's own words) as a "joke," a "farce," or "an escapade" in which "everything [is] mocked" became something far more serious and elaborate. Among other things, *Orlando* is a semi-biography of "Vita [Sackville-West]; only with a change about from one sex to another" (*Diary* 114–115), as well as a history of her ancestors.[2] It incorporates aspects of autobiography in its depiction of Woolf's own struggles as a woman and a writer and, according to Madeline Moore, in its veiled expression of the love affair between Virginia and Vita, which takes the form of the biographer in pursuit of his/her elusive subject and displaces lesbian feelings onto the androgynous figure of Orlando (see Moore Ch. IV).

On another level, *Orlando* is a social and literary history of England, examining in general the "spirit" of its ages from the Renaissance to the modern period, as well as tracing the cultural construction of gender roles in each. For some feminist critics its scope is ultimately more concentrated: DuPlessis reads the book as a "feminist apologue" in which "the Ages of England have become the Ages of Woman" (61), and Sue Roe sees Woolf attempting to make "a serious point about literary inheritance" and using Orlando's sex change as a way of documenting "the appearance of the woman within the story of the literary tradition" (93–94). Being a story of women's experience and women's writing as much as it is a representation of androgyny and its relationship to literary creation, *Orlando* is a kind of fictional workshop for the exploration of Woolf's literary ambitions. Finally, the book is also a delightful and witty parody of all of the above, calling into question the patriarchal projects of biography, literary history, and gender construction and refusing to allow them to be taken too seriously.

A Room of One's Own, based on a series of highly imaginative lectures in which Woolf directed herself to the task of giving an account of "Women and Fiction," also resists easy labeling. Like *Orlando*, it is a hybrid of many forms or genres, including aspects of biography, autobiography, history, fantasy, literary criticism, and more; its style is anecdotal, informational, suggestive, didactic, satiric, and utopian. Central to most of *A Room of One's Own* is the experience of women: as sisters and mothers, as friends and lovers, as objects of study, and as potential and actual writers. Throughout the book, Woolf asserts women's difference, at one point forcefully proclaiming: "It would be a thousand pities if women wrote like men, or lived like men, or looked like men" (*Room* 88), and asserting that "[t]he book has somehow to be adapted to the body" (78). In the final chapter, however, Woolf proposes her androgynous ideal, which seems to fly in the face of the sex-specific recommendations which precede it. Needless to say, Woolf's shifting goals and points of view in this work place her theories of women's writing and androgynous creation in a complicated position: they are by no means part of a logical or systematic treatise but of a wandering, multi-purposed (and, at times, seemingly cross-purposed) exposition of women's issues. As Catharine Stimpson puts it, "*A Room* is an agitating series of gestures that forbids complacency, security, and premature intellectual closure" (130).

Despite their classification by some critics as belonging to separate literary genres (i.e., the novel and the essay), *Orlando* and *A Room of One's Own* share numerous formal qualities which embody Woolf's literary ideas on gender. First of all, in their fictive depictions of the largely unrecorded experience of women in relation to the male literary establishment, both works blur the boundaries between fiction and nonfiction in order to represent the effects of the masculine gendering of literary history and tradition. Woolf announces her eccentric method early in *A Room of One's Own* in explaining why she will argue her theories about women and fiction by means of stories: "Fiction here is likely to contain more truth than fact. Therefore I propose, making use of all the liberties and licenses of a novelist. . . . Lies will flow from my lips, but there may perhaps be some truth mixed up with them" (*Room* 4). According to Beth A. Boehm, the "marriage of fact and fiction" in both texts by means of the biographical fables of Orlando, Judith Shakespeare, and Mary Carmichael "is particularly necessary if one is to write narratives about women's lives, since nonfictional narrative forms have left unrecorded the facts of women's lives, while fictional narratives have distorted or ignored the real conditions of female existence" (193).

The combination of fact and fancy or biography and fantasy in both books serves other purposes besides making women visible in a man's world. Woolf's use of fantastic elements (such as her hyperbolic depiction of male-dominated literary periods and methods and her creation of a transsexual writer who transcends generations and literary forms) enables her not only to amend the patriarchal history of literature but also to reconceive such history from a woman's point of view by formally upsetting its linear and scientific thrusts. Her generic innovation here is both parodic and utopic in that it playfully mocks phallocentrically selective historical and biographical methods and hopefully rewrites women's literary lives and reimagines their literary possibilities for the future. The infiltration of biography and the essay by fantasy, especially in *Orlando*, also enables Woolf to represent bisexual and homosexual desires that are forbidden or foreclosed by the constraints of traditional literary forms (a project that is similar to that of E. M. Foster in his fiction). As Rosemary Jackson presents it, "fantasy characteristically attempts to compensate for a lack resulting from cultural constraints: it is a literature of desire" (3).

The playfulness or whimsicality shared by these works is another important formal quality through which Woolf subverts traditional constructions of history, gender, and sexuality. Minow-Pinkney says that this playfulness "does not mean secondariness or unseriousness, but is a necessary detachment and disguise, a deliberate narrative politics by which she can express what she otherwise prohibits herself" (120). The masquerading quality of the texts is particularly manifest in the multiple plots and complexities of their narrative structures. *Orlando*'s layerings of literary history and parody with love stories and poems and *A Room of One's*

Own's juxtaposition of academic lectures and anecdotes with sketches of real and fictional literary personae serve Woolf's multiple aims to subvert what she sees as conventional masculine forms (e.g., literary history, realist fiction, biography, and the essay) and create new gender- and genre-bending ones. In both cases, there is at work what Boehm calls "a self-conscious metafictional play" which problematizes the reader's "expectations about the relative status of fiction and truth" (194 & 197) and thereby renders the reader open to new (feminist and/or androgynous) stories and truths.

By virtue of their playful hybridity, both *Orlando* and *A Room of One's Own* confront the relationship of authorship and sex and embody Woolf's desires for the creation of specifically female artistic forms and the development of writing produced by the reconciliation of genders in an androgynous mind. As it traces its protagonist's numerous attempts over the ages to write a poem, *Orlando* serves as a fictional laboratory for the exposition and investigation of Woolf's theories about the relationship of gender to aesthetic creation, which are articulated more explicitly in *A Room of One's Own* and other literary essays. In the sections which follow, I will elaborate upon and illustrate the primary issues Woolf raises with regard to the connection between gender and the novel through a comparative look at these two representative pieces of Woolf's practice and theory at its height. In particular, I will focus on material from *Orlando* and *A Room of One's Own* (and other related essays) which, in a playfully serious and generically unique way, discusses and represents nineteenth- and twentieth-century literary history and the quest for the woman writer to find not only a room but a form of her own within the exclusive world of English literature.

WOOLF'S TAKE ON THE MALE NOVEL TRADITION: REALISM AS ERECTION

As a parody of English literary history, *Orlando* is wickedly clever in its representation of each period's dominant atmosphere and writing style, which is often expressed in gendered terms. Reflecting Woolf's deep frustration with the patriarchy of her social and cultural inheritance, the narrator's depiction of the degeneration of the Victorian age is both humorous and insightful. Ushered in by a great, damp cloud, the period is described as a "garish erection," a "conglomeration . . . of the most heterogeneous and ill-assorted objects [crystal palaces, bassinettes, military helmets, etc.], piled higgledy-piggledy in a vast mound" (*Orlando* 232–233). The cultural tumescence of the age is paralleled in its prose style: "sentences swelled, adjectives multiplied, lyrics became epics, and little trifles that had been essays a column long were now encyclopaedias in ten or twenty volumes" (229–230). At one point Orlando immerses herself in stacks of Victorian literature, written by a "mass" of unknown men, "all vocal, clamorous, prominent, and requiring as much attention as anybody else," and she finds it to be "corpulent . . . dry . . . respectable . . . [and] delicate"

(290–291). This cultural and literary inflation has the direct and contrary effect of repression on society at large and woman in particular: "Love, birth and death were all swaddled in a variety of fine phrases. . . . No open conversation was tolerated. . . . The life of the average woman was a succession of childbirths" (229).

The Edwardian period does not fare any better in Woolf's hands. In the novel, Orlando passes briefly through the age, a time in which "Everything seemed to have shrunk" and each house is "precisely the same as the other." The notable characteristic of the period is that it intensifies Orlando's powers of sensation: "her thoughts became mysteriously tightened and strung up . . . her hearing quickened . . . and she saw everything more and more clearly" (296–298), and this enables her to notice in an almost scientific way even the most minute of the physical details around her. As with much of the literary parody in *Orlando*, the style of this passage is written in imitation of the dominant mode of the age, in this case, the empirical technique of Edwardian novelists.

Orlando's literary critique even touches one of Woolf's male contemporaries, setting its sights on D. H. Lawrence in the following passage, which describes the potential intrusion of love ("woman's whole existence") upon Orlando's attempt to complete her poem as a woman:

> Surely, since she is a woman, . . . she will soon give over this pretence of writing and thinking and begin to think, at least of a gamekeeper. . . . And then she will write him a little note . . . and make an assignation for Sunday dusk; . . . and the gamekeeper will whistle under the window—all of which is, of course, the very stuff of life and the only possible subject for fiction (268–269).

Noteworthy is the fact that this apparent reference to Lawrence's work in *Lady Chatterley's Lover* is included in the windy biographical account of the Victorian phase of Orlando's life, thus linking Lawrence retroactively with his realist forebears, a link he himself would probably dispute (as we shall see in chapter four). Siegel sees this satiric moment as a critique of Lawrence's "return to conventional novelistic plotting and values" (97). Woolf goes on further to skewer such love tales with a marked attack on Lawrence's ideal of "tenderness": "But love—as the male novelists define it—and who, after all, speak with greater authority?—has nothing to do with kindness, fidelity, generosity, or poetry. Love is slipping off one's petticoat and—But we all know what love is" (269).

The literature of the Victorian and Edwardian ages that Woolf lambastes is dominated by the realist tradition, and she makes her indictment of this patriarchal force more directly in her critical essays. In one of her later pieces, "The Leaning Tower" (1940), she accuses nineteenth-century authors, most notably Dickens and Thackeray, of being liars and suppressors because they never told the "unpleasant truth" about themselves ("to admit that one is petty, vain, mean, frustrated, tortured, unfaithful, and unsuccessful"), thereby "crippling themselves, diminishing their material, [and] falsifying their object" (*Essays 2:* 177). Woolf took on the Edwardians (whom she terms "materialists" or "truth-tellers") with full force in "Modern Fiction" (1919), decrying the ways in which "they are concerned not with the spirit but with the body" and "write of unimportant things [... and] spend immense skill and immense industry making the trivial and the transitory appear the true and enduring" (104–105).

Woolf takes this argument even further in one of her most famous essays, "Mr. Bennett and Mrs. Brown" (1924), in which she criticizes the Edwardian style as too narrowly preoccupied with external detail ("the fabric of things"—332). She claims that authors like Wells, Bennett, and Galsworthy "were never interested in character in itself; or in the book in itself" but in "something outside," usually a social or political agenda they wished to promote, making the reader feel that, in order to complete their books, "it seems necessary to do something—to join a society, or, more desperately, to write a cheque" (326–327). The patriarchal quality of their myopic method is illustrated in Woolf's construction of a scene on a train which, as Makiko Minow-Pinkney points out, demonstrates the male Edwardians' inability to take notice and tell the real story of the main character, an apparently insignificant old lady named Mrs. Brown, that represents a typical woman whose voice, "'protesting she was different', has been silenced or ignored" in their novels (7).

Several of Woolf's essays are full of references to nineteenth- and early twentieth-century male authors as writing out of a specifically male tradition based on men's experience and values. In *A Room of One's Own*, Woolf theorizes that Galsworthy and Kipling write "only with the male side of their brains." She uses phallic imagery to describe the emotion these writers generate in their work: "It is coming, it is gathering, it is about to burst on one's head," and in response to figures like Kipling's "Sowers who sow the Seed, ... one blushes ... as if one had been caught eavesdropping at some purely masculine orgy" (*Room* 101–102). "Women and Fiction" (1929) speaks in general of men as the "arbiters" of literary convention and of the "order of values in life," which are established by men and prevail in fiction "to a very great extent." Their control also extends to the structure of the accepted prose style: it is "a sentence made by men; it is too loose, too heavy, too pompous for a woman's use" (*Essays 2:* 145–146). *Orlando* and *A Room of One's Own* suggest that there is even a masculine persona or ego which dominates the writing of this period in the form of an "I" whose shadow crosses the page of both Orlando's writing and Woolf's reading. According to Gillian Beer, this "I" is the written sign of the male first-person consciousness or "the phallic oppressiveness of the opinionated male writer" which is so characteristic of the literary tradition Woolf has inherited (88).

Although the phallic oppressiveness of this male "I" might appear to some feminist critics as a fitting description of Lawrence's work (as we shall see), Woolf's critical opinions on Lawrence's writing are ambivalent, as she shifts between liking and disliking his work. On the one hand, as Siegel shows, Woolf's identification with Lawrence in "The Leaning Tower" and some of her private writings shows that, perhaps by virtue of his lower-class status outside the majority, "Lawrence slipped across the border between the genders in Woolf's mind" (90). Despite her critique of much male fiction, she sees that Lawrence's work has "the freedom from predetermined form and received ideas that Woolf increasingly both valued and associated with women's writings" (92). On the other hand, as her satirical critique of *Lady Chatterley's Lover* in *Orlando* demonstrates, Woolf felt that there was "something wrong with Lawrence, which makes him brood over sex" (*Letters 2*: 476). Also, Siegel suggests that, just as Woolf found in the fiction of Charlotte Brönte, Lawrence's work contained "an angry self-consciousness Woolf sees as antithetical to art" (93).

Constructing a Women's Literary History

Not only does Woolf characterize literary convention as male-dominated, she also presents it as antagonistic to women writers. In *Orlando*'s fictional account of English literary history, as traced through Orlando's literary efforts from the Renaissance to the "present moment" of the publication of the novel in 1929, the latter half of the novel is a chronicle of the difficulties undergone by women in their struggles to become authors. Unsuccessful in his male attempts at aesthetic creation (embodied in the numerous aborted versions of his poem, "The Oak Tree"), Orlando flees to the exotic Eastern land of the "Other" in Constantinople. Rendered hysterical by anxieties generated by his masculine duties as lover, statesman, and poet, Orlando takes ill and dies into a woman's body, literally becoming "otherized" in the process. Orlando's sex change occurs during the late eighteenth century, the period when women like Aphra Behn first began making their mark in literature. After her transformation, each literary age confronts Orlando with new challenges that mirror the experience of her feminine contemporaries who sought to write.

Orlando's initial encounter with the literary world as a woman is anything but fortuitous. During the eighteenth century, she is first relegated by her sex to being a hostess or mere ornament at literary tea parties, only allowed "to pour out tea, and ask my lords how they like it" (*Orlando* 158), and in this role she falls prey to the enchantment of "great writers" like Dryden, Addison, and Pope. Under their tutelage Orlando learns the elements of Augustan literary style (toward which Woolf is largely sympathetic), but she is also treated with the authors' masculine disdain for women, including being insulted in the "Characters of Women," and, as a result, is never given a space within which to write. Fortunately, close personal contact with these distinguished mentors allows Orlando to judge them from a woman's perspective as being "much like other people" (208) and to lose her illusions about their transcendence as human beings. Here Woolf directly relates Orlando's inner life to her gender role, as when the necessary change of clothes which accompanies Orlando's change of sex not only alters the way she is perceived but also alters the way she perceives, equipping her with a "sidelong glance" which enables her to view the patriarchal world with "subtlety" and "suspicion" (188).

Only in the nineteenth century does Orlando once again take up her poem, this time as a woman, but her efforts to write in this period are largely futile because the spirit of the Victorian age is "antipathetic to her in the extreme, and thus it took her and broke her" (244). The obstacles to success are represented in hyperbolic moments in which Orlando either suffers forms of writer's block, when she is "impeded by a blot, which spread and meandered round her pen," or logorrhea, when "the pen began to curve and caracole with the smoothest possible fluency," flowing "in cascades of involuntary inspiration" which yield only "insipid verse" (237–239). Like so many Victorian women, Orlando can only progress if she agrees "to yield completely and submissively to the spirit of the age, and take a husband" (243). This action is suitably ridiculed through Woolf's depiction of Orlando's engagement-at-first-sight to Count Shelmerdine followed by a chaotic, rushed marriage, which is so noisy that "no one heard the word Obey spoken or saw, except as a golden flash, the ring pass from hand to hand" (262) and is left unconsummated because Shelmerdine abandons Orlando immediately after the ceremony in order to return to his independent masculine exploits. The one redeeming quality of the event seems to be that Orlando has found a similarly androgynous partner, as evidenced in this realization that is nearly simultaneous with their proclamation of their love: "'You're a woman, Shel!' she cried. 'You're a man, Orlando!' he cried" (252).

Some feminist critics view Orlando's androgynous marriage to Count Shelmerdine as a "social façade" or "defense" through which she gains access to literary production and triumphs over Victorian literary restraints. Perhaps the strongest of these voices is that of Maria DiBattista, who believes that an "introversion of the narrative" occurs at this point in which Orlando retreats indoors after the wedding and is actually able to "write of love in her own way," using "a feminine wile that deceives the guardians of 'customs' by feigning conformity and by masking the satirical, cynical, and psychological urges in her art" (139–140). This positive view of Orlando's literary progress is backed up by the fact that, through marriage, she finally acquires "a room of her own" and the leisure with which to collect her thoughts and write, apparently in a way which preserves her identity: "she need neither fight her age, nor submit to it; she was of it, yet remained herself. Now, therefore, she could write, and write she did. She wrote. She wrote. She wrote." (*Orlando* 266).

Such freely flowing and prodigious work points toward the successful conclusion of Orlando's goal, until the fate of her completed poem is considered. When the "blood-stained" manuscript (281), the product of a few hundred years' toil, is finally finished, it brings with it a feeling of "dissolution" and a need to "be read" (and, therefore, published by the male establishment) rather than a sense of fulfillment (272), thus revealing Orlando's continued dependence on the patriarchal literary world. A further irony emerges in the fact that the poem is entrusted to a pompous literary critic, Nicholas Greene, who embodies all the worst characteristics of the male literary establishment and has previously satirized in print Orlando's life and creative talent. There is also a troubling link between the poem and the baby she delivers at about the same time, which is manifested in the similarity of their fates. The delivery of the baby is presented as an unimportant detail or an after-thought; as Rachel Bowlby points out, it "emerges almost parenthetically: in the formal style of a newspaper announcement, and from the hands of another woman rather than from Orlando's own body" (61). No further mention is made of the child, and its apparent insignificance possibly reflects the way in which women's literature and, hence, Orlando's literary "baby," the poem, was treated in the Victorian era. As Madeline Moore sees it, hard as Orlando may try, "[a]s a woman trying to break with convention in the nineteenth century," she "cannot transform traditional forms" and ends up writing in the same vein (104).

Given the fact that the primary channel for Woolf's own literary efforts is the novel, it seems odd that she has Orlando seek to make his/her mark as a poet, but Woolf's discussion of poetry in *A Room of One's Own* helps to explain this paradox. First of all, Woolf gives poetry a special place in her claim that the "original impulse was to poetry" (*Room* 66) and in her effusive and sometimes jealous appreciation of the poetic accomplishments of earlier periods. However, using language that directly relates to *Orlando*, Woolf also recognizes that "masterpieces are not single and solitary births; they are the outcome of many years of thinking in common" (65). In her attempt to piece together the undocumented history of women, Woolf shows how they lacked the material conditions necessary for creating poetry, which requires a "concentration" that was impossible in the interruption-filled "common sitting-room" of the nineteenth century, and the literary training available was "training in the observation of character" and "in the analysis of emotion" (66–67), qualities Woolf sees as more conducive to novel writing. The absence of material conditions and a common literary tradition for women at this time makes it nearly impossible that Orlando, working on a poem with a solidly masculine English subject like "The Oak Tree," will succeed as a poet in feminine terms.

Orlando's plight as a woman writer in the nineteenth century is described outright as an enslavement to patriarchal convention in Woolf's other critical writing. In "Modern Fiction" she uses a damning image to describe the pressures placed on modern writers by the male establishment: "The writer seems constrained, not by his own free will but by some powerful and unscrupulous tyrant who has him in thrall, to provide a plot, to provide comedy, tragedy, love interest, and an air of probability embalming the whole. . . . The tyrant is obeyed; the novel is done to a turn" (*Essays* 2: 106). Woolf states bluntly in *A Room of One's Own* that of all nineteenth-century women writers, only Jane Austen and Emily Brontë had the "integrity . . . in the midst of that purely patriarchal society, to hold fast to the thing as they saw it without shrinking" (*Room* 74). However, they could do so only by writing novels even though they showed talent for other genres.

Another powerful representation of this literary coercion is found in Woolf's famous figure, "The Angel in the House," who demonstrates the subtle ways in which patriarchal desires are assimilated by women. In "Professions for Women," Woolf gives a personal account of writing a piece of literary criticism on a book written by a man, during which the "Angel" appears and offers the following submissive advice: "Be sympathetic; be tender; flatter; deceive; use all the arts and wiles of our sex. Never let anybody guess that you have a mind of your own. Above all, be pure" (*Essays* 2: 285). This deferential strategy serves as an adequate summary of the expectations that Woolf believes are placed on women by the "extreme conventionality of the other sex," which is why she insists in "Women and Fiction" that the Angel must be killed so that, as we shall now see, women can "explore their own sex [and] write of women as women have never been written before" (146).

WRITING A WOMAN'S SENTENCE . . . AND NOVEL

Orlando achieves her proper stance as a writer only in the twentieth century, and her experience of "the present moment" (*Orlando* 298), which coincides with the writing of her biography, serves as an illustration of the new possibilities and forms open to women writers of the modern age. Having "dropped" both baby and poem, Orlando is relieved of the burdens of motherhood and her patriarchal literary past and experiences a fuller degree of freedom. Her liberation is symbolized in her hopping into a car for a spin around London in order to take in "[t]he very fabric of life" (300) and revel in the sights, sounds, and smells of a department store while on a shopping spree. Probably for the first time, she is able to immerse herself in the moment, allowing sensations, emotions, and memories to flow through her mind and convey a sense of the many "selves of which we are built up" (308).

Orlando's life is not all "ecstasy" at this moment, however. While attempting to summon up her "Captain" or "Key self," she feels a deep sense of the fragmentation of her inner self and her age. This disorienting experience is paralleled in the broken prose of the passage, at times resembling

Woolf's own "stream of consciousness" style, as it conveys to the eavesdropping reader Orlando's "rambling talk, disconnected, trivial, dull, and sometimes unintelligible" (310). The narrator/biographer later describes this state of disjunction as a particularly feminine experience: "when we write of a woman, everything is out of place—culminations and perorations; the accent never falls where it does with a man" (312). The potential climax of Orlando's personal and aesthetic search is located in a suitably ironic place. Only when she spots a "wild goose" (313) does she get in touch with herself in a special way, described in language which suggests a return to a pre-Oedipal state. It is "as if her mind had become a fluid that flowed round things and enclosed them completely" and "words . . . are plumped out with meaning" (314–315), as is every movement and action.

Woolf's depiction in *A Room of One's Own* of the writing of Mary Carmichael, a fictional contemporary novelist, parallels Orlando's disruptive and unprecedented experience almost to the letter. While reading Carmichael's first novel, appropriately entitled *Life's Adventure*, Woolf notices that: "something was not quite in order. The smooth gliding of sentence after sentence was interrupted. Something tore, something scratched. . . . First, she broke the sentence; now she has broken the sequence" (*Room* 80–81). The difference is not only one of grammar or syntax; Mary Carmichael also has the courage to "break the content" by writing about how "Chloe liked Olivia," thereby violating Victorian heterosexual conventions and opening up an unspoken realm of women's experience. As DuPlessis sees it, for Woolf: "breaking the sequence can mean deligitimating the specific narrative and cultural orders of nineteenth-century fiction—the emphasis on successful or failed romance, the subordination of quest to love, the death of the questing female, the insertion into family life" (34–35) and, externally, the orders of literary history. Orlando's bisexual/androgynous state (mirroring Woolf's own experience) frees her to move beyond literary convention to new forms.

The womb-like imagery of Orlando's final, ecstatic experience suggests that she has finally gotten in touch with life (which is gendered here as feminine, since it comes through her body and experience as a woman) and is on the brink of being able to write from that site. Paradoxically, Orlando does not produce any written work in this final stage of her journey, but through the unsatisfactory experience of her poem's publication, she has learned that writing has nothing to do with "praise and fame" but is "a secret transaction, a voice answering a voice" (*Orlando* 325) inside herself. Woolf leaves the fulfillment of Orlando's literary quest open-ended (like her own)[3] in the final scene, as Orlando leaves her book "unburied and dishevelled on the ground" and gazes on the world around her, caught up in a vision of "ecstasy" when her husband and the wild goose appear on the horizon.

Woolf leaves Orlando gazing out into the future to represent Woolf's own view on women's writing at the time the novel was written, a perspective that is further developed in several of her essays. In "Professions for Women," Woolf takes pride in the fact that she, like Orlando, has killed the "Angel in the House," but she admits that she has not solved the problem of "telling the truth about my own experiences as a body" and recognizes that for women there are still "many ghosts to fight, many prejudices to overcome" (*Essays 2*: 288). Despite these obstacles, Woolf notes in "Women and Fiction" that progress has been made and that "women's fiction at the present moment" is "courageous" and "sincere," it "keeps closely to what women feel" and "is not bitter." Also, in a paradoxical statement hovering between constructionism and essentialism, Woolf claims that such writing "does not insist upon its femininity," but it is also "not written as a man would write it" (146–147). Bowlby attributes a good deal of this progress to Woolf's own pioneering fiction, which produces a prose that is characterized by ellipses, dashes, parentheses, omissions, interruptions, and gaps. In other words, Woolf herself has created a woman's sentence ("the dotted line"), which "breaks open or leaves incomplete the masculine sentence" and which cannot "make sense or be heard as reasonable within the structure as it is" (169–170).

Although *Orlando* and *A Room of One's Own* seem largely concerned with issues of women's experience and writing, Woolf clearly does not wish to exclude men from the new styles and forms of writing she advocates. This is perhaps the motivating force behind her theory of androgyny that calls for writers to "be woman-manly or man-womanly." In *A Room of One's Own* she talks of numerous past male authors who fit her androgynous ideal, including Shakespeare, Keats, Sterne, Coleridge, and Proust (although he is described as "a little too much of a woman" (*Room* 103)). Woolf's early criticism includes male writers of the Georgian generation (including Joyce) among those who "attempt to come closer to life" and "discard most of the conventions which are commonly observed by the novelist" (*Essays 2*: 107) so that they can write of the present moment.[4]

Woolf paints herself into a bit of a logical corner here. In an attempt to get beyond gender difference, Woolf develops her idea of androgyny with its "marriage of opposites" that is necessary for creative production. Because her motive here is formalist as well as feminist, she sees that "modernism" is not exhaustively correlated with femaleness. However, her feminist claims for women in their relationship to writing seem to rest on an essentialism that conflicts with her androgynous purposes. If the two are to be even partially reconciled theoretically, then Woolf's argument must be seen as a "feminine" position that is based on cultural rather than biological difference. As Pamela J. Transue puts it, it "will be the gift of the woman artist to rejuvenate the novel through correcting this one-sidedness [i.e., the dominance of masculine values] and providing us with a more harmonious vision" (8).[5]

Considering Woolf's Peers: Gendering the Novel as Well?

Having outlined Woolf's pioneering efforts to articulate and represent issues of gender in relation to the novel, I intend, in the rest of this book, to discuss three of Virginia Woolf's novel-writing contemporaries about whom little has been written examining the connection of gender issues to their formal and thematic innovations in the English modernist novel. There are a number of reasons for considering E. M. Forster, May Sinclair, and D. H. Lawrence in the same light as Woolf concerning the relationship of gender and genre. First of all, the peak period of their writing careers was nearly simultaneous; all four authors wrote most of their innovative novels during the same period of time—the 1910s and 1920s. Secondly, in addition to making original contributions to the development of the modern novel, all four wrote significant nonfictional texts that develop a theory of the novel in which the categories of gender and sexuality (consciously or unconsciously) play a significant role, albeit it very different ways. As significant contributors to English literary culture during the "gender crisis" of the early twentieth century, their theory and practice are marked, often intensely so, by the conflicted rhetoric of degeneration and renovation that characterized the discourses surrounding gender and sexuality in their time.

Besides these chronological and generic connections, a consideration of the relationships among all four authors creates an intricate web of personal and literary connections, not all of which can be detailed here.[6] On the personal level, Forster had a somewhat intimate but uneasy friendship with both Woolf and Lawrence. Forster became a part of the Bloomsbury set in 1910, giving a paper on "The Feminine Note in Literature" which met with Virginia's approval. Two years later, he entered into a friendship with Leonard Woolf, in which the latter "cast himself in Forster's eyes . . . in the role of the manly man," and gradually developed a "friendly, if not intimate" relationship with Virginia, who "was impressed by his penetration and vision" and "became very dependent on his opinion" (Furbank 1: 217 & 2: 17–18). Their friendship continued until her death, although it had its ups and downs during the days when they critiqued one another's work.

Woolf and Forster's ongoing literary relationship was generally cordial but occasionally tense. Each of them admired the other's early work, with Woolf enjoying "the cleverness, the sheer fun, the occasional beauty" of *A Room with a View* (*Letters 3*: 221), and Forster finding *The Voyage Out* "[a]mazingly interesting, and very funny"(*Selected Letters 1*: 223). Their public literary discussion began with Forster's article on "The Early Novels of Virginia Woolf" in 1925 which praises "her own wonderful new method and form" but faults her treatment of character, criticizing her for not allowing "her readers to inhabit each character with Victorian thoroughness" (*Abinger* 114).

The debate intensified with Woolf's review of the published lectures which made up *Aspects of the Novel*, for which Forster had enlisted Woolf's advice to make up for the gaps in his novel reading, and her essay on "The Novels of E. M. Forster" (both from 1927). In the review, which was later published as "The Art of Fiction," Woolf takes Forster to task for his casual synchronic approach to the novel, saying that he does not really "theorize about fiction except incidentally," and for his "arbitrary" definition of the "Life" which he claims is the focus of the novel (*Essays 2*: 52–53). As Ann Henley represents it, in this literary to-and-fro "each forced the other to clarify his or her conception of the novel," with Forster emphasizing character and Woolf stressing artistic vision. As the debate plays itself out, Forster defends "the novel as a perpetuator of traditional values and a transmitter of belief," while Woolf "becomes increasingly the champion of an objective, self-sufficient, endlessly experimental art form" (Henley 74).

Forster had a more intimate and complex relationship with Lawrence, whose opinion of Forster and his work underwent a series of changes. During an initially warm but very brief period of friendship in 1915,[7] Lawrence eventually became obsessed with Forster's lack of sexual feeling and experience. In a letter of the time, Lawrence reflected his belief that sexual frustration was the source of Forster's distress with modern society and literature ("Forster does not believe that any beauty or any divine utterance is any good anymore") and sexual continence had deleterious effects on his work. Lawrence posits a (hetero)sexual solution to Forster's *Weltschmerz*: "Forster knows that his implicit manhood is to be satisfied by nothing but immediate physical action. He tries to dodge himself—the sight is pitiful. But why can't he act? Why can't he take a woman and fight clear to his own basic, primal being?" (*Letters* 2: 283).[8] As can be imagined, Forster was offended by Lawrence's harsh and intrusive judgments of his inner life, and he reacted in kind in a letter to Florence Barger: "I do not like the deaf impercipient fanatic who has nosed over his own little sexual round until he believes that there is no other path for others to take, he sometimes interests & sometimes frightens & angers me, but in the end he will bore him merely, I know" (*Selected Letters* 1: 219). Forster ultimately felt that "Lawrence ignored his own homosexual side" (Furbank 2: 12), so the friendship quickly faltered.

Lawrence's assessment of Forster's work was as mercurial as their relationship. He was initially impressed by *The Celestial Omnibus* but found too much "splitness" in the stories. Not surprisingly, his favorite Forsterian character was the working-class underdog, Leonard Bast, in *Howards End*. He was also favorably disposed to *A Passage to India* when it came out in 1924 (it led him to call Forster: "about the best of my contemporaries in England" (*Letters* 5: 91)), but he did not accept Forster's apparent rejection of human relations in the novel's conclusion. For some mysterious reason, Lawrence's accolades turned sour three years later. In response to reviews of *Aspects of the Novel*, Lawrence wrote: "Judging from the notice of Forster's last book, he must be rather a piffler just now. And I read the *Celestial Omnibus* again—and found it rather rubbish. Those things don't wear" (*Letters* 6: 225). Although Forster approached being that rare commodity in Lawrence's life, a respected literary peer, the intense affect of Lawrence's reactions to Forster suggests that he touched nerves and issues, especially sexual ones, that Lawrence did not want to acknowledge.

Forster's written commentary on Lawrence's work is minimal but appreciative, and he assigns Lawrence a special place in *Aspects of the Novel* as "the only prophetic novelist writing today . . . the only living novelist in whom the song predominates, who has the rapt bardic quality." However, Forster also criticizes Lawrence for being "an excessively clever preacher who knows how to play on the nerves of his congregation." Forster finds that Lawrence's talent for "irradiating nature from within, so that every colour has a glow and every form a distinctness which could not otherwise be obtained" is especially evident in *Women in Love* (*Aspects* 143–144). Despite their drifting apart as friends, Forster maintained literary contacts with Lawrence and was among the greatest of Lawrence's champions after his death, proclaiming him "the greatest imaginative novelist of our generation" yet also recognizing that he "became more didactic and mannered" with age ("Letters" 888, 109).

The only personal contact between Woolf and Lawrence was some business correspondence concerning the possibility of Woolf's renting his cottage on the Cornish coast and her sighting of Lawrence from a carriage in Italy, and their literary connections were slight. As Earl Ingersoll puts it, "Lawrence's letters provide little evidence that he was aware of Woolf's existence" while hers "indicate that she was very much aware of his presence on the literary scene" (125–126). Although Woolf issues only several passing comments on his work in her diary, letters, and essays, usually marked by frustration at his depiction of women, in one letter she recognizes his accomplishments in *Women in Love*: "I can't help thinking that there's something wrong with Lawrence, which makes him brood over sex, but he is trying to say something, and he is honest, and therefore he is 100 times better than most of us" (*Letters* 2: 476). Also, in a letter written after his death, she calls him "a man of genius . . . but genius obscured and distorted I think" (*Letters* 4: 315).

It appears that Sinclair met Lawrence only once (they shared a literary agent, Curtis Brown), but it cannot have been a warm encounter, as Lawrence later offered this reaction to her: "You should see her . . . a little humped up scrawny woman. Oh, married, of course, but she could never be anything but a spinster" (Nehls 412), and his comments on her work were disparaging. On the literary level, Sinclair did not write any extended criticism of the other authors' work, but she was certainly as familiar with their novels as they were with hers. Forster penned a review of one of Sinclair's novels, *Mary Olivier*, which he calls "a notable experiment, unattempted hereto" that, unlike realism, "allows our imagination and sentimentality a little play," but he also found its style "jerky and monotonous" and "austere almost to bleakness" ("Moving" 8). Her writing also seems to have had some direct effect on the work of Lawrence and Woolf. First of all, Sinclair's novel *The Three Sisters* bears some thematic similarities to *The Rainbow* and *Women in Love*, and it seems to have directly influenced the revision of one of Lawrence's short stories, "Daughters of the Vicar" (Zegger 74–77). Secondly, she, like Woolf and Forster, lent her voice to the defense of Lawrence's work against censorship. Finally, Sinclair's critique of Dorothy Richardson's novels was a source of inspiration for Woolf's essay, "Modern Fiction" (Allen 5).

All in all, there was plenty of personal and literary interaction among these authors to warrant a comparative study of their work. The limited space of this book makes it impossible to cover four vast literary careers as they relate to the topic of gender and genre in the novel, so my approach consists of treating each of the remaining authors in a separate chapter which draws from a selection of their novels and nonfiction writings in order to identify some aspect(s) of their innovative work in the modern English novel as it relates to the categories of gender and, in some cases, sexuality. As we shall see, all of these authors rely in some way upon gendered language and imagery in their articulation of their literary theory and projects, although some are more conscious and active than others in their participation in the "gender crisis" or "gender wars" of the modernist period. For example, all four writers employ androgynous or bisexual terms when speaking of the creative imagination, and three of them (Woolf, Forster, and Lawrence) apply the language of gender to formal aspects or techniques of the novel, but only Woolf and Lawrence use gender as a category through which to map literary history and envision regenerations of the novel tradition. What follows is an account of the intersection of gender (and sexuality) and literary theory in the work of Forster, Sinclair, and Lawrence and its relationship to innovation(s) in the form or subject matter of their novels.

Given the overlapping and diverse nature of their literary connections and publishing careers, it is difficult to come up with a neatly chronological or systematic approach to the remaining authors. Therefore, by way of proceeding, I will consider them in terms of their radial relationship to Woolf, highlighting significant perspectives on or relationships to gender issues which they share with Woolf and showing how these are manifested in their novel theory and practice. What will emerge in each case may seem, at times, to be incommensurate with the others since their approaches are so different and sometimes even opposed, yet I hope to show that, beyond sharing links to Woolf, the work of all three writers exemplifies the interpenetration of gender discourse and genre practice that was so central to the modernist age.

I will begin with a consideration, in chapter two, of E. M. Forster, who is arguably the least innovative of these authors, but whose links to Woolf's writing and ethos are strong. In addition to personal and philosophical ties fostered by the Bloomsbury set, Forster shares some artistic similarities with Woolf, most especially his innovative employment of fantasy within the novel. In a move that illustrates the slipperiness of sex-gender discourse, Forster uses the category of gender to describe fantasy as an androgynous (sometimes male, sometimes female) aspect or submode of the novel, but his deployment of fantasy serves a sexual purpose as well. Inspired by his reading of Carpenter's sexual theory, Forster, like Woolf, uses fantastic elements within his novels to allow himself a safe place in which to locate and enact conflicted homosexual desire and also offer a critique of the sexually intolerant society which generates such conflict. As part of his literary masquerade, he too includes double narratives and androgynous characters as devices for representing gendered and sexual identities (often conflating the two) that fall outside of patriarchal, heterosexist cultural norms and literary forms.

As a fellow feminist, May Sinclair shared a number of Woolf's political goals, and as a woman writer, she encountered the same kind of frustrations Woolf met in her efforts to find a place in the male literary establishment in which to represent women's experience. In chapter three, I will show how, somewhat like Woolf, Sinclair represents creative genius in conversely gendered or androgynous terms and trace the path of formal development in her novel writing, which moves away from the Victorian patriarchal confines of romance and realism toward modernist innovations in terms of narrative style. Although writing contemporaneously with Woolf and Richardson but not sharing their theoretical project of creating specifically gendered (i.e., feminine) literary forms, Sinclair still produces a series of experiments which eventually yields a version of the "stream of consciousness" novel that seems most suited to female subject matter in its depiction of the struggles of her modern heroines in the clash between genius and gender role.

The writings of D. H. Lawrence serve as a complementary bookend to Woolf's work in terms of the relation of gender and genre. In chapter four, I will show how Lawrence was an integral participant in the modernist "gender wars," albeit in a conflicted and inconsistent way. Although he sometimes includes seemingly feminist elements in his early work, Lawrence's ultimate quest to create a "phallic novel" serves as a fascinating contrast to Woolf's feminist literary project and a perfect example of the inconsistency of gender discourse since, in total opposition to Woolf, Lawrence portrays the tradition of the nineteenth- and early twentieth-century novel as a degenerative feminizing and emasculating force. Further indicating the contradictory nature of his work, Lawrence's novel of "phallic consciousness," his proposal for the renovation of the enervated modern novel, is represented in equitable heterosexual terms but is fraught with strains of misogyny and homophobia. Lawrence's conflicting theories about gender and sex roles (as well as the tensions they generate) influence numerous formal aspects of his novels, including their often fractured or unresolved structures, but I have chosen to focus on the ways in which his sex-gender ideas are represented through innovative developments in representing character and sexual relations. Lawrence's reverence for the novel's power to change the world is reflected in his description of it in biblical terms as the "Book of Life" for the modern age. A consideration of his novel career demonstrates how his history of salvation takes place in the novel primarily on the level of the sex-gender struggle because he believes that "[t]he great relationship, for humanity" is "the relation between man and woman" (*Phoenix* 531).

The writings of each of these authors use sex-gender categories in very different ways both to identify their literary ideals and describe the formal developments in their novels which are meant to embody those ideals. Whereas Woolf articulated an androgynous or bisexual ideal of thinking and writing which she represented in gender- and genre-bending texts, Lawrence posited a heterosexual model based on sexual difference which he embodied in phallocentric novels. Forster directed gender confusion and homosexual desire into the fantasy submode while Sinclair channeled gender role frustration and female creative energy into the stream of consciousness technique. Without erasing the obvious differences in the meanings and methods of each author, these brief studies will, I hope, bear out the contention of Woolf and numerous other critics that, in the turbulent, convention-shattering modernist period of English literary history, sex-gender issues both instigated and provided a language for revolutionary changes in the genre of the novel.

CHAPTER TWO

Pursuing (a) Fantasy
E. M. Forster's Doubled-Up Fiction

INTRODUCTION

> The general tone of novels is so literal that when the fantastic is introduced it produces a special effect: some readers are thrilled, others choked off: it demands an additional adjustment because of the oddness of its method or subject matter. . . . fantasy asks us to pay something extra. (*Aspects* 108–109)

> Fantasy . . . flits over the scenes of Italian and English holidays, or wings her way with even less justification towards the countries of the future. She or he. For Fantasy, though often female, sometimes resembles a man. (*Omnibus* v)

When read with a knowledge of his sexual history, E. M. Forster's characterization of fantasy, one of the seven topics or "aspects" of fiction he discusses in his 1927 lectures and book, yields "queer"[1] possibilities. Described in almost orgasmic terms as thrilling or choking its readers and categorized by the "oddness" of its method or subject matter, fantasy, conceived by Forster as an alternative to realism in fiction, becomes suggestive of alternative desires and identities as well. In his understanding, fantasy is a double-natured and -gendered beast: expressing some aspect of reality through an element of the supernatural, fantasy can take on the guise of male or female. This "aspect" is central to Forster's creative production: from his very first fictional effort, "The Story of a Panic," to his final novel, *A Passage to India*, and his posthumously published homoerotic writings, Forster's fiction is usually punctuated by elements of the fantastic. On a surface level, Forster's use of mythic or magical figures and places reflects a literary fashion of his day. As he put it in a radio talk, in those days Pan was "in the air" (Colmer, *EMF* 29), and popular Edwardian fiction is full of pastoral fantasy tales, populated by satyrs and nymphs and

25

set in magical woods and dells.[2] Fantasy is much more than a faddish pursuit for Forster, however.

Fantasy's queer duality is a significant quality for Forster because he himself experienced a tremendous sense of being split in both his emotional life and his writing. As a young Englishman coming to terms with homosexual attractions while forging a career in the heterosexually coded world of early twentieth-century fiction, Forster found that his life and work were constantly marked by tensions between his (then) illicit desires and social and literary conventions.[3] Most of his novels were written during a time of sexual confusion and frustration, during which Forster wrestled with but barely acted upon his desires, never having a physically consummated homosexual experience until 1916.[4] Because Forster believed that "it is the function of the novelist to reveal the hidden life at its source" (*Aspects* 45), he needed a means by which to express his desires and experience (or lack thereof) of that secret life. Fantasy provided a pathway through which Forster could negotiate, sometimes unconsciously, the conflicting demands of sexuality and respectability, but not without generating compromises and failures in the midst of his literary triumphs.

Forster's use of the "aspect" of fantasy and its doubling structures yields novels marked at times by numerous contradictions, gaps and inconsistencies that not only express his struggles with same-sex desire but also offer a subtle critique of the society which produces such conflict.[5] Although many modernist works (Woolf's *Orlando* among them) might be said to share these paradoxical qualities, all of Forster's novels (to a greater or lesser degree) can also be considered "queer" texts. Similar to what Annamarie Jagose describes as "queer . . . gestures or analytical models," Forster's novels "dramatise incoherencies in the allegedly stable relations between chromosomal sex, gender and sexual desire" (3). Expressing what Michael Warner calls a "dissatisfaction with the regime of the normal" (xxvii), these novels use fantasy elements to queer the literary form that is the repository of the Edwardian "normal," i.e., novelistic realism.

In Northrop Frye's form criticism, fantasy appears as a submode analogous to romance, which Frye places in an oppositional relationship to realism: "In the fiction-writing of the last four or five centuries there has been a kind of reversible shuttle moving between imagination and reality. . . . One direction is called 'romantic,' the other 'realistic'" (37). In the eighteenth and nineteenth centuries, the novel served as "a realistic displacement of romance" (38), but in the late nineteenth and early twentieth century, writers like Oscar Wilde heralded a "new age in literature" that turned "away from the descriptive use of language and correspondence form of truth" of realism and back toward the use of "mythical and romantic formulas . . . with great explicitness" (46). Of particular relevance with regard to placing Forster's work within this modal shift is Frye's claim that: "Fiction in the last generation or so has turned increasingly from realism to fantasy, partly because fantasy is the normal technique for fiction writers who do not believe in the permanence or continuity of the society they belong to" (138).

Because post-Wilde Edwardian society disapproved of homosexuality, Forster used fantasy (at times unconsciously) to construct a realm in which same-sex desire could be covertly acknowledged and expressed. In this chapter, I will elucidate the relationship between gender and genre in Forster's theory and practice by tracing how he increasingly incorporates the double-gendered and sexually fluid mode of fantasy into his seemingly realist novels, showing that the "oddness" of fantasy's "method" parallels the "oddness" of its primary "subject matter" for Forster. Although Forster sometimes uses fantasy in the service of heterosexual love, he more often and more successfully uses it to represent homosexual love in particular and sexual tolerance in general. As Frye notes, to its critics, "romance appears to be designed mainly to encourage irregular or excessive sexual activity" (24). It seems appropriate, then, that Forster employs the related submode of fantasy to construct a subversive, utopian space in which "irregular" same-sex love can be represented, with the potential effect of "thrilling" some readers and "choking off" others.

The interrelatedness of content and form in Forster's "fantastic" approach to the novel is evident in what might be called a queer use of a few key structural components in his fiction. First of all, tensions generated in Forster's personal struggles with gender identity and sexual orientation are reflected in his use of fantasy's dualistic elements (especially godlike characters, magical spaces, and coincidental events) in conjunction with a double-plot (of varying degrees of development) in most of his novels. As Judith Herz notes, "[t]here is always another story beneath the surface of the story he is telling," and she sees Forster's "greatest novelistic strength" as being his "ability to control and manipulate the tensions generated by the collision of surface plot [relating a heterosexual romance] and under plot [expressing the desire for male friendship and/or homosexual love]" ("Double" 85).[6] Forster's employment of the double-plot is a potentially subversive practice that Scott R. Nelson calls "narrative inversion," in which a homosexual "subtext" is submerged into and sometimes upends the "Edwardian 'master narrative' of heterosexual, homosocial (and necessarily misogynist) desire" (311). These "alterations in the narrative contract" through the insertion of the homosexual subtext is Forster's significant contribution to the modern novel, entitling him to a place among his modernist peers, although it is a structural innovation as opposed to the "stylistic innovation" of people like Woolf, Joyce, and Proust (320).

Another structural element that works within fantasy to reflect the sexual and social tensions of Forster's novels is his use of pairs and triangles of characters to enact various emotional, psychological, and social conflicts. Usually structured on the surface as conventional love triangles, these character combinations not only dramatize sexual struggle but often act out the "dividings of personality" (*Aspects* 112) that Forster considers one of the expressions of fantasy, which works largely in a psychological way here and is clearly influenced by Carpenter's writings on the "intermediate sex." In each triangle, there is generally a Forster-like character (male or female) torn between two other characters who serve as dualistic markers of one or more categories,[7] e.g., gender (masculine or feminine), sexuality (hetero- or homo-),[8] race (English or European, Western or Eastern), social status (levels of class and education), and temperament (aesthetic or physical).[9] One of the lines of progress or failure in each of Forster's novels is the pivotal figure's ability to integrate his/her gender identity, sexuality, and personality, a process that is more often thwarted than fulfilled (at least for the males) in Forster's Edwardian settings.

Beginning with Forster's theoretical writings on the novel and then moving through his six novels, I will now show how he subverts the conventions of realism by means of the "something extra" that fantasy provides in order to incorporate into his novels the world of homosexual desire and relations which the realist tradition ignores. Forster's use of fantasy follows a somewhat parabolic path over the course of his career, and the degree to which fantasy is present in each novel is roughly proportional to its level of homosexual content. In the earliest novels, *Where Angels Fear to Tread* and *A Room with a View*, there are latent traces of homoerotic desire represented in a few characters and scenes that bear touches of the fantastic. Moving deeper into the realm of the sexual, *The Longest Journey* is suffused with both homoerotic feeling and fantasy elements, albeit in a confused and conflicted way, that register Forster's own sexual inexperience and frustrations at the time it was written.

Forster's career seems to take a sudden turn with the writing of *Howards End*, marked by a shift in focus to a female perspective and an apparent backing off from homosexual content, yet the novel ends with what is (to that point in his career) Forster's most utopian and sexually tolerant vision. Riding on the success of *Howards End* but desiring to move away from the conventional heterosexual love plot of the novel, Forster decided to write his most explicitly homosexual yet still fantastic novel, *Maurice*, but his inability to publish it for fear of censorship became a lifelong source of disenchantment for him. The arc of Forster's fantasy career takes a downward turn with *A Passage to India*, which has its own share of fantastic characters and sites but whose vision of male relationships is his most pessimistic, reflecting the continued frustration of Forster's public efforts to represent homosexual desire within the heterosexually constructed form of the novel. In the end, Forster's results are mixed: while the elements of fantasy in his novels sometimes create an idyllic sense of love and personal freedom for Forster's eccentric and/or homosexual characters, the world of fantasy is ultimately incompatible with the social reality of early twentieth-century England, and this is finally reflected in Forster's abandonment of novel writing altogether.

ASPECTS OF FANTASY

Attempting to speak of Forster's theory of the novel generates problems and ironies because Forster eschewed attempts to universalize the process of novel writing and had limited respect for the act of criticism. His resistance notwithstanding, Forster loosely articulates such a theory in *Aspects of the Novel*, first presented as a series of lectures that were "informal, indeed talkative, in their tone" (*Aspects*, "Note"). Its approach is familiar and anecdotal, much like Woolf's *A Room of One's Own*, but Forster's analytic "method" differs sharply from that of his peers. In contrast to both Woolf and Lawrence, Forster was "deliberately anti-historical" because he had a limited background in the area of literary tradition (Colmer, *EMF* 175), and he genuinely believed the maxim, "History develops, Art stands still" (*Aspects* 21).[10]

Adopting a synchronic method (which Woolf directly critiques in her review), Forster invites his readers to "visualize the English novelists . . . seated together in . . . a sort of British Museum reading-room—all writing their novels simultaneously" (9). Believing that the core of a novelist's art is the timeless force of "inspiration" rather than social or historical conditioning, he juxtaposes passages from novelists of different periods and emphasizes their similarities across the historical divide. It should be noted here, however, that Forster's perspective and selections are not completely ahistorical or gender-blind. Forster recognizes that there was "a close association between fiction in England and that [Women's] movement in the nineteenth century" but, in a move reflecting the discourse of degeneration, finds the assumption that "[a]s women bettered their position, the novel . . . became better too" to be: "Quite wrong." (20). This attitude, along with his minimal appreciation of women's texts in *Aspects*, shows how Forster, "[l]ike many other men of letters in the universities and elsewhere . . . is also concerned to construct a version of the 'tradition' which writes out all but the most exceptional of women" (Pykett, *Engendering* 70).

Forster recognizes the obstacles inherent in a study of the novel, which he describes as an "amorphous" and "formidable mass" that is "one of the moister areas of literature," sometimes resembling a "swamp" or a "spongy tract" (*Aspects* 5–6). (The proliferation of aquatic metaphors—a kind of Irigarayan language before its time—suggests that the novel, which Forster sets off against "History," is a more feminine genre.) Treating all novels on the same level for analysis, Forster arranges his ideas topically and dissects the novel into seven "aspects," a term meaning "both the different ways we can look at a novel and the different ways a novelist can look at his work" (24). These aspects are broken down into two groups:

the first three are easily recognized and shared by most novels ("The Story," "People," and "The Plot"), while the other four are treated in pairs ("Fantasy and Prophecy" and "Pattern and Rhythm") which are defined oppositionally by Forster and do not reside in all novels.[11] An important consideration in appreciating each aspect includes "considering the sort of demand it makes on the reader" (107).

"Fantasy" and "Prophecy" are initially presented in mysterious terms; each is something "more" in the novel "than time or people or logic or any of their derivatives, more even than Fate" but which "includes them, embraces them." Forster's primary metaphor for the function of fantasy or prophecy in a novel is a "bar of light" that "cuts across" the other aspects of the novel and "is intimately connected with them at one place and patiently illumines all their problems, and at another place shoots over or through them as if they did not exist" (106–107). Exhibiting what Forster calls an "intermittent realism" (and thus moving away from conventional Edwardian fiction), fantasy and prophecy serve as illuminators and intensifiers of the material world. The author, writing as a fantasist or prophet, "manipulates a beam of light which occasionally touches the objects so sedulously dusted by the hand of common sense, and renders them more vivid than they can ever be in domesticity" (135). The two aspects operate diametrically in relation to one another, as seen in Forster's image of placing certain novels along "the fantastic-prophetical axis," with novels like *Tristram Shandy* on the "fantastic" end and Herman Melville's *Moby-Dick* on the "prophetic" one (107). Although the image of an axis suggests numerous positions on the "fantastic-prophetical" spectrum and offers the possibility of hybrid forms, the novels Forster considers in these terms are placed at one pole or the other.

A primary distinction between Forster's conception of fantasy and prophecy is on the level of structure, which James McConkey articulates in terms of duality versus unity. Fantasy involves "a double structure; what we see about us is transformed by placing it in operation within another framework," i.e., its "mythology" (McConkey 46), which serves as a "kind of backdrop against which . . . character is placed." By means of this backdrop, the author achieves "a liberation from the phenomenal world," but this involves a "distortion" in which some things, like objects or characters, "will have a value which is not the value imposed by phenomenal reality" (44). The combination of "liberation" and "distortion" allowed by fantasy's doubleness enables Forster to represent the usually repressed and marginalized "reality" of homosexual desire within conventionally heterosexual realist fiction, yielding emotionally and stylistically queer results. Forster contrasts prophecy's singular "accent" or "tone of voice" (*Aspects* 125) with the scattered, almost promiscuous (and queer) quality of fantasy: prophecy's "face is towards unity, whereas fantasy glances about. Its confusion is incidental, whereas fantasy's is fundamental" (136).

Forster also distinguishes prophecy from fantasy in terms of the affective discipline that each requires of both reader and author. "[H]umility and the suspension of the sense of humour" (126) are necessary for the reader to listen to the voice of the prophet, who "has gone 'off' more completely than the fantasist, he is in a remoter emotional state when he composes" (136). In contrast, by virtue of its odd method and subject matter, fantasy "compels us to an adjustment" (108) and its "appeal is specially personal" (111). The sexual suggestiveness and emotional immediacy with which Forster associates fantasy point toward its greater potential as a medium through which to represent homosexual desire.

As for its meta-realist properties, fantasy may involve the supernatural,[12] but never the supranatural, which is the realm of prophecy. As Forster puts it: "The power of fantasy penetrates into every corner of the universe, but not into the forces that govern it . . . and novels of this type have an improvised air, which is the secret of their force and charm" (*Aspects* 110). Among the devices employed in fantasy, Forster includes: "the introduction of a god, ghost, angel, monkey, monster, midget, witch into ordinary life; or the introduction of ordinary men into no man's land, the future, the past, the interior of the earth, the fourth dimension; or divings into and dividings of personality; or finally the device of parody or adaptation" (112). In particular, fantasy's "dividings of personality" are suited to Forster's negotiation of sexual desire and character relations, found especially in his polysexual character triangles. The most famous examples of fantasy novels Forster cites are *Tristram Shandy* and *Ulysses*.

In contrast to the doubleness of fantasy, prophecy is "a tone of voice" that "may imply any of the faiths that have haunted humanity—Christianity, Buddhism, dualism, Satanism, or the mere raising of human love and hatred to such a power that their normal receptacles no longer contain them" (125–126). For McConkey, prophecy is "a bardic quality" which in its mythology "suggests unity, a mingling of physical reality with some universal element," but the mythology "has no artifice about it, no framework which is *arbitrarily* (and hence intellectually) established around the people and the normal world" (46). As examples of prophecy, Forster "can only think of four authors to illustrate it—Dostoevsky, Melville, D. H. Lawrence, and Emily Brontë" (*Aspects* 137), especially in the following novels: *The Brothers Karamazov*, *Moby-Dick*, *Women in Love* and *Wuthering Heights*.

Although fantasy and prophecy are similar in what McConkey calls their "sense of mythology," another distinction between them is found in "the kind of mythology each possesses" (45) or, as Forster puts it, "They are alike in having gods, and unlike in the gods they have." Their difference is essentially a hierarchical one. In a list that is queer in both literary and sexual terms, fantasy invokes "all beings who inhabit the lower air, the shallow water, and the smaller hills, all Fauns and Dryads and slips of the memory, all verbal coincidences, Pans and puns." In contrast, prophecy calls upon "whatever transcends our abilities, even when it is human passion . . . the deities of India, Greece, Scandinavia and Judaea" (*Aspects* 109–110). There is a suggestion here that fantasy is allied with a primitive polytheism whereas prophecy is linked with more institutional religion. Forster's choice to invoke the pagan gods of fantasy in most of his work may be a reflection of his own agnosticism as opposed to the institutional belief systems (which outlaw homosexuality) connected with the gods of prophecy. The difference in mythology may also point toward a difference in form which places prophecy closer to the realist impulse in its engagement of organized or official religion.[13]

As mentioned at the beginning of the chapter, Forster considered fantasy to be largely a female form, but he felt it could sometimes take a male shape. An examination of the Greek gods to whom Forster fittingly appeals in his theory of the novel (Pan, Demeter, and Hermes) helps to illustrate the androgynous and queer qualities of fantasy that are often embodied in his fiction. Among other things, the polysexual aspect of these figures is emblematic of Forster's sexually inclusive utopian vision. First of all, the half-goat, half-god Pan was a reigning force of fantasy in the early Edwardian period. Forster includes a Pan figure in a number of his early stories and novels, usually a member of the lower class who possesses a strong link to nature. Patricia Merivale points out that, in late nineteenth- and early twentieth-century fiction, the qualities of Pan are usually divided "into the beneficent and the terrifying" (134). In Forster's work, these attributes are combined, and Pan's approach "reveals the inner world to those capable of perceiving it, while the representatives of ordinary insensitive humanity are forced to flee in terror" (181). Pan is a strongly male god, and in Forster's work he is identified with the "instinctual man, one who is close to the earth and who thus—like some of D. H. Lawrence's characters—is devoid of hypocrisy and capable of right relations with other men" (McConkey 7).

Pan's identity and purpose is complicated by the fact that his power, as "the guide into a profound mystical experience, which has as concomitants the emotions of terror and ecstasy" (Merivale 180–181), is an intensely sexual power in Forster's fiction.[14] Judith Herz notes that Pan is "a figure of sexual awakening" for Forster ("Narrator" 19), and many critics, from his friend Edward Garnett onward, draw connections between Forster's sexual fears or frustrations and his use of Pan figures for sublimation.[15] Samuel Hynes considers Pan to be "Forster's presiding deity . . . of a homosexual world, or a world in which homosexuality is natural . . . because, in Forster's Sawston-and-Cambridge world, homosexual love could not be a force in itself; it was only by supernatural intervention that direct emotion could find expression" (116–117). The figure of Pan and its ironic double function (in configuring both natural forces and "unnatural" homosexual ones) illustrate the queer confusion of gender and sexuality that emerges in Forster's version of fantasy: Pan paradoxically serves as a marker of manly qualities and a repository of feminized homosexual desire. These apparently contradictory qualities are found in the way Forster, like Lawrence, "often use[s] foreign men, and on occasion feminized, foreign (especially southern European or Mediterranean) men, as [Pan-like] agents of social and psychological renovation" (Pykett, *Engendering* 122).

Further sexual doubling and queerness is evident in Forster's treatment of the goddess Demeter, an Earth-Mother and icon of fertility who, Frederick Crews notes, is "an embodiment, not just of pastoral gaiety, but of suffering and hope, of disappointment and salvation combined" (135). The statue of the Demeter of Cnidus in the British Museum was a kind of idol for Forster, and his reflections on seeing the original in Greece reveal its power of attraction: "Demeter alone among gods has true immortality. . . . to her, all over the world, rise prayers of idolatry from suffering men as well as suffering women, for she has transcended sex" (*Abinger* 176). According to P. N. Furbank, Demeter represented for Forster "the reconciliation of male and female in his own nature" (1: 102), and Herz says that Forster (perhaps as one of those "suffering [homosexual] men") took from Demeter "the special comfort of her double sexuality" ("Narrator" 18).

In Forster's novels the Demeter figure is usually an androgynous, spinsterish character resembling his maiden great aunt, Marianne Thornton, who helped raise him. This character (e.g., Charlotte Bartlett, Ruth Wilcox, and Mrs. Moore) helps bring about fantasy's utopian vision by tolerating difference and uniting characters in love. Besides being an androgynous figure, however, Demeter embodies the largely sublimated sexual concerns in Forster's fiction, reflecting the idea inherited from Walter Pater that "the central myths of Greece which can be re-enacted in modern England are those of Dionysius and Demeter, the priest-consort and the earth-mother; and that what the myths convey, in only barely concealed form, is a homosexual romance" (Martin, "Paterian" 102). Forster's use of Demeter figures reveals an indebtedness to "[t]he mysticism of both the decadents and some of the New Woman writers" in his adoption of "[t]he idea that women have a sacred mission to mother the race, or to rescue it from decline and/or destruction" and his creation of "stories [that] repeatedly enact the renovation of, or escape from, a masculinized bourgeois culture, by means of feminine (or at least not conventionally masculine) forces" (Pykett, *Engendering* 74).

A final god associated with Forster's idea of fantasy is Hermes, "the beautiful young friend and guide" (Herz, "Narrator" 18), whose statue in the British Museum also attracted Forster's attention. Hermes is Forster's queerest god, and he occupies a special position in Forster's theory, as the quotation excerpted at the beginning of this chapter goes on to show: "For Fantasy, though often female, sometimes resembles a man, and even functions for Hermes, who used to do the smaller behests of the gods—messenger, machine-breaker, and conductor of souls to a not-too-terrible hereafter" (*Omnibus* v). Herz argues that, particularly in the early stories,

Hermes serves the function of narrator because "[h]is true space—and the one most frequently evoked in Forster's stories—is the space between worlds" ("Narrator" 20), especially those of love and death or male and female. He assumes the position, in the words of Karl Kerenyi, of a "trickster," one who "operates outside the fixed bounds of custom and law" (185), "the psychopomp, . . . the hoverer-between-worlds who dwells in a world of his own" (189). In a way, Forster himself is a Hermes figure, embodying both masculine and feminine qualities and telling stories on the edge of sexually permissible desire but somehow remaining a detached observer. The emotional conflict of Forster's contradictory position is repeatedly enacted in his novels, especially as embodied in characters like Philip Herriton, Rickie Elliot, and Clive Durham.

Following from his sense of the need for artistic distance, Forster's theory of the creative imagination is portrayed in asexual or metasexual terms, calling to mind Woolf's summons to the woman writer to "unsex" herself for the sake of creation. In an essay extolling "the divine tendency toward anonymity" in literature, Forster presents the imagination in a paradoxical way: it is "the immortal God which should assume flesh for the redemption of mortal passion. . . . our only guide into the world created by words." For Forster, the state of imaginative creation is an anonymous and therefore non- or asexual one: "there are no names down there, no personality as we understand personality, no marrying or giving in marriage" ("Anonymity" 595).

The duality of sex in Forster's theory of fantasy and its link to the imagination also has roots in the homosexual theory of his day. Forster was acquainted with the work of the sexual psychologists Havelock Ellis and John Symonds but was most strongly influenced by ideas of Edward Carpenter, especially in two ways. First of all, he was very familiar with Carpenter's writings on "the intermediate sex," which John Fletcher describes as "a highly idealized account of the homosexual temperament as a synthesis of masculine and feminine attributes" (73). It was Carpenter's idea that their combination of gender qualities made homosexuals more likely to possess the sensitivity and creative imagination of artists, and Forster's character triangles often play out the tensions between such gender qualities. Secondly, Carpenter's theories made a concrete impact on Forster during a visit to Carpenter and his lover George Merrill. At one point, the latter touched Forster's "backside" and, as Forster put it: "The sensation was unusual . . . [and] seemed to go straight through the small of my back into my ideas, without involving my thoughts. If it really did this, it . . . would prove that at that precise moment I had conceived" (*Maurice* 249). Forster attributes the spontaneous creation of *Maurice* to this physical incident. Although Forster's notion that creativity can be transferred through physical contact is dubious at best, homosexual desire is powerfully at work in Forster's literary production, especially in his use of fantasy, as we shall now see in more detail.

WHERE HOMOSEXUALITY FEARS TO TREAD: THE ITALIAN NOVELS

Whereas Forster was unafraid to immerse his characters in the supernatural in early short stories like "The Celestial Omnibus" (which travels on a route to heaven) and "The Curate's Friend" (who is a satyr), each of his novels employs fantasy in a less overt way, suggesting forces that seem mystical or magical rather than actually including incidents which transcend nature's laws. Most of these novels exhibit Forster's strategy to contain the sexual energy in his writing through "the creation of a fantasy landscape . . . the place where one encounters one's true nature, where one is allowed one's real sexual identity" (Herz, "Double" 85). In both *Where Angels Fear to Tread* (1905) and *A Room with a View* (1908), Italy is the exotic and intoxicating locale in which Forster tries to bring about love connections and insights among his muddled, middle-class characters which would be impossible to achieve in their sexually staid and convention-bound England. As Margaret Goscilo puts it, both novels are "queer," in that, Forster, drawing on a tradition of European homoerotic writing since the 1750s, "codes foreignness, and particularly Italianness, to include the tabooed 'Otherness' of homosexuality, displacing onto nationality some of the themes that he tackles directly in *Maurice*" (193). Although *The Longest Journey* (1906) was published between them, in a sense these two novels can be linked together as Forster's earliest because *A Room with a View* had its beginnings in 1902 as the "Lucy novel," his earlier but aborted effort at a longer fiction piece.

Based on observations from Forster's tour of Italy in 1901–1902, his representation of the land and its culture in both novels contains an aura of romance, mystery, and threat that serves to simultaneously attract and repel his English characters and draw them deeper into the "hidden life" (in this case, of romantic love and sexual desire) which Forster describes as the aim of the novel. Its status as a potentially queer site is underlined by Forster's homosocial (and homoerotic) description of socialist Italy as "a delightful place to live in if you happen to be a man" where "the brotherhood of man is a reality" and men might "become as David and Jonathan" (*Angels* 47). Although they are not as fully developed as some of the later novels in terms of plot and characterization, these two "Italian" novels contain hints of fantasy which point to the sexual conflicts of more complex novels like *The Longest Journey* and *A Passage to India*. In each novel I will show how the double plot and character triangles join with the elements of fantasy to problematize the novel's realist and heterosexual conventions. Forster's use of fantasy characters and locales is often fleeting or underdeveloped in these early novels, but they reveal the nascent homosexual desires which are more fully developed in his later work.[16]

The initial plot of *Where Angels Fear to Tread* traces the somewhat conventional pattern of a frustrated, recently widowed Englishwoman, Lilia Theobald, who escapes the constraints of family, class, and country by traveling to romantic Italy, marrying a swarthy dentist's son, Gino Carella, for love and offending her English in-laws in the process. However, the conventional love plot disintegrates as the marriage descends into patriarchy and infidelity and Lilia dies delivering a son. The rest of the novel traces the attempt by Lilia's English in-laws to retrieve the baby and revolves around the bizarre love triangle that is formed among her brother-in-law, Philip Herriton; her friend Caroline Abbott; and Gino. Philip and Caroline are challenged and changed by the strange Italian culture, which they see as barbaric, and the earthy but charismatic Gino, a Pan figure[17] whom they view as a boy in a manly guise. At base, the triangle is a romantic one, albeit unrequited on Gino's part, with both Philip and Caroline falling in love with Gino.

In its representation of this love triangle, Forster negotiates the narrative in a double-sexed and -structured way.[18] The "surface plot" operates on a heterosexual level as Philip becomes attracted to Caroline in their common quest for the baby, only to find that she has fallen for Gino in the process. Difficulties emerge here because of Philip's voyeuristic temperament. As Caroline so aptly tells Philip: "you're without passion; you look on life as a spectacle; you don't enter it; you only find it funny or beautiful" (*Angels* 181). (In many ways, these words capture Forster's own personality, bearing out Bristow's suggestion that one of the male characters in each novel is usually an aesthete like Forster.) In the end, both Philip and Caroline remain unhitched, overturning what could have been a standard comedy denouement and reflecting what John Colmer sees as a primary goal of Forster's literary project: "the ironic juxtaposition of the false values associated with conventional marriage and the true values associated with personal relations" ("Marriage" 118), particularly homosexual ones.

The questions raised by the frustration of the heterosexual love plot cannot be answered without taking into account the novel's "under plot," which operates on a homosexual level that shows Philip's deepest attractions to be directed toward Gino (and toward the violence and amorality that is linked to Gino,[19] i.e., the "terror" side of the Pan figure), although the signs in the text are covert. Philip's initial impression of Gino is that he was "a young man who might eventually prove handsome and well-made" (*Angels* 29), with a face that "was not merely beautiful, but had the charm which is the rightful heritage of all who are born on that soil." However, the issue of class (a source of intense homosexual desire and conflict in all of Forster's work) complicates the attraction, for while Philip enjoys the sight of the brutal Gino's face, he "did not want to see it opposite him at dinner. It was not the face of a gentleman" (31).

Philip's homoerotic passion moves from the visual to the physical in an altercation with Gino that is played out beside Philip's pensione bed as he tries to financially seduce Gino out of the marriage. Their scuffle ends with Gino giving him "an aimless push, which toppled him on to the bed" (39). This violent action initially enrages Philip, but later in the novel he finds himself "suffused with pleasure" at his thoughts of the event (another sign of the sadomasochistic strain in his desire), believing that "romance had come back to Italy; there were no cads in her" (111) because he anticipates an apology from Gino. The final physical consummation, what Goscilo describes as "a high point of passionate release in the book" (199), comes when Philip visits Gino to apologize for stealing the baby. Offering himself as a sacrifice ("You are to do what you like with me" (*Angels* 168)), Philip enters into a struggle with Gino that fluctuates between pain and pleasure, moving from Gino's piercing pinches of Philip's broken arm to Philip's loving efforts, after a blow to Gino, "to raise him up, and [prop] his body against his own . . . filled with pity and tenderness," and finally ending with Gino nearly choking Philip to death in a heated "moment of oblivion" (169–170). The fight is followed with Caroline, who seems to Philip "like a goddess" (172), insisting that both men drink from the pitcher of the baby's milk which she herself does not drink, a ritual of sorts that serves as "a variation on both blood brotherhood and seminal exchange" (Goscilo 199).[20] In an ironic twist, Forster never appreciated the sexual power of this scene until much later, as he stated in 1935: "if my novels were analysed they would reveal a pretty mess. . . . There are things in my earlier stuff which are obvious enough to me now, though less so when I wrote them—e.g. . . . Gino's savaging of Philip in . . . Where Angels" (*Selected Letters* 2: 129).

The doubling of plot in the novel goes hand-in-hand with its triangulation of character, a quality that marks all of Forster's novels in some way. The Caroline/Philip/Gino triangle is Forster's first attempt to work out the tensions of race, class, gender, and sexuality which continue to occupy him throughout his career. In all of his novels, a sexually ambiguous character usually bearing similarities to Forster (in this case, Philip) is attracted to and caught between masculine and feminine qualities personified in two other characters (Gino and Caroline). This love triangle is an example of Eve Kosovsky Sedgwick's theory on the enactment of male homosocial and -sexual desire,[21] but with two twists. In this case, the role usually played by the woman (the apex of the triangle) is split between the two men: Gino is the mutually desired body, making the love competition take place between a man and woman, and Philip is the one torn between two potential lovers, albeit unknowingly. Further complicating the triangle is the fact that Gino differs in both race and class and thus serves as the attractive and repulsive "Other" of English middle-class hetero- and homosexual desire. The lack of a resolution to the triangle other than an admission of attraction by the unrequited parties (naively revealed on Philip's part) shows that Forster had a long way to go in creating a balanced portrait of such split desire (reflecting Forster's own sexual conflicts), a task he handles more adeptly, and with the increased aid of fantasy, in each new novel.

Where Angels Fear to Tread's ambiguous ending complicates Italy's function as a fantasy landscape, undercutting the conventionally held image of its power to generate the magic of heterosexual love, as none of the male-female relationships proves lasting. Initially, Italy is a land of romance, but a very different sense of its atmosphere is represented in Lilia's discovery of the patriarchy of Italian society. This is exemplified in the "delightful luxury" of its Socialism, whose "equality of manners," shared only by men, is "accomplished at the expense of the sisterhood of women" (*Angels* 47). As Alan Wilde puts it, "the passage goes on to envisage the possibility of a relationship between men that is as close as David and Jonathan" ("Depths" 259) because it is free from "feminine criticism and feminine insight and feminine prejudice" (*Angels* 47). This is the first of several instances in which Forster uses the masculine rhetoric of politics, usually represented as some form of "comradeship," to encode homosexual love (just as Lawrence does in several of his novels). It seems that, in this novel, the fantastic locale is not a place for sustaining love between men and women. Forster employs the language of Socialism to articulate a fundamental conflict between male friendship and female presence in Italy, revealing a misogyny in the narrative (most strongly exemplified in the characterization of the shrewish, grasping Harriet) which destroys all possibility of lasting (heterosexual) love and the life it engenders. As we shall now see, Forster enacts a similar threat in *A Room with a View* but with decidedly different results.

From many perspectives, *A Room with a View* is a conventional romance novel of the boy-meets/loses/gets-girl variety. The core relationship of the surface plot is between the two aptly named romantic protagonists: Lucy Honeychurch, a young middle-class Englishwoman with aspirations which stretch her beyond the conventions of her class; and George Emerson, the "ill-bred" son (*Room* 6) of a free-thinking Socialist father of working-class origins. Their romance is enkindled in Italy, torn asunder by Lucy's fear and her initially disapproving female companion, Miss Charlotte Bartlett, and then fulfilled after overcoming various obstacles in England. Although the novel's "queer coding becomes dispersed among four males"—George, Freddy, Cecil and Mr. Beebe (Goscilo 203), the primary challenges to this union come in the attitudes and actions of the latter two effete male characters with ambiguous sexual inclinations (they belong to "the strongly feminine atmosphere" of the novel rather than "the one normally associated with men" (Cavaliero 94)), each of whom is involved in a triangular relationship with Lucy and George. Their effeminate qualities and homosexual desires point toward the under plot operating beneath the main love story, through which Forster (unconsciously) attempts to work out the tensions between hetero- and homosexual desire and once again reveals his favoring of male friendship over marriage.

The most obvious and conventional obstacle to the union of Lucy and George is the existence of a rival for Lucy's affections, Cecil Vyse, her upper-class fiancé who has the approbation of both families for the marriage but who is "an aesthete who sees Lucy as a desirable painting" (Dowling 50). The love triangle on the level of the surface plot is lopsided, however, because Cecil could not be more different from the manly and modern-minded George, setting up another Forsterian aesthete-athlete conflict. Uninterested in sports and games, Cecil is represented as a fop who is awkward at love and more comfortable with a book in hand than a lady. Everyone but Lucy grasps his asexual character: the celibate Reverend Mr. Beebe says that Cecil "is an ideal bachelor. . . . he's like me—better detached" (*Room* 98), and George proclaims that Cecil is "only for an acquaintance" and "should know no one intimately, least of all a woman" (193). In eunuch-like fashion, Cecil cannot stir up passion in Lucy or himself, which ultimately dooms their relationship, and he becomes "cynical" about women in the end.

The more serious threat to Lucy and George's relationship comes through the machinations of the Rev. Mr. Beebe, whose sexual attraction to George sets up an inverted love triangle (similar to the Caroline/Gino/Philip dynamic in *Where Angels Fear to Tread*) and motivates his attempt to sabotage their engagement. Initially, Forster portrays Beebe as an open-minded man who encourages Lucy to live with passion and excitement and blesses her engagement to Cecil, but toward the end of the novel he rejects her when she truly decides to marry George. The crux of this shift in Mr. Beebe's personality is found in the event that precipitates what Herz calls "the collision of [the] two story lines, the surface heterosexual romance and the interior homosexual romance" ("Double" 87): the humorous and revealing all-male bathing scene in the "Twelfth Chapter" of the novel, which Colmer describes as "Forster's attempt to anglicize the Pan motif" (*EMF* 50). Hynes claims that "no physical scene between the lovers is treated as vividly" as this one and finds it "so reminiscent of the pederastic bathing of Victorian homosexual writing and photography" (116).

Inspired by Edward Carpenter's idea of nature as a "crucial force in saving one's body and soul" (Goscilo 204), Forster sets the scene at a pond in the "pine-woods," a lush, fantastic landscape which calls to mind other woodland settings in his short stories and the infamous "greenwood" of *Maurice*, secret places in which male love is explored and celebrated. In *A Room* the underlying dynamic is no different: when Freddy bluntly invites George to "Come and have a bathe," Mr. Beebe says it is "the best conversational opening I've ever heard. But I'm afraid it will only act between men" (*Room* 145). He goes on to give "a thinly disguised plea for homosexual love" that is reminiscent of Walt Whitman (Meyers, *Homosexuality*

92) by proclaiming: "We despise the body less than women do. But not until we are comrades shall we enter the garden [of Eden]" (*Room* 146).

At first Beebe is a voyeur, only watching while the others disrobe and bathe, and in the description of what he sees, the connections between the fantasy setting and homosexual desire are clear. Meyers makes note of the way in which "Forster hellenizes nature to blend with the classical ideal of manly love" (*Homosexuality* 93), using images like "the seeds of the willow-herb dance chorically" and the Pan-like George standing "Michelangelesque on the flooded margin" (*Room* 150) to create an idyllic and erotic tone. Finally giving in to the playful spirit of the moment, Beebe divests himself and enters the pond, engaging in boyish frolics like splashing and racing naked around the pond with Freddy and George until their homoerotic idyll[22] is shattered by the intrusion of the effeminate Cecil and the Honeychurch women, once again revealing the incompatibility of male love and female presence. The narrator sums up what Meyers calls the "enduring influence" of the incident on Mr. Beebe, "ironically described in ecclesiastical imagery" (*Homosexuality* 94): "It had been a call to the blood and to the relaxed will, a passing benediction whose influence did not pass, a holiness, a spell, a momentary chalice for youth" (*Room* 153).

According to Meyers, in this scene "Beebe's latent homosexuality has been released and he has fallen in love with George" (*Homosexuality* 94), which explains Beebe's reactions in the events which follow and demonstrate the "symbolic" conflict "between him and Mr. Emerson over the soul of Lucy" (Herz, "Double" 88). Beebe's sympathies appear anti-romantic when the news of the engagement's termination stirs his "belief in celibacy" and the narrator states that "he never heard that an engagement was broken off but with a slight feeling of pleasure" (*Room* 219). His final uncharitable stance toward Lucy and George (he "will never forgive" or "be interested" in them again (243–244)) undermines his altruistic Christian position of sexual self-denial and reveals it to be driven by more negative forces.[23]

There is an obvious connection between Beebe's (and Cecil's) chastity and his repressed homosexuality and not-so-veiled misogyny. Myers sees Beebe's piety-cloaked stance as reflecting "a fundamental questioning of the value of heterosexual love [that] is recurrent in Forster's works," in which Forster is "essentially sympathetic to Beebe's views" because he is "unwilling or unable [in 1908] to endorse homosexual love directly" and therefore has "to present his views obliquely and ambiguously, to deflect them through a clerical guise" (*Homosexuality* 95 & 99). Forster's treatment of homosexuality is clearly conflicted at this stage in his career: Beebe's cruel, pseudo-Christian stance toward love is a misguided expression of homosexual desire, but the bathing scene provides a brief, positive alternative. It seems to me that, whether consciously or not, Forster best achieves the indirect communication of homosexual love in the novel through his use of a fantasy environment in which all trappings of the official culture (including religion) can be thrown off in a fleeting moment of Pan-like eros, and he develops this environment more fully in his more obviously homoerotic novels.

However one interprets the issue of Forster's position in the novel's debate on passion versus restraint, the novel's use of fantasy is divided, with two different fantastic landscapes yielding two very different atmospheres and experiences of sexual love. In sharp contrast to those of *Where Angels Fear to Tread*, the Italian scenes which frame *A Room with a View* serve as both the originating and the consummating points of the heterosexual romance in the mainstream plot of the novel. Here the fantasy of a lasting love match between a man and woman proves true, ironically accomplished through the Demeter-like ministrations of Miss Bartlett, the original obstacle to the union who comes to see the blessings of the couple's love. Forster does not achieve the final harmony of the novel without cost, however; the other locus of fantasy in the novel, the pine-woods outside suburban England, provides a briefly idyllic but ultimately troubling moment of male comradeship and covert homoerotic love in an under plot which cannot exist in harmony with the surface love story. At this point in his career, Forster's engagement with fantasy has not yet provided a way in which to articulate the "hidden life" of homosexual relationships within a genre which is constructed around the attainment of heterosexual love. In many ways, the tension between his eccentric homosexual subject matter and the conventional ways of the heterosexual romance plot come to a head in what is considered his most problematic (and perhaps his queerest) work, *The Longest Journey*, in which the elements of fantasy are a dominant if confused force.

Fantasy in Conflict: *The Longest Journey*

Reflecting upon *The Longest Journey* some fifty-three years after it was published, Forster described it as "the least popular of my five novels [*Maurice* had not yet been published] but the one I am most glad to have written" because, "in it I have managed to get nearer than elsewhere towards what was in my mind—or rather towards that junction of mind with heart where the creative impulse sparks." Forster goes on to speak of the novel's origin and creative process in what might now be considered queer terms, calling it "the only one of my books that has come upon me without my knowledge." His highly charged language suggests a spontaneity and uninhibited quality that "excited" him and even extended to what might be called inspired mistakes: "sometimes I went wrong deliberately, as if the spirit of anti-literature had jogged my elbow" ("Aspect" 1228).[24] These comments are both telling and ironic because, despite Forster's pride in the novel, it is probably the one which has received the most negative assessment by critics as being over-ambitious, confused, and lacking in authorial distance, yet even those who find fault with the novel's structural qualities are usually drawn in by its unique spirit.[25] Forster's own words reveal the paradoxical nature of the book in relation to his conflicted sexuality. Because he had not personally achieved "that junction of mind with heart where the creative spark speaks," the novel embodies, in both form and matter, the split characteristics and tensions of its creator's struggles and serves as possibly the best example of the connection between Forster's use of fantasy and the homosexual spirit behind it.

Symptomatic of the novel's structural troubles and queerness, its plot is schematic yet confusing. On the surface, the novel operates as a kind of *Bildungsroman*, tracing the "lame" (5) and "effeminate" (87) Ricky Elliot's entry into manhood. It begins with his naive undergraduate days, moves through an ill-advised marriage and disastrous teaching and writing career, and ends with a reconciliation with his newly discovered half-brother and a tragic yet heroic premature death. Reinforcing the progress of the plot, the significant stages of Ricky's life are programmatically set in three sharply contrasting locales (the intellectual and homophilic halls of Cambridge, the domestic and repressive suburb of Sawston, and the fantastic and passionate site of Wiltshire), each of which represents a different social, philosophical, and emotional position that Ricky adopts in an attempt to locate his true identity and achieve balance (between head, heart, and imagination) in his life.[26]

The presence of an under plot in which Ricky struggles with but never becomes conscious of (and therefore never settles) his homosexual feelings strongly complicates the surface action and overtly expressed themes of the novel. Rickie's obsession with creating a stable family, first through heterosexual union with Agnes and then through half-blood brotherhood with Stephen, is undermined by his homosexual desires. As a result, the significant love triangle is found not in the apparently heterosexual relations of Rickie; his future wife, Agnes; and her first love, Gerald; but in the suppressed homosexual links among Rickie; his aesthetic classmate, Ansell (drawn from Forster's own homophilic relationship with Hugh Meredith); and the athletic Gerald, who is later replaced by Rickie's equally masculine half-brother, Stephen.

Although its story takes place completely in England, *The Longest Journey* resembles the Italian novels in that Forster employs the devices of fantasy in several ways to register the desires and tensions of the novel's homosexual underside. First of all, they appear in Rickie's perception of those he loves most as deities participating in a world of romance that he feels incapable of sharing because of his deformity, a clubfoot that is emblematic of his homosexuality.[27] Secondly, two of the novel's primary locations are steeped in an atmosphere of fantasy, and they function for Rickie and Stephen as sites of liberation from society's expectations of their manhood and places in which male bonding can occur. Finally, in a self-reflexive movement, a number of striking parallels to Forster's early career and personal relations emerge in the novel as it traces the progress of Rickie's

Pursuing (a) Fantasy

writing (largely in the mode of fantasy) which mirrors his emotional and sexual struggles.

Several of the characters, while presented primarily in a realistic vein, take on the queer qualities of the "lesser gods" of fantasy in Rickie's (and the narrator's) perception of them, and the distance set between them and him is a primary obstacle to Rickie's achieving psychosexual maturity. Central to Rickie's pantheon is his Demeter-like mother, Mrs. Elliot, the victim of a loveless marriage and premature death whom Rickie "worshipped" and for whom he held an unwavering sympathy despite the fact that "[s]he was afraid of intimacy" and "held her son at a little distance" (*Longest* 26). Mrs. Elliot's spirit hovers over the novel and is embodied in a tattered picture of Demeter hanging in Stephen's bedroom.

Forster's linking Mrs. Elliot to a goddess of the earth and human fertility generates a couple of ironies that are tied to Rickie's physical deformity and, by extension, his status as what would then be called an "invert." First of all, of her progeny, the illegitimate one (Stephen) is healthy and able to continue the maternal family line while the legitimate son is crippled and can only pass on the deadly deformity of his paternity. Secondly, Rickie's attraction to his mother as a figure of health and potency rests in his own lack of wholeness and vitality and is further explained by Forster's description of "the people who love" Demeter as all "so weak-chested and anaemic and feeble-kneed" (*Abinger* 176). Fantasy operates here in a more psychologically developed way than in his earlier work (and Forster gets closer to expressing his own personal desires) as the novel revolves around Rickie's need to make peace with the unhealthy images and influences of his childhood, one of which is this idealized image of his mother. Much of his turmoil emerges from futile attempts to recover the lost mother, first in his creation of a new family romance with Gerald and Agnes, and then in his quest to "cure" Stephen of his drinking problem.

Rickie's fantasies about life and love blossom in his perception of Gerald and Agnes, in whose union he gets entwined through his conflicted attraction toward both parties, whom he exalts in divine terms. The rugby-playing Gerald, the novel's first Pan figure,[28] is the primary object of Rickie's attention in his adolescent days. From Rickie's viewpoint, Gerald has "the figure of a Greek athlete and the face of an English one. . . . Just where he began to be beautiful the clothes started" (*Longest* 37). This physical allure is complicated by the "shadow" of their previous relationship as "[t]he bully and the victim" (41) in their public school days when Gerald tortured Rickie. Crews notes the "spirit of masochism" of Rickie's feelings for Gerald and his brutal treatment (similar to Philip's attraction to the violent Gino in *Where Angels*), a dynamic which is transferred to Agnes and her bullying in their marriage (134–135).

At the heart of Rickie's fantastic view of Gerald and Agnes is a scene in which he stumbles upon them in the "lovers' bower" of the garden (38) "locked in each other's arms" and becomes transfixed by "the sight burnt into his brain" (42). This voyeuristic moment (in which Rickie, as if assuming Agnes's position in the embrace, focuses primarily on Gerald's action) later takes on the qualities of a heavenly vision, having "invaded his being and lit lamps at unsuspected shrines." As Rickie limps away from the scene, he stores the image of this "priest and high priestess" who "had got into heaven" in his memory as an encounter with divinity (43–44). As Martin notes, "Rickie's response to the scene and his own voyeurism . . . is to propose marriage—to *both* Gerald and Agnes" by offering them the money they need to get started ("Umbrella" 261–262). Even the usually obtuse Gerald sees this as inappropriate: "I can't stand unhealthiness. . . . Did you ever hear such blasted cheek? Marry us—he, you and me" (*Longest* 53).

Rickie continues his process of deifying Gerald and Agnes (and deflecting his homosexual desires) after Gerald's sudden death at a rugby match. Turning the holy embrace into a monument of "Love" which can never be equaled, Rickie uses it as a source for his writing, further blurring the lines between reality and fantasy. As the text puts it, in writing a new story inspired by the severed couple, Rickie "deflected his enthusiasms" for the "gods and heroes" of his stories and "transfigured a man who was dead and a woman who was still alive" (65). Projecting his attraction to Gerald into a call to emulate his heterosexuality, Rickie convinces himself that he is in love with Agnes. The link between Rickie's fantasy and his homosexual desires is evident in the hopeless way he calls up a memory of Gerald and Agnes's embrace to prod his passion but is uncomfortable with putting himself in Gerald's position: ". . . [Rickie] dreamt that she lay in his arms. This displeased him. He determined to think a little about Gerald instead" (71). Rickie's inability to take up the role of the heterosexual lover is later revealed in his unsettled married life with Agnes and his inability to sire a healthy child.

In the second half of the novel, Rickie's desires are transferred to a much safer character endowed with mythic and fantastic significance, his half-brother, Stephen Wonham, "the Pan-like figure so frequently encountered by the hero once he has passed over the threshold into the world of his adventure" (Thomson 135). A "powerful boy of twenty, admirably muscular" (*Longest* 94), Stephen is frequently represented as a creature of the earth. His expulsion from public school for stealing and his scapegrace existence on his aunt's Wiltshire farm underline his resistance to civilizing influences. In the published version of the novel, Stephen's links to Pan are evident in his frequent raucous exploits in the Wiltshire countryside, but his identification with the nature god is most obvious in what Forster called "a long fantasy chapter" which he "cancelled" from the final version of the novel.[29]

Upon discovering that Stephen is his half-brother, Rickie sees him as "a person . . . that is symbolical" and "stands for some eternal principle" (149), and believes that he can accept life by embracing and rehabilitating

Stephen. Even after Rickie realizes that Stephen is the bastard child of his mother rather than his father, he insists on "sentimentalizing him into a symbol of his mother" (Rahman 59). In a sense, both Rickie and Stephen serve as Dionysian figures, lost children of their mother Demeter, a connection Forster most likely adopted from Walter Pater. As Martin sees it, in the novel "the mourning mother goddess" is "comforted by the return to her of Rickie/Dionysus, whose death in turn frees Stephen to assume his role as the new child, the summer Dionysus" ("Paterian" 108). This revitalization is furthered by Stephen's siring of a girl child who is named after her grandmother, thus completing the circle of the maternal. Finally, Rickie himself is somewhat symbolical or mythological in the way he serves as a Hermes figure, both as a go-between in relation to Gerald and Agnes and in his writing projects, which attempt to convey a message of love but from a detached observer's position, delivered in denial of his sexual feelings.

Forster develops the relations among these queer quasi-fantastic figures against the backdrop of a few settings that are imbued with magical or mythical overtones, which also reflect Forster's struggles with gender identity and sexual desire. Besides being places of enchantment, they are the only sites where Rickie's primary desires, i.e., male companionship and making peace with his past, can be fulfilled. The first of these is "a secluded dell" outside of Cambridge which Rickie discovers in "the brief season of its romance . . . its divine interval between the bareness of boyhood and the stuffiness of age." This "holy" and expansive site on the edges of that time (late adolescence) and place (tradition-bound Cambridge) in which English manhood is formed becomes a sanctuary for Rickie, "a kind of church . . . where indeed you could do anything you liked, but where anything you did would be transfigured." Similar to a dell near Forster's childhood home, Rooksnest, the dell is a haven where Rickie brings his male friends and even "people whom he did not like" as he tries to "attain the intimate spirit of the dell" (*Longest* 19–20).

Two incidents that serve as omens of his adult life occur in the dell. In the first, Rickie has a confabulation with Ansell and two other aesthetic Cambridge classmates. Rickie is accused of "trying to destroy friendship" among his aesthete friends in his Carpenterian attempts to foster fraternity (and fulfill an unconscious sexual need) by linking them with "the beefy set" (21) of rowers at Cambridge. In the heat of the argument, as Rickie asserts his inability to hate anyone, his friends bring up the sensitive topic of his feelings toward his father. At this disruptive moment, the sight of the sun striking "the white ramparts of the dell" gives Rickie the inspiration to tell the story of his home life, a tale of "great loneliness" which reveals the background of his conflicted emotional and sexual state. His psychologically stereotypical account of a "weakly and lame" father and a "beautiful" and "dignified" mother trapped in a loveless marriage that ends in illness and premature death highlights Rickie's need for a male figure in his life. Bereft of his parents' affections, he is tortured by the seemingly hopeless question, "Shall I ever have a friend?" and the knowledge that he shall never have a brother (23–26). Only in the magical, therapeutic space of the dell, among a coterie of male companions, does Rickie have the freedom and courage to share his inmost homophilic feelings and experience some of the affection he has lacked. Tellingly, Ansell's assessment of Rickie's behavior in the dell is that he "had been rather queer" (22).

The other significant encounter in the dell is a violation of its sacred homophilic space that foretells Rickie's doomed marriage. On a country walk with Agnes while discussing his writing, Rickie offers to show her the dell, the inspiration for his Dryad story. However, as he approaches the dell and feels the "quiver in its enchanted air," Rickie finds it "too beautiful" and "perilous" and passes by it because he "dared not enter it with such a woman" (79). A seductive tug-of-war ensues, as the strong-willed Agnes goes in and calls his name "with the tones of an angel" to follow her, while Rickie resists the "devil" in her cry and invokes the name of Gerald to ward off her allure. Lacking a "sign" from Gerald's spirit, Rickie finally enters and places his head on Agnes's lap "for a moment before he went out to die." A queer admission comes when Rickie, in response to Agnes's playful suggestion that he hoped she had become a Dryad, says, "I prayed you might not be a woman" (80). Ending with a kiss and Rickie's desperate reminder of Agnes's transcendent love for Gerald (which gives her a "sense of something abnormal" (81)), the scene marks the intrusion of a woman and the threat of heterosexual love in a place that Rickie has invested with his desires for male companionship and love, portending the ill-fated marriage which follows.

A second important fantasy site in the novel is Wiltshire,[30] where Rickie has a final chance for personal integration and happiness. Traversed by a river named "Cad" and a "great wood" that looks as if it "needed shaving" (137), the manly seeming Wiltshire embodies "the redemptive influence of earth" (McDowell 78) and represents the last hope and bastion for the survival of England's spirit. The centrality of this locale signals a shift in Forster's fiction away from Italy as the primary site for the fulfillment of fantasy. As the narrator, describing Rickie's panoramic view of the area from the apex of the Cadbury Rings, states: "Here is the heart of our island.... The fibres of England unite in Wiltshire, and did we condescend to worship her, here we should erect our national shrine." In Rickie's mind, Wiltshire is set in contrast to the "spiritual fatherland" of Italy, which he conceives of "as something exotic, to be admired and reverenced, but not to be loved like these unostentatious fields" (*Longest* 137–138).[31]

The heart of Wiltshire and the spiritual center of the novel is the Cadbury Rings, "a double circle of entrenchments" (105) erected in the pre-Christian era that pale in comparison to Britain's more famous pagan sites like Old Sarum yet command an impressive view of the area. Like the dell, the Rings are the fantastic site of two key scenes in the novel, this time marking the progress of Rickie's relationship with his half-brother Stephen, the spiritual child of the Rings. Rickie's first visit to the site unleashes its significance as a place of mysterious power and male union. While reading a passage from Shelley's *Epipsychidion* (a favorite poem from his Cambridge days, and the inspiration for the novel's title, that speaks out against embarking upon "the dreariest and the longest journey" of marriage), Rickie's reverie is disturbed by the appearance of Mrs. Failing (his aunt) and Agnes, with Stephen in tow. Initially deaf to Mrs. Failing's cryptic allusions to Stephen as Rickie's half-brother, he finally appreciates her revelation at the center point of the shrine, while "gazing at the past" which "gaped ever wider, like an unhallowed grave . . . encircled him," and led him to "faint among the dead." Upon his recovery, Rickie responds with "a cry, not of horror but of acceptance" and calls out to Stephen, but Agnes rushes in to block their union (142–143). The conflict articulated in the poem takes flesh here, as Rickie cannot make a connection with his brother and achieve his ideal of same-sex friendship until the obstacle of his exclusive heterosexual bond is removed.

The second mysterious incident in Wiltshire occurs during Rickie's exodus to the environs of the Rings after he rejects his nightmarish heterosexual existence in Sawston, and it enables him to come as close as possible to fulfilling his unconscious homosexual desires. Once he learns that Stephen is the bastard child of his revered mother rather than his loathed father, Rickie abandons his marriage and returns to Wiltshire. He does so in hopes of establishing the comradeship that was lacking in his marriage by residing with Stephen in the countryside and curing him of his drinking problem. Stephen, recognizing Rickie's action as an attempt to restore his mother's reputation and use himself as "a symbol for the vanished past" (274), rejects this domestic arrangement and invites Rickie to join him on the road in a non-familial relationship, "as a man . . . not as a brother" (276). Stephen's unconventional invitation points up the numerous contradictions inherent in this queer text and leads to its conflicted resolution. Nelson shows that, this attempt at an alternative bond notwithstanding, "Forster displaces the homoerotic elements of their 'friendship' by making them half brothers and thus eliminates the possibility of Rickie's ultimate self-understanding" (319) and any earthly connection between them. The result is the novel's overdetermined heroic ending, in which Rickie sacrifices his life (and gets his crippled leg removed in the process) by rescuing the drunken Stephen from on oncoming train, leaving him to carry on the maternal line and benefit from Rickie's posthumous literary success.[32]

A final connection between fantasy and homosexual desire in the novel emerges in the representation of Rickie's writing career, which in some ways mirrors Forster's own. Forster was writing the novel on the heel of his early short stories, many of which are fantasies that include a great deal of "allegorical classicism" (Crews 68). What initially seems to be a self-reflexive critique of Forster's own early career and inexperience, however, becomes more complicated as Rickie's literary project and financial success are tied to his pursuit of heterosexual subject matter and realistic form in his fiction. Some of the queerest and most contradictory moments in the novel appear as, on one the hand, Forster links the limitations of Rickie's fantastic short stories to his inexperience in life and love (which Forster himself shared) and, on the other hand, he allows Rickie a measure of success only after enduring a loveless marriage, a failure to propagate, and a tragic death. It seems that Forster has written Rickie into a corner: unable to admit and pursue his homosexual desires and unsuccessful at channeling them into fantasy, Rickie is also prevented from reaping the rewards of a heterosexual union and mainstream literary career. (The frustration of plot and characterization here is possibly an indicator of Forster's own sense of sexual paralysis in this period, during which he struggled with his own unexpressed erotic desires for his beloved friend Syed Ross Masood.)

Rickie's first attempts at fiction consist of "trying to write little stories," that he calls "[s]illy nonsense" and "bad" because the events in them "can't happen" (*Longest* 15 & 77).[33] Further suggesting an autobiographical connection, among these fantastic tales is a story like Forster's "Other Kingdom," in which "a lovely young lady" turns into a Dryad in order to escape her engagement to a "vulgar man" and live in "[f]reedom and truth" (77). The story also has parallels to Forster's homoerotically charged tale, "The Story of a Panic," which recounts how an effeminate young Englishman, Eustace, is liberated through what the narrator calls a "promiscuous intimacy" (*Omnibus* 22) with the Pan-like fisher-lad, Gennaro. Rickie eventually amasses a "pile of little stories," as he puts it, "all harping on this ridiculous idea of getting into touch with Nature" (*Longest* 78), which he hopes to publish in a collection aptly called *Pan Pipes*.

Rickie's writing career soon takes a wayward course that is caught up in his rival relationships with Agnes and Stephen and reflects his conflicted sexual desires. His early writing is dominated by Agnes who, driven by ambition, fails to appreciate Rickie's aesthetic concerns (and the desires which inspire his fantasies) and constantly pressures him to "make something" of his talents ("I want you to plunge") in his writing, expressing things "plainly" or "people might miss the point" (78–79). (Note the phallic, heterosexual imagery Forster uses here and its link to simpler, realistic prose.) Her ignorance is evident in her flattening of one of his tales into a "neat little resume": "Allegory. Man = modern civilization (in bad sense). Girl = getting into touch with Nature" (131). In the midst of his married life at Sawston, Rickie has "a curious breakdown" and spends a period of time "partly in bed . . . partly in the attempt to get his little stories published" (153). However, an editor finds that Rickie's work "does not convince as a whole" (157) because he has not seen enough of life. There is an underlying incompatibility between Rickie's homoerotically inspired fiction and his heterosexual milieu, to which Forster adds a further ironic twist: Rickie considers a trip to the fantasy land of Italy or Greece because "[p]erhaps life would be there" and he could "be delivered from the shadow of unreality that had begun to darken the world" (165) since his marriage.[34]

By turning to an emotional relationship with Stephen and changing his lifestyle and fiction style, Rickie approaches emotional peace and literary success, but this too operates in a paradoxical way. The uneducated but instinctual Stephen has a much more accurate sense of Rickie's early work, labeling the Dryad story as "a production" and "cant" and letting it "fall into the gutter" as he falls asleep while reading it (131). Freed from the constraints of his hellish marriage and suburban life, and surrounded by the companionship of Stephen and the Wiltshire countryside, Rickie finally pursues in his writings the "enthusiasms" which first inspired him in the snatched glimpse of Gerald and Agnes's embrace. The result is a "long story... [a]bout a man and a woman who meet and are happy" (296) that is also inspired by his mother's affair with her earthy, lower-class lover Robert. However, Rickie's shift to a more realistic and heterosexual mode in his writing yields a work that is still a fantasy; it is a product of his imagination rather than his lived experience because his own attempt at heterosexual love was a "catastrophe" (296). Mrs. Failing underlines the paradox of the relationship between Rickie's life and his writing: "so you are abandoning marriage and taking to literature. And are happy" (297).

The queerness of the novel erupts as its final scenes pile contradiction after contradiction that violates the conventional norms of the optimistic (and heterosexist) realist ending. Rickie's escape from an unsuitable marriage and pursuit of a male friendship with his half-brother are prerequisites for his writing successfully about a heterosexual love affair. However, Rickie cannot share the happiness of his story's ending: publication and financial success only come posthumously and incongruously. Although previously labeled a failure, his collection of stories becomes marketable for a few contrary reasons, first of all, in light of Rickie's heroic, masculinizing death and a biographical "introduction" filled with "wrong details" about his life (305). Further aiding the sale is the erasure of Rickie's male muse: although Stephen has played an instrumental role in Rickie's work, Agnes's brother "crossed out the dedication" to Stephen and "tidied" him "out of the introduction" (307). In a final ironic twist, a change in literary fashion makes the publishing of the once scorned *Pan Pipes* a guaranteed seller, providing a delayed reward for Rickie's repression (and perhaps some wish fulfillment for Forster in his own career—his first collection of short stories, *The Celestial Omnibus*, was to come out four years later).

Poetic justice seems to triumph in the end as Stephen becomes the primary beneficiary of Rickie's financial success and settles into domestic bliss, but there is something unsettling about the details of this "happy" heterosexual ending that sees Stephen's monetary gain coming in tandem with his settling down to a domestic life with a (glaringly invisible) wife and child. The final tableau of the novel (which has Stephen looking out toward the Rings, saluting his daughter and contemplating how Rickie has "bequeathed him salvation" (311)) implies a healthy continuation of the family in Stephen's marriage and the naming of his daughter after his mother. However, the relegation of Rickie to death and Stephen's wife to the sidelines (she is represented as "a pleasant voice" offstage (309)) has both homophobic and misogynist overtones and seems to obliterate all sexual relations by the end of the novel. The sexual conflict of the novel ends in a situation in which neither homophilic nor heterosexual desire is allowed a central place.

Forster's representation of the relationship of life and art appears inconsistent here. Despite its flukish success at the end of the novel, the use of fantasy as a literary genre and outlet for constrained homosexual desire seems outmoded and ill-fated in light of conventional (i.e., realistic and heterosexual) form and subject matter. Yet the novel's artist figure, who attempts both literary styles, is a physically and emotionally crippled homophile that must die in order to succeed at either. To add a final paradox, this mixed message is itself enclosed within a novel that employs the devices of fantasy to represent the failure of heterosexual love and the fatality of homosexual desire. All in all, Forster has created a very queer text in which the norms of Edwardian realist fiction fail to hold together and a stable conclusion is impossible.

The contortions of the novel's ending clearly indicate Forster's continued conflict in representing sexual desire, so perhaps it is understandable that he turned back at this point in his career to finish his "Lucy" novel. Completing *A Room with a View* gave Forster a chance to return to a "bright and merry" story with a happy heterosexual ending that he felt would "gratify the home circle" (Furbank 1: 154 & 165). His next novel, *Howards End*, appears to follow the same safe heterosexual path as *A Room* but, as we shall see, its final destination is far from the sexual confusion of *The Longest Journey*. In a sense, Forster transforms Rickie's unconscious quest to write fantasy fiction that expresses homosexual desire into Margaret Schlegel's conscious crusade to unite the "prose" of English utilitarianism with the "passion" of German idealism, yielding Forster's most sexually tolerant vision ever.

Fantasy Rerouted: *Howards End*

Unaware of *Maurice*, critics writing before 1970 located the final chapters and the apex of Forster's career as a novelist in the publication of *Howards End* (1910) and *A Passage to India* (1924). Most of these critics pair the two novels together as exemplifying a substantial turn in Forster's work to deeper reflection on the psychological and political aspects of personal relations. McConkey sees the shift as one which reflects the order of Forster's *Aspects*: "Fantasy, largely artifice, inclines toward prankishness and does not require the voice of prophecy, nor nearly so extensive a vision; and as might be presumed, Forster's progression is from fantasy toward prophecy" (48). The presumption of a clearly demarcated movement in Forster's novels that parallels his theory is a reductive one because, while both *Howards End* and *A Passage to India* seem more concerned with the "universal" view of prophecy, they also contain elements of fantasy that are more than holdovers from a previous phase of Forster's career.

Forster intended *Howards End* to be his "condition of England" novel and, therefore, broader in scope and more realist in its subject matter than his earlier love tales, but it still conjures up the spirit and elements of fantasy in service of its goals. Although these aspects of the novel are difficult to trace directly to homosexuality,[35] they contribute to a final vision that is probably Forster's most optimistic and sexually accepting.[36] Also, as Bakshi points out, although the novel "does not encompass relations between men, the effect of the author's discourse on personal relations . . . is to modify and de-centre the primacy of heterosexual love" (156).

Largely following the path and style of realist fiction, *Howards End* tells the tale of Margaret's movement toward integrating reason and emotion through a union of the Wilcox and Schlegel families. Unlike previous novels, it contains no apparent under plot and its "love" triangle, if it can be called that, seems more philosophical or metaphysical than physical, with Margaret poised between and attempting to reconcile the values (and genders) represented by her husband Henry and her sister Helen. In addition, Bakshi notes the operation of a Sedgwickian homosocial triangle forming as "Margaret's strong defence of Leonard [Bast] excites Mr. Wilcox" (167). However, the novel still contains characters and settings that are clear descendants of Forster's earlier fantasies. The relative paucity of fantastic elements as compared to *The Longest Journey* reflects Forster's characterization of the fading of the previous age, in which, "The Earth as an artistic cult has had its day, and . . . [o]f Pan and the elemental forces, the public has heard a little too much" (*Howards* 108). *Howards End* depicts the last gasp of what Forster sees as England's halcyon days and "the strange degenerative disease of modern English life" through the portrayal of "a divided society whose problems are represented . . . in terms of gender imbalance and a polarization and/or confusion of conventional gender roles" (Pykett, *Engendering* 117–118). The novel's remnants of fantasy, particularly the house itself, contribute to Forster's pan-gendered attempt to create a prose that includes all manner of passion.

The guiding spirit of the novel is embodied in the person of Mrs. Ruth Wilcox, the proprietress and spirit of Howards End who functions as a Demeter figure, understanding all the characters and reconciling the sexes after her death much in the same way as the divinized Mrs. Moore does in *A Passage to India*. According to McConkey, both figures "suggest the potentialities of the feminine spirit" and "elude not only all dimensional categorization but the distinction of sex itself, existing . . . more as wisps of spirit than as corporeal substance" (29–30). Forster represents Mrs.

Wilcox as an Earth-Mother (Thomson 192), walking through garden and meadow, her long dress trailing over the grass and her hands full of hay, and he sets her off in direct contrast to the men of the novel who have hay fever (Finkelstein 101). Identified with Howards End from the start, Mrs. Wilcox seems "to belong not to the young people and their motor, but to the house, and to the tree that overshadowed it," and possesses "the instinctive wisdom the past can alone bestow" (*Howards* 22). In her reconciliation with Helen, Margaret comes to appreciate Mrs. Wilcox's omniscient, goddess-like quality: "I feel that you and I and Henry are only fragments of that woman's mind. She knows everything. She is everything" (313). This unifying spirit, representing "a sort of female priesthood" that includes the "role of mothering and saving the race" (Pykett, *Engendering* 121), is gradually transferred to Margaret through her marriage to Henry and her eventual inheritance of Howards End.

Functioning as an even more obvious fantasy element in the novel is the house itself, which is the privileged site around which the plot and its characters gradually circle in a centripetal pattern. An old farmhouse located on the edge of the rapidly approaching London suburbs, Howards End stands in sharp contrast to the two primary city dwellings of the novel, Wickham Place, the "female house" of the idealistic and artistic Schlegel sisters and their effeminate brother, and Ducie Street, the "irrevocably masculine" residence of the practical and materialistic Wilcoxes (*Howards* 44). Representing a space apart from these single-sexed domiciles, Howards End has an androgynous air about it that is most clearly represented in its relation to the mystical wych-elm tree which overhangs it and serves as "a symbol of the promise which the past holds for the present . . . [and of man's] relation through the mysterious natural flux to all time and to divinity" (McConkey 128). Embedded with pigs' teeth that are believed to "cure the toothache" (71–72), the wych-elm possesses a "peculiar glory" which, by means of its embrace with Howards End, both combines and rises above gender. Margaret sees this upon her first visit to the house: "It was a comrade, bending over the house, strength and adventure in its roots, but in its utmost fingers tenderness. . . . House and tree transcended any similes of sex. . . . to compare either to man, to woman, always dwarfed the vision" (*Howards* 206). The sexually ambiguous character of the house is further underlined in the Wilcoxes' rejection of the house after Mrs. Wilcox's death (Finkelstein 113) because, as Henry puts it, "we feel that it is neither one thing nor the other" (*Howards* 136). Howards End represents more than a union of sexes or genders, however; it is also "the single emblem for Forster's ideal of harmony between the spiritual and the physical" (Crews 112).

A final space of fantasy in the novel is the area of Six Hills, "six Danish tumuli that stood shoulder to shoulder along the highroad, tombs of soldiers" (*Howards* 15),[37] which overlooks Howards End and operates (like the Cadbury Rings in *The Longest Journey*) as the setting for two climactic

Pursuing (a) Fantasy 53

and fantastic moments. Observed from afar throughout the novel, these "[c]urious mounds" (204) are the backdrop for the scene in which Margaret asks Henry to finally "connect" by allowing herself and the pregnant Helen to stay one night at Howards End before she returns to her self-imposed exile on the Continent. Throughout this tense scene Margaret deliberately stands in view of Six Hills, as if they provide her with the inspiration she needs to call upon Henry's sense of compassion as she compares his past infidelity with Helen's sexual indiscretion. After her entreaties fail, Margaret briefly seeks succor from "the Six Hills, tombs of soldiers, breasts of the spring" (309), which are "suggestive of her soldier father, of the earth, of the past, of the unseen, and of androgyny" (Summers 133).

Only toward the very end of the novel are the hills physically broached, when Margaret and Henry sit upon their ground to discuss their future after the crisis of Leonard's death. On this spot Henry reveals Charles's impending trial for manslaughter, in reaction to which, "Margaret drove her fingers through the grass. The hill beneath her moved as if it was alive." The consequent emotional breakdown on Henry's part, after which "a new life began to move" (*Howards* 334) for Margaret and Henry, seems to emerge from the power of the Six Hills to draw things together and leads to the novel's ambiguous conclusion.

The pastoral scene at Howards End which closes the novel contains a utopian vision in which the forces of "prose" and "passion" are finally connected by Margaret. In the wake of Henry's breakdown, Margaret takes him "to recruit at Howards End" (334), along with the pregnant Helen. The novel's final tableau occurs fourteen months later on a lush June day during the cutting of the meadow, presenting, on one level, an apparent reconciliation of class and gender. Helen has delivered her baby, whom one critic calls a "Blakean child" (McDowell 85), the offspring of lower and upper classes who makes fast friends with the local farmer's boy and is, in sharp contrast to his male relatives, comfortable playing in the hay. Hearkening back to the infants in *Where Angels Fear to Tread* and *The Longest Journey*, the baby is a symbol of the union of forces which Forster has set in opposition throughout the novel,[38] male and female, upper and lower class, past and present, city and country, etc.

The baby's function as harmonizer notwithstanding, there is a way in which the final androgynous reconciliation is undercut in favor of a single-sex vision which, uncharacteristically for Forster, is a female one.[39] Aside from the baby, all of the significant males in the novel have been either eliminated or marginalized: Leonard has been killed off, Charles is in prison, Tibby is pursuing his aesthetic ideal at Oxford, and Henry is quarantined in the house because of his hay fever. In the end, only Margaret and Helen have really been able to "connect," a process which begins with their taking over Howards End for a night together, turning it into a "feminine sanctuary" and amusing themselves "over the masculine spoliations of the past" (Stone 265). As Barbara Rosecrance puts it, the "eclipse of Margaret and Henry by Margaret and Helen" shows how the novel "takes its impetus from the failure of a heterosexual relationship and finds vindication in the success of a single-sex one" (120).[40] To this end, the baby can be seen as the result of "a search on Forster's part for a queer kind of begetting that can lead to the construction of a queer 'family'" (Martin, "Umbrella" 272).

While many read this scene as a feminist triumph, Stone believes that the bonding of Margaret and Helen at Howards End suggests something much deeper: "The only convincing love scene in the book is that between Margaret and Helen, alone at last, exchanging endearments in the temple from which men have been excluded. It is almost incestuous, a love that has cast off all connections except those within the family—and with God's representative, Ruth Wilcox" (Stone 265). Although the atmosphere surrounding Howards End is configured as a metasexual one, the fact that the strongest bonds at the end of the novel are single-sexed ones suggests that Forster's concerns are still very much within the realm of the sexual. The language of comradeship throughout the novel calls for a transcending of sexual boundaries, yet the same kind of language functions as code in the homoerotic subtexts of his earlier novels, as well as in the novels to come. Although he has switched sexes here, on one level Forster is still constructing a homosexual idyll. As Charu Malik notes, "*The Longest Journey*, *Howards End*, and *Maurice* all struggle for heirs of same-sex lovers who would inherit the earth, inherit England. And all resort to fantasy to achieve this end" (229–230).

Ultimately, Forster's achievement of a sexually tolerant England within the world of Howards End seems to be an exercise of what Stone calls "fictional transvestitism" on Forster's part, in which he abandons "[t]he attempt to compete as a man" as in *The Longest Journey* and "takes shelter in female bodies that men do not normally strike" (237). In a less obvious way, Forster still uses fantasy as a means by which to present his homosexual ideal, this time by taking on the mantle of "the female predicament" or "the powerlessness of women" (Rosecrance 120). Whereas in previous novels, there was usually some kind of identification with the female heroine on Forster's part (especially in her appreciation of the handsome hero), the portrayal of Margaret goes much further. Forster represents her in androgynous terms from the start, and her "sexuality, such as it is, actually lessens as the novel progresses" (McConkey 32). In her struggles to foster a connection with (and within) Henry, there are "echoes of the melioristic notion advanced by Carpenter and Dickinson of the emergence of a 'third sex,' a new synthesis that will transcend sex" (Stone 257). I agree with those critics who see Margaret's intermediary position as linked to a position of tolerance. According to Summers, "Forster's celebration of pluralism . . . is undoubtedly influenced by his acceptance of his own homosexuality" (Summers 137), and Finkelstein sees Margaret's ministrations as revealing an "acceptance of sexuality, [and] the role of women (and by extension of homosexuals) in society" (Finkelstein 91). This positive attitude leads into the creation of his next and most homosexually affirming novel, *Maurice*.

From Phobia to Fulfillment: *Maurice*

The time after the publication and tremendous success of *Howards End* was a personally turbulent one for Forster, both because of the joys and stresses of his newfound fame and because his frustrations with heterosexual fictional conventions came more fully to the surface. In 1911 the following entry appeared in his diary: "Weariness of the only subject that I both can and may treat—the love of men for women & vice versa. Passion and money are the two main springs of action (not of existence) and I can only write of the first & of that imperfectly" (Furbank 1: 199). As an emotional outlet, Forster wrote and shared privately with a few friends the first of what was to be many overtly erotic homosexual short stories. Further frustration came with Forster's attempts from 1911–1912 to start a new novel to be called *Arctic Summer* that was to contrast two types of men ("the civilized and socially useful man" and the "chivalrous man, the knight errant" (199)) and include some homoerotic material. However, he soon dropped this effort because its approach was too close to the "style of patient, synoptic comment on social issues" (210) of *Howards End*, a genre he no longer wished to pursue.

A much-needed hiatus in India from 1912–1913, followed by the aforementioned "stirring" visit to Carpenter and his lover, gave Forster the patience and focus he needed to write *Maurice*, which tells the tale he might have told in *The Longest Journey* but had neither the self-awareness nor literary confidence to present honestly and clearly in the earlier novel. Described as "the one classic portrayal of 'masculine love' . . . and the one explicitly homosexual *Bildungsroman* produced within the mainstream English literary tradition by a canonical author" (Fletcher 64), *Maurice* was first written from 1913–1914 and revised in 1932 and 1959 but only published posthumously in 1971, according to Forster's wishes. Because it is an overt exploration of homosexuality, it would appear that the novel has no need to employ a double-plot, with a homosexual under plot running simultaneously to the action of the heterosexual surface plot. In a sense, though, there are still two plots in the novel, but this time they run almost sequentially as the title character undergoes two attempts at forging a lasting same-sex relationship. This produces a "doubling" quality in the text, seen most noticeably in the two voices of Maurice and his two radically different male lovers (Nadel 182).

Some critics find fault with Forster's more straightforward approach in the novel, claiming that its lack of complexity and largely realistic style flattens the narrative and renders it devoid of charm.[41] This is a reductive position, however; *Maurice* is both more complex and less realistic than it appears. In fact, although its open exploration of homosexuality might seem to eliminate the need for the subversive mode of fantasy used in the other novels, the novel is in many ways written as a fantasy. Forster's employment of fantastic elements points to a continued tension within himself and the text, as well as the seeming impossibility of writing a realist novel about a homosexual relationship, at least in his day. Another obstacle to a realistic treatment of this situation is Forster's continued inexperience in matters of homosexual physical intimacy.[42]

Forster's articulation of the genesis of *Maurice* reveals its primary status as a fantasy for Forster. Immediately responding to the inspiration of the Carpenter visit, Forster channeled his energies into a work which would help him escape the dead-endedness of his surface heterosexual fictions yet was not a complete departure from them. In the "Terminal Note" of the novel, his projection for the novel's basic situation and outcome reflects his intention to retain the conventional structure of romantic fiction while reorienting its subject matter: "A happy ending was imperative. I shouldn't have bothered to write otherwise. I was determined that in fiction anyway two men should fall in love and remain in it for the ever and ever that fiction allows, and in this sense Maurice and Alec still roam the greenwood" (*Maurice* 250). Despite the realistic vein that runs through *Maurice*, in the end Forster was still writing a tale about the threatened love that inhabits "the dell" of *The Longest Journey*; he was creating yet another fantasy of homosexual love by representing an impossible pairing within the social conditions of his day. This is reinforced by the fact that he felt constrained not to have the novel published until after his death.

While not as predominant as in *The Longest Journey*, elements of fantasy appear in significant moments of *Maurice*, beginning with some telling omens in Maurice's childhood. Chapter 3 contains two emotionally opposed dreams Maurice has at school which take up an active role in the text; the narrator intends that "they will interpret" Maurice. The first dream involves Maurice's "playing football against a nondescript whose existence he resented," but with concentration he is able to turn the figure into George, the garden boy who, Pan-like, "headed down the field towards him, naked and jumping over the woodstacks." Just as Maurice is able to collar the boy, he "turns wrong" and "a brutal disappointment" wakes Maurice up, leaving him thinking "he was going to be ill, and afterwards that it was a punishment for something." Echoing Ricky Elliot's quest for a male friend, the second dream is more obscure: "He scarcely saw a face, scarcely heard a voice say, 'That is your friend,' and then it was over, having filled him with beauty and taught him tenderness." Lack of details aside, the dream generates the feeling that Maurice "could die for such a friend . . . ; they would make any sacrifice for each other, and count the world nothing." After unsuccessfully persuading himself that the friend is Christ, Maurice recognizes that it is just a man, and he "would never

Pursuing (a) Fantasy 57

meet that man nor hear that voice again, yet they became more real than anything he knew" (*Maurice* 22–23).

Maurice's childhood dreams, which the narrator describes as "part brutal, part ideal" (23), reveal a masochism and predilection for athletic, lower-class males seen in earlier novels, and the intersection of these dreams with reality becomes, in essence, the motivating force behind the novel.[43] The second dream points toward Maurice's pursuit of an ideal, chaste male friendship with Clive, while the first dream foretells the physicality and crossing of class of his relationship with Alec, who ultimately proves to be the true "friend" Maurice is seeking. Highlighting what is perhaps Forster's most developed psychological use of fantasy's dividing of personality, John Fletcher's reading sees the two dreams giving Maurice "a distinctive psychic profile" (84) and illustrating his quest for a "land through the looking glass" (Clive's phrase for homosexuality, *Maurice* 242–243) that "constitutes a dream of obscure and shifting relations between the desired boy, the Ideal Friend, and the mourned-for lost father, non-descript and resented. If Alec enters into the heritage of the naked garden boy, Clive moves from the position of the Ideal Friend to take over the burden of that shadowy paternal absence" (Fletcher 88).

Maurice's search for an ideal male love takes place within the usual Forsterian tension between the harsh world of Edwardian England and a couple of safe fantastic landscapes. On one side is Maurice's futile attempt to remain within the "norms" of English society by entering into dialogue with its most respected institutions, each one of which is represented by a key scene in which Maurice encounters and ultimately rejects the advice of a male authority figure. As Cavaliero puts it, "in order to reach the greenwood where he can be free to love another human being in the way his nature dictates," Maurice "has to pass the four guardians of society—the schoolmaster, the doctor, the scientist, and the priest" (137). The scenes—a sex education talk by Mr. Ducie, a physical exam by Dr. Barry, an attempt at hypnotic cure by Mr. Lasker Jones, and a catechetical chat on sexual irregularities with the rector, Mr. Borenius—all serve to underline the bankruptcy of English culture in the face of homosexuality.

Offsetting the rigid institutions of the novel and their patriarchal representatives are occasional places of refuge for Maurice in which he is able to pursue his fantasy of male love and eventually bring it to fulfillment. In this novel the world of Cambridge is an even more openly homophilic milieu than it is in *The Longest Journey*. To a degree, Maurice's friendship with Clive (another character inspired by Hugh Meredith) is allowed to blossom in the halls and rooms of the colleges, yet under some constraint. Liberation comes through a youthful jaunt outside of the city which has the mood of a fantasy and helps to seal their relationship.

In a manner that is suggestive of Rickie's trips to his sacred dell, Maurice and Clive play hooky from class one day to go for a drive in the countryside that serves as "an ironic Forsterian pastoral" (Grant 200).

Motoring off into the distance, they enact a version of Maurice's second dream: "They cared for no one, they were outside humanity, and death, had it come, would only have continued their pursuit of a retreating horizon." Eating on a "grassy embankment" amid the "song of the lark" (*Maurice* 76), the pair laugh, touch cheeks, and wrestle playfully (one of Forster's—and Lawrence's—favorite images of male love). In a telling moment that hearkens back to *A Room with a View*'s pond frolic, only Maurice feels free to bathe in the waters of a nearby dike. After stepping into the water, Clive retreats (he had "no idea" of how "deep" it was (77)) and chooses the voyeuristic role of carrying Maurice's clothes while watching him bathe. The escape into a homoerotic arcadia is short-lived, however; Maurice's absence from a lecture leads to his being sent down, and this forces him and Clive to secretly pursue their relationship in the intolerant heterosexual worlds of suburban and upper-class Edwardian England.

Perhaps most symbolic of the tension between the spheres of male friendship and English social convention in the novel is Clive's home at Penge, an upper-class estate which is surrounded by woods "in a remote part of England on the Wilts and Somerset border" (86). Initially a site for chaste yet affectionate encounters between Maurice and Clive which last for two years, the world of Penge takes on a darker and more passionate character after Clive has decided to marry the aptly named Anne Woods and provide an heir,[44] and Maurice begins to see his identity as that of "an outlaw in disguise" like "those who took to the greenwood in old time" (135). On Maurice's second series of visits to Penge, the woods and the dark sexuality they represent encroach upon his previously ordered and sheltered upper-class world in the person of Alec Scudder, the gamekeeper of the estate and the only developed fantasy character in the novel. Although he "sprang . . . of a respectable family," Alec appears in one scene "as an untamed son of the woods . . . [who] liked the woods and the fresh air and water . . . better than anything" (219), conjuring up an image of Robin Hood and his merry men. Alec is an obvious descendent of other Forsterian Pan figures like Gino and Stephen, and his plan to emigrate in pursuit of a freer life in the Argentine reinforces his outsider status.

In an effective blending of fantasy setting and character, the relationship of Alec and Maurice begins on the border between two very different social and physical worlds which are finally mingled in the crucial bedroom scene at Penge. At this transgressive moment, Alec literally becomes the answer to Maurice's dreams by climbing through a window from the outside and crossing the threshold of class and sexuality by entering Maurice's bed after he has cried "Come" in his sleep. (The scene has an earlier parallel in Maurice's entry of Clive's Cambridge rooms at night to kiss Clive in response to his calling out "Maurice" in his sleep.) Although they violate the sanctity of Penge's image in this act, the scene is only a brief victory over English propriety; from this point on, Maurice and Alec must withdraw into secret settings, a boathouse and a "strange hotel" in London (228), to share their passion.

Forster does his best here to present an open and realistic alternative to the coded male-bondings of his previous novels, but in the end the relationship of Maurice and Alec is necessarily forced beyond the borders of English society into the fantasy land of the greenwood, a place which Alan Wilde calls "oddly vague" and "a space of fictional absence" ("Desire" 117–118). Their future is actually left to the imagination because, in the final scene of the novel, Maurice, after confronting Clive with the truth of his love for Alec and intention to remain with him, "disappeared . . . leaving no trace of his presence except a little pile of the petals of the evening primrose" (*Maurice* 246), never to return except in Clive's nostalgic memory. A vague suggestion of the fate of Maurice and Alex appears in the previous scene when Maurice realizes that Alec is not taking the boat to Argentina: "He knew what the call was, and what his answer must be. They must live outside class, without relations or money; they must work and stick to each other till death. But England belonged to them. That, besides companionship, was their reward" (239). In the end, Wilde notes, "it is the irony of Forster's most overtly sexual novel that it fails at the last quite literally to embody its abstract ideal" ("Desire" 118).

Forster qualifies this ambiguous ending, however, in an "epilogue" he wrote but never published, which "took the form of Kitty encountering two woodcutters some years later and gave universal dissatisfaction" (*Maurice* 254). The epilogue displays a dark sense of irony: after meeting Maurice on her "old-maidish weekend" in the woods (*Selected Letters* 2: 158), Kitty begins to reflect on what she imagines is his happiness with Alec in light of her own "trivial existence" (97), as Elizabeth Wood Ellem puts it. Their apparently idyllic greenwood "is not a place of joyous freedom," however, because "[w]hile Kitty is thinking about them and realizing that they live only for each other, the two are huddling together in the cold woods, deciding that they must flee in case Kitty should report that she has seen them and they be hunted down. From one wood to another they flee, from one refuge to another" (Ellem 97).

In either case, the conclusion of *Maurice* has been the subject of much critical attention questioning its status as a "happy" ending and its suitability in relation to the rest of the story.[45] With hindsight, Forster himself recognizes the datedness of the novel: "it belongs to an England where it was still possible to get lost. It belongs to the last moment of the greenwood . . . [which] ended catastrophically and inevitably" with the advent of the "great wars" (*Maurice* 254). Given the social reality of the enforcement of anti-sodomy laws and the court battles over censorship during the time *Maurice* was written, it seems that Forster had no choice but to mix fantasy with reality in this overt celebration of homosexual love on the margins. Of course, the fact that Forster himself had not yet experienced a physically consummated homosexual relationship may also explain the novel's mode of fantasy and its deferral of a more stable sense of gratification. Although Forster's vision cannot be fully realized, the fantasy spaces of the novel provide Forster with a momentary satisfaction of his desires.

A final way of assessing the novel and its ending comes through a consideration of the triangular conflict among the main characters, which in itself is an expression of fantasy. As Grant points out, in *Maurice* "we have Forster's most clearly defined story of the double, one of those 'divings into and dividings of personality' Forster distinguishes as one of the devices of the writer of fantasy" (199). The love triangle is best interpreted in light of early twentieth-century theories of homosexuality, which were at the forefront of Forster's mind as he wrote the novel. Robert Martin offers a schematic view of *Maurice* as opposing "two kinds of homosexuality"— the first, "identified with Cambridge and Clive," is "dominated by Plato and, indirectly, by John Aldington Symonds and the apologists for 'Greek love'"; and the other, "identified with Alec and the open air" is "dominated by Edward Carpenter and his translation of the ideas of Walt Whitman" ("Carpenter" 35–36). The progress of the novel in Martin's schema sees Maurice moving through three stages: first, accepting "homosexuality as an idealized friendship"; second, accepting "lust in the physical expression of homosexuality"; and third, accepting "the social and political consequences of homosexuality" (42).

John Fletcher's more convincing and nuanced argument finds that Martin's dualistic interpretation leads to an "over-polarizing of both the novel and its genealogy." Because "Symonds as much as Carpenter is concerned to defend the physical expression of homosexual love" (66), the novel cannot be so neatly split into two parts enacting competing theories of homosexuality. Fletcher posits that "[t]he three male figures form the nucleus of the novel's character system, and the combination and substitution of terms their story plays out, is the working through of highly conflicted and overdetermined psychic and ideological material necessary for the novel's 'imperative' happy ending to be put into place" (67). In concrete terms, Fletcher sees Clive as a Forster figure who is left out of the final union of Maurice and Alec (just as Forster was in the Carpenter-Merrill relationship) because he represents a "debilitating intellectuality" or "male femininity" that cannot be incorporated into "[t]he motif of the thinking body . . . [that] is characteristic of literary theories of the period" and is embodied in the "cross-class democratic harmony between upper middle-class intellectual and working man" (68 & 70).[46]

In the end, the "happy" ending of *Maurice* comes at the expense of Clive's (and Forster's) own participation, as "the formation of the masculine couple requires the exclusion of the unmanly intellectual with his disavowed paternal affiliation" (90). This interpretation is in line with Bristow's argument that Forster's fictions steer clear of effeminacy in their attempt to merge the "aesthete" and "athlete." For all of its sexual openness, *Maurice* ultimately fails to fulfill Forster's desire for a happy homosexual novel because it leaves a character like him in the cold. This was not to remain true for Forster on a personal level, however, as in 1917 he was to establish a sustained relationship with a working-class Egyptian named Mohammed, whom he met while on war duty in Alexandria. Once Forster found such love, one might assume that the realization of his long-thwarted passion would inspire a work that would improve upon *Maurice*'s failings, but this was not to be. What followed was a ten-year fictional drought that ended in Forster's pessimistic return to representing male union covertly in his final novel through the use of another homosexual under plot, but this time with a racial and political twist, to demonstrate that the realization of male comradeship and love in the world of the novel, as well as in life, was still little more than a wishful thought.

From Fantasy to the "Not Yet" of Reality: *A Passage to India*

Forster's final attempt to make sense of personal relationships in a novel came with the publication of *A Passage to India*, a much-delayed accomplishment coming after a series of personally devastating experiences. First of all, the long-awaited 1921–1922 return to his beloved India as a Maharaja's secretary was a major disappointment for Forster, exemplified in his cynical attitude toward the superficially cordial change in Anglo-Indian relations he encountered, which he described as the result of "tragic resignation" to Britain's fading influence there (qtd. in Furbank 2: 92). Doubly devastating was the fact that his liberating five-year love relationship ended with the tragedy of Mohammed's death by consumption while Forster was abroad, after which Forster suffered months of depression and a case of writer's block that he tried to end symbolically by burning his homoerotic stories.[47]

Plagued by this series of personal blows and numerous fits and starts in writing the novel, which he had begun in 1913, Forster published *A Passage to India* in 1924. It is considered "the most prophetic of Forster's books" (Stone 340) by many critics because it is more deeply philosophical and mythic in its content and style, and its cross-cultural dynamic sets the stage for Forster's most universal statement of human relations. Yet for all of its lofty aspirations and apparent dissimilarities to his earlier and lighter work, the novel still includes elements of fantasy in service of a homophilic and covertly homosexual plot. As George Steiner sees it, Forster "saw that sexual eccentricity could be isolated in racial or caste terms. The encounters between white and native . . . in *A Passage to India* are a brilliant projection of the confrontations between society and the homosexual in *Maurice*" (481). Malik reads an even stronger queer agenda into the novel, stating that, through the Aziz-Fielding relationship, the novel "implies that a shift in the paradigm, which privileges heterosexuality as 'normal,' to include same-sex relationships could help eliminate the structure of dominance prevalent in the meeting of two races" (231).[48]

Isolating the central plot is a tricky undertaking: on one level, the dramatic core of the novel revolves around the alleged sexual scandal in the Marabar caves and the ensuing trial, but on another level, the novel charts a spiritual quest that transcends racial and religious differences, beginning with Mrs. Moore's open-hearted visit to the Moslem mosque and ending with the participation of her children in the Hindu feast of the birth of Krishna. However, as Dowling sees it: "The novel is essentially a love story—not that of Aziz and Mrs. Moore, or Ronnie and Adela, or even Mrs. Moore and India, but that of Aziz and Fielding." Not exactly an under plot, as in Forster's early novels, the story of their relationship threads its way throughout the novel, whose central "question is whether friendship . . . can flourish between individuals of different backgrounds and beliefs." By translating the setting to the multicultural and pan-religious world of India, Forster is able "to return more directly to the issue which concerned him in *Maurice*, but without feeling limited by the sexual debate within the mores of one restrictive society." Once again Forster tries to create a same-sex relationship which transcends sex, only to end his novel career with yet another tale of "the unfulfilled urge towards a homosexual friendship" (Dowling 74–75).

While most of the characters in the novel fall on one or the other side of the English/Indian ethnic and cultural divide, two figures, Mrs. Moore and Professor Godbole, emerge from the text in a fantastic and tolerant light.[49] A descendent of Mrs. Wilcox in *Howards End* and an avatar of Christian values, Mrs. Moore begins as a hymeneal figure escorting her son Ronny's prospective wife to India to witness their nuptials, but she is gradually "transformed into a Hindu version of Demeter" (Summers 217) by novel's end. Her spiritual qualities are evident from the start of the novel in her visit to an Islamic mosque during which she shows unexpected acceptance and reverence by removing her shoes, observing silence, and acknowledging the presence of the divine ("God is here" (*Passage* 18)).[50] The result is a cross-cultural friendship with Aziz (who proclaims her an "Oriental") that demonstrates Mrs. Moore's gift for "connecting and bridging cultures [and] suggests a corresponding bridge over arbitrary sexual differences" (Finkelstein 124), pointing toward a Demeter-like androgyny.

Mrs. Moore's potential divinity and the novel's early optimism about bridging differences are shattered by the visit to the Marabar Caves. Her experience of the caves' nihilistic, "terrifying echo" (a "boum" sound which robs "infinity and eternity of their vastness" and murmurs, "Everything exists, nothing has value") makes her irritable and she does not "want to communicate with anyone, not even God" (*Passage* 165–166). Adela's rape charge disrupts her psyche and undermines her confidence in the powers of love and marriage. As the chaos surrounding the accusation rages, Mrs. Moore becomes more withdrawn, and when she does speak, it is with the "cynicism of a withered priestess" (231). The novel's destructive tide turns only when she attempts to flee from India. In one of the plot's

Pursuing (a) Fantasy

most fantastic moments, Mrs. Moore's death occurs simultaneously with the turning point in Aziz's trial. Her divinization occurs when a Hindu version of her name ("Esmiss Esmoor" (250)) is chanted by the natives in the courtroom, initiating a kind of trance through which Adela proclaims Aziz's innocence in the caves and leading to "the beginning of a cult" (285) complete with legends about Mrs. Moore's death and two different tombs containing her remains. Mrs. Moore's divinity is ultimately represented in the completion of her hymeneal task in her daughter's marriage to Mr. Fielding and in the coming of the monsoons, which bring "to the sere landscape soothing rains and renewed fertility" (Summers 218).

The other character who takes on fantastic significance is Professor Godbole, a Hindu teacher who appears "as if he had reconciled the products of East and West, mental as well as physical" (*Passage* 77) and is sometimes sage, sometimes buffoon in his appearances throughout the novel. Functioning as both a source of wisdom and a parody of a religious guru, Godbole also acts as a Hermes figure, a summoner of the gods, mystically setting the stage for the novel's climax during the all-embracing Hindu feast of the birth of Krishna and acting as a catalyst for the novel's fleeting experience of connection across race, sex, and religion. Godbole holds a position of honor in the ceremony, leading a chant and religious ritual which seems to non-Hindu eyes "a muddle . . . a frustration of reason and form" (319). There is a synthetic or syncretistic aspect to the ceremony, which incorporates myriad objects, images (including a memory of Mrs. Moore), lights, and sounds, during which the singers "loved all men, the whole universe, and scraps of their past, tiny splinters of detail, emerged for a moment to melt into the universal warmth" (321).

The spiritual experience at Mau is the culminating manifestation of Forster's use of India as a fantasy locale.[51] India's resonance in the novel is as an exotic place apart from the Western norm, much like the English and Italian countryside of his earlier novels. The link to these earlier fantasy locales is made explicit in Fielding's impressions on his first journey in India: "To regard an Indian as if he were an Italian is not, for instance, a common error, nor perhaps a fatal one, and Fielding often attempted analogies between this peninsula and that other, smaller and more exquisitely shaped, that stretches into the classic waters of the Mediterranean" (64). As in *The Longest Journey*, Forster divides the novel into three sections, each centered around a "foreign" (to Westerners) locale which represents one of the mysterious facets of Indian belief: a Moslem mosque, the Marabar caves, and the Hindu festival. One can read this tri-partite setting as an attempt by Forster either to merge the seemingly disjointed cultures of India or to indicate a progression in the novel's spiritual quest, from the restrictions of institutional religion (the mosque) through a deconstruction of religious certitude (the caves) to a paradoxical unity amid the chaos of traditions and cultures (the festival). In all of these places, the Westerner is never really at home, and each site embodies a mysterious "other" force that cannot be fully understood or penetrated by imperialist efforts, which contributes to the novel's air of fantasy. As the narrator puts it, "How can the mind take hold of such a country? . . . She has never defined. She is not a promise, only an appeal" (150).

Robert K. Selig injects a note of caution and levity into the debate over the interpretation of Forster's use of religious myth and symbolism as a prophetic gesture by drawing attention to the author's ironic intentions in treating his spiritual material, representing the idea of union with God as a fantasy or practical joke in itself (471, 476–477). The text seems to have it both ways here. Forster's agnostic leanings notwithstanding, there is something reverential about his treatment of Hinduism in contrast to his exposure of the limitations of both Christianity and Islam through the uncharitable acts of his British and Muslim characters. However, the great synthesis of the diverse cultures during the Hindu ceremony is finally symbolized by the collision of two boats carrying the "four outsiders" (Fielding, Aziz, and Mrs. Moore's children), which revolve "like a mythical monster" and capsize, throwing their occupants together into the warm water amidst a "tornado of noise" made by artillery, drums, and elephants. The narrator calls this scene "the climax, as far as India admits of one" (*Passage* 353–354), and it is possible to see it as a kind of baptism, but it is also certainly one of Forster's best depictions of a comic muddle.

Set within this fantastic landscape and quest for unity is the story of Fielding and Aziz, another Forsterian friendship plot that is laden with homoerotic elements. Both men are outcasts, of a sort, and thereby rendered open to a same-sex friendship. In the wake of his wife's death, Aziz has sworn off future heterosexual contacts: "no woman could ever take her place; a friend would come nearer to her than another woman" (57), and until the end of the novel, his dealings with women are marked by an air of condescension and misogyny. Fielding is a "disruptive force" in the colony because he has "no racial feeling." In this oppressive imperialist society one cannot cross the lines of both race and gender and retain respect: "He had discovered that it is possible to keep in with Indians and Englishmen, but that he who would also keep in with Englishwomen must drop the Indians." As a result of his transgressive beliefs, the English men only "tolerated" him and the women "disliked" and "took no notice" of him (65–66). Cavaliero finds that "Fielding's ostracism by the Club draws strength from the author's own sensitivity to society's ostracism of the homosexual" (154).

Although there is no love triangle as such in the novel, as Elaine Freedgood notes, "Aziz and Fielding negotiate their intimacy through homosocial triangles, triangles that are based not on a common desire for women, but on a common rejection of women." On the surface, Fielding and Aziz's relationship is based on gentlemanly respect and a desire for brotherhood, particularly as demonstrated in Aziz's breaking of purdah by showing his wife's photograph to Fielding. However, almost immediately, this "small

Pursuing (a) Fantasy

bridge toward intimacy . . . is then kicked away" (Freedgood 133), and homosocial bonding is facilitated as Aziz dismisses the photo ("Put her away, she is of no importance, she is dead" (*Passage* 126)), and Fielding goes on to put down the local English women as "much nicer in England. There's something that doesn't suit them out here" (128). At certain points in the novel, the relationship is marked by latent homosexual desire. The most obvious example of this is the scene in which Aziz lends Fielding his collar stud, a gesture laden with not only erotic but also sadistic and anti-colonial overtones in its suggestion of forced sodomy: "Let me put in your stud. I see . . . the shirt back's hole is rather small and to rip it wider a pity" (69).[52]

Two women (Adela and Stella Moore) become obstacles to the Aziz-Fielding friendship, by virtue of misunderstandings, as the text would have it. First, Adela's unjust accusation of Aziz erodes his relationship with Fielding, who empathizes with Adela after the trial by sheltering her at the College and recommending Aziz's leniency toward her. Aziz's resentment later assumes delusional proportions as he imagines that it is Adela (rather than Stella Moore) whom Fielding has married. Secondly, as Fielding's wife, Stella becomes another female obstacle to the friendship, but her representation at the novel's end seems to support the homosexual undertones. One critic reads Fielding's marriage as an antidote to Adela and Ronny's failed engagement because it represents "a true marriage of the rational and the intuitive" (McDowell 121). However, similar to the erasure of Stephen's wife at the end of *The Longest Journey*, there is an "indirect hint of homoeroticism" in "the novel's total evasion . . . of the task of presenting the beautiful Stella," who is "never physically described" and "never speaks a word" (Selig 486).

The troubled quality of the male-female bonds in the novel indicates the misogyny still present in Forster's work and apparently favors the development of same-sex friendship, but the emotional turmoil enacted in the novel ultimately leads to a suspicion of all personal relationships, as represented in the concluding scene. After the apparently unifying (or muddling) events of the festival, Fielding and Aziz go for a final horse ride that degenerates into a squabble over politics. Ironically, Aziz has now taken up the cause of women by writing feminist poetry, and he is much more overtly political in his feelings about colonialism. After "half-kissing" Fielding, Aziz insists that their friendship must be put on hold until India has its independence, whereupon Fielding, "holding him affectionately," makes this plea: "Why can't we be friends now? . . . It's what I want. It's what you want." Forster concludes this, his final novelistic depiction of male love, with two pessimistic signs: the horses shy away from one another to indicate they "didn't want it," and the earth joins the chorus, as rocks, temples, birds and others reply, "in their hundred voices, 'No, not yet,' and the sky said, 'No, not there.'" (*Passage* 362). It would seem that, for Forster, the current situation is no place for cross-racial or same-sex unions, and the same homosexual and homosocial fantasy fleetingly represented in *Maurice* is unrealizable in a foreign, colonialist locale.[53]

The resolution of Forster's final novel must have been tinged by the double disappointment of losing his beloved Mohammed and the India he once knew. One cannot but feel that these two intensely negative experiences had something to do with Forster's abandonment of novel writing at the mid-point of what was to be a long life. This is a mystery that Furbank attributes to three possible causes: (1) some deep-seated anxiety about Forster's success in life and an unwillingness to tempt fate, (2) frustration with writing about heterosexual love and his inability to publish *Maurice*, and (3) the loss of his inspiration, which may have come "all at once, in early manhood," so that he had no more to write (Furbank 2: 131–132). Forster himself, remarking in a 1966 letter to Stone, wrote: "Why did I stop writing fiction after *The Passage* came out? . . . I can only suggest that the fictional part of me dried up. As far as I can remember I did not even think of writing either a novel or short stories" (*Selected Letters* 2: 289).

Forster's decision to stop writing novels is most likely related to his disappointments with *Maurice* because the truth is that he did not completely stop thinking about or writing fiction after *A Passage to India*. Over the remainder of his life, Forster wrote a number of explicitly homosexual short stories (of varying degrees of aesthetic quality), which indicates that he was still very much taken up with the idea of representing same-sex love in fiction. These might be explained away as literary diversions, but Forster's rejection of the novel as the form by which he could express homosexual desires suggests that, at least in his mind, it was incompatible with his aims. Although, for Forster, fantasy seemed to be the best means by which to represent that which could not be accepted, its inclusion within the realist novel was never an easy fit. The homosexual spirit behind much of his fiction, uncontainable within realist norms, had to spill over into the world of fantasy with queer, sometimes fascinating and sometimes confusing, results. In the end, it was not enough to inject the sexually ambiguous and fluid mode of fantasy into a genre that, in Forster's day, brooked no tolerance for sexual transgression. Because this world was publicly unrealizable in Edwardian society, it remained, like fantasy itself, the stuff of the lesser gods and fairies, a queer diversion that Forster once tellingly compared to "a sideshow in an exhibition" (*Aspects* 109). Our next author, May Sinclair, also takes up a sexually challenging position toward the conventions of the novel, but her focus is largely directed toward the experience of women and her attempts to break the novel's patriarchal mold are carried out through innovations in narrative style.

CHAPTER THREE

The Sexing of Genius
May Sinclair's Experimental Novels

Introduction

> Among all artists there is a strain of manhood in every woman, and of womanhood in every man. (*Audrey Craven* 92)

> He denied perversely that genius was two-sexed, or that it was even essentially a virile thing. The fruitful genius was feminine, rather, humble and passive in its attitude to life. It yearned perpetually for the embrace, the momentary embrace of the real. (*The Creators* 14)

> Doesn't it look . . . as if genius were the biggest curse a woman can be saddled with? It's giving you another sex inside you, and a stronger one, to plague you. When we want a thing we can't sit still like a woman and wait till it comes to us. . . . We go after it like a man; and if we can't get it peaceably we fight for it. . . . And because we fight we're done for. And then, when we're down, the woman in us turns and rends us. (103)

The possession of creative genius, at least as characterized by May Sinclair in *The Creators* and a number of her other novels, can lead to a serious case of gender confusion. In a move that goes beyond the Romantic notion that "[t]he genius was a male . . . who *transcended* his biology" in a kind of "psychological femininity" (Battersby 3) and that predates Woolf's "androgyny of the mind," Sinclair portrays genius as an oppositely gendered force within a person which creates an interior conflict that is considerably more troubled for a woman than a man. One of the recurring themes in Sinclair's fiction is the strife encountered by the artistic genius, whose life is continually caught between creative pursuits and social expectations. Although Sinclair represents the tensions of the creative life as shared by artists of both sexes, male artists in her fiction generally have an easier time exercising their "feminine" genius without threatening their gender role.

Sinclair's women artists, however, suffer from the "gender bias in the concept of genius" (Battersby 7) as they struggle intensely with their "manly" genius in a repressive world that offers few acceptable outlets for their creativity and demands enormous efforts of self-sacrifice. Telling their tales yields Sinclair's most effective work.

Blessed by a lengthy writing career, Sinclair had numerous opportunities in which to articulate the experiences and passions of the artist's tortured plight and the conditions which rendered it so. Her fiction-writing career spanned thirty years (1897–1927) and included twenty-four novels and six collections of short stories. A fascinating array of late-Victorian, Edwardian, and Georgian or modernist "psychological" styles, the course of her fictional writings can, on one level, be viewed as a quest to find the most appropriate form of the novel in which to represent the life of the genius or gifted person (especially female) in the modern world. Hrisey D. Zegger helpfully divides Sinclair's prodigious novel career into three phases which reflect the concerns and forms of their ages. In the first (1897–1906), Sinclair wrote "novels that were deeply influenced by philosophical idealism dealing with religious ethical questions and spiced with romance and melodrama," and the second stage (1907–1913) saw her "writing realistic, social-problem novels in the manner of H. G. Wells." Sinclair's career finally evolved into a modernist period (1914–1920) in which she produced what critics almost unanimously consider her best work, found in her "psychological novels" (Zegger 9), including several examples of a literary style which was named by Sinclair herself in an essay on Dorothy Richardson, the "stream of consciousness" mode.

In an article on May Sinclair's approach to women, Diane F. Gillespie points out that, unlike Dorothy Richardson and Virginia Woolf, "Sinclair does not suggest, in either her essays or her fiction, that women artists should evolve artistic forms suitable for the expression of women's values" ("Muddle" 243). However, at the same time, as Jane Eldridge Miller puts it, Sinclair "strove for . . . a narrative form and style that would allow her to depict the reality of women's lives as truthfully as possible" (188). In this chapter I contend that while Sinclair did not claim in theory to be engaged in developing a particularly female form of the novel, nonetheless, like her literary sisters, her practice reveals strongly gender-determined connections between her method and her matter. Sinclair's shift away from romance and social realism to more experimental forms of the novel runs concurrently with significant developments in her philosophical and literary thinking.

Immediately before and during her "psychological novel" period in the 1910s, Sinclair became deeply engaged with feminism, imagism, and psychology, and this involvement yielded some of her most successful non-fiction prose, especially in the areas of philosophy and literary criticism. In a move that resembles aspects of Woolf's theory, Sinclair genders "life" as feminine in several of these works and also puts forth the essentialist thesis that, by virtue of their procreative connection to the "Life-Force," women blessed with genius are capable of intense experiences of reality, particularly in contact with the world of nature. She also attributes to women a naturally placed superiority over men in moral matters, a female spirituality that is fueled by the burden of sacrifice and suffering. Like other writers in this period of "gender crisis," Sinclair is not always consistent in her theorizing about gender, so it is unclear whether she wishes to maintain in these writings her earlier sense of female genius as being "manly." However, at times it seems that there is an ironic way in which, if a woman artist forgoes motherhood through sublimation of her sexuality, her genius can provide the seed by which these intense encounters with reality will bear works of art that reflect a distinctly female experience of fulfillment which rivals that of motherhood.

It was not long before Sinclair's theory influenced her practice, and the result is a series of novels focussed on the interior life of one central character and written in a freer and sometimes more poetic style. Although Sinclair applied this style to both male and female protagonists, suggesting that she did not see interiority as a solely female realm, Sinclair's version of the "stream of consciousness" novel (what she later calls the "synthetic psychological novel") seems more conducive to representing the conflicts between individual identity and gender roles that women experience in the early twentieth century. As Sydney Janet Kaplan argues, Sinclair "put what she had learned in other fields immediately into a fictional form" (48) and, in her best novels, constructed a "feminine consciousness . . . primarily involved with the search for reality, reality as it can be perceived only by a woman" (70). In doing so, she reflected the "pressures of heredity and environment and natural drives" on such a woman while also communicating her possibilities for freedom and fulfillment through the sublimating expression of creative genius (58). Miller concurs, saying that "[a]lthough neither Sinclair nor Woolf characterized this new kind of novel of consciousness as a particularly feminine mode, it is obvious from their fiction that it was nevertheless uniquely suited for depicting those whose inner life dominated the outer" (195).

In this chapter, I will show how gender and genre are strongly linked in May Sinclair's practice of novel writing if not in her consciously articulated theory of the novel. I will begin with a brief look at characteristic examples of fiction from Sinclair's philosophical idealist and social realist periods to illustrate early concerns and styles which undergo significant change as her writing progresses. My primary focus will be on the third and most innovative phase of her career, which emerges out of and draws its form from early twentieth-century philosophical, social and literary developments in which Sinclair was actively involved. As a means of illustrating some of the significant ideas and forces behind Sinclair's formal shift, I will show how a pivotal novel, *The Three Sisters*, contains embryonic aspects of novels to come.

Within this period I will examine what are arguably Sinclair's finest "psychological" novels, *Mary Olivier: A Life* and *The Life and Death of Harriet Frean*, which serve as a diptych portraying the inner life and experience of two modern women and the radically different ways in which they manage the tensions within their largely repressive, biologically and culturally determined lives. These works will be set in contrast to two attempts by Sinclair to apply the same novelistic form to the lives of modern men, *Arnold Waterlow: A Life* and *The History of Anthony Waring*, works whose "stream of consciousness" style seems ill-fitted to the characters of the protagonists. Curiously, Sinclair's representation of their experience as men, although subject to many of the same repressive forces, lacks the inner conflict and complexity of their female literary counterparts. At her best, Sinclair uses her version of the "stream of consciousness" to yield a feminine form of the novel (at least as she constructs it) that is particularly suited to depicting a woman's struggle with the conflicting demands of genius and society.

TALES OF IDEALISM AND REALISM: SINCLAIR'S EARLY NOVELS

Dividing May Sinclair's novel career into distinct periods with characteristic styles is a reductive but necessary exercise for the purposes of this study.[1] Sinclair wrote nine novels before the period with which I am concerned and, while I cannot cover the full range of their styles and subject matter, I think it will be useful to touch upon two of them to articulate some of her early concerns and formal strategies. First, it will be helpful to outline Sinclair's fundamental framework of philosophical idealism, a theoretical position she maintains throughout her career with various qualifications based on developments in philosophy and her own personal experience.

Like other writers of late nineteenth-century England, Sinclair was impressed by the work of T. H. Green, an idealist philosopher who wrote in answer to the empiricism and utilitarianism which had become so influential in British philosophy. Countering the idea that all reality can be reduced to material things and processes, Green upheld the primacy of mind and spirit in the order of being, and his writings take on a mystical quality in promoting the concept of an ultimate spirit in which human consciousness participates. On the level of ethics, Green rejects the hedonistic notion that the individual's actions are based on a mechanistic calculus of pleasure and pain and, instead, he ascribes motives or ends (which are not "natural phenomena") to human action which move the individual beyond him/herself to embrace the good of others. His "primary ethical category" is that of "self-realization" (Zegger 19) which, given the individual's links to society and God or "Ultimate Spirit," often demands self-denial in the service of others' needs, a dynamic which is repeatedly played out in Sinclair's fiction.[2]

The tenets of philosophical idealism are not the only theoretical ideas upon which Sinclair builds her early fiction; in a paradoxical way, Sinclair incorporates elements of the very naturalism with which philosophical idealists did battle. Her first novel, *Audrey Craven* (1897), asserts that "Custom, Circumstance and Heredity are the Three Fates that weave the web of human life" (4), and its subject matter, the struggles of the title character with her "defective heredity," reflects the influence of naturalism and eugenics. Kaplan notes that Sinclair brought to her fiction "the burden of her extensive reading in philosophy and biology," including "the nineteenth-century mixture of science and sociology, with its notions of the survival of the fittest, the respect for power, and the determinism of organic development carried over into the realms of philosophy and politics" (56–57). Throughout her fiction, one can see "how these concepts from Naturalism are [especially] involved with the feminine character and the behavior of women in her novels" (59). However, Sinclair's attitude toward the reigning climate of determinism is not a fatalistic one in her early novels; as Theophilus E. M. Boll puts it, "[w]hile she accepts the fact of heredity, she resists the Victorian surrender to it as the force of destiny and the judge passing doom upon the unfortunate inheritor" (164). According to Suzanne Stark, "May Sinclair's basic concern is . . . to free the individual from his entanglements with the race and to make him a self-contained being which is not driven by determinism but has the possibility of free choice" (277). Her eccentric fusion of naturalistic conditions with idealistic solutions characterizes all of her work to a degree, but it is most present in the early novels.

Perhaps the best example of Sinclair's mixture of the battle against heredity and the pursuit of idealism is found in her most popular novel, *The Divine Fire* (1904), which "[i]n an allegorical fashion" depicts "the way a man can reach his highest self and the divine through self-sacrifice, through struggling against the evils in his environment, and through service to others" (Zegger 22). Combining the passions of artistic struggle and romance (along with a heavy dose of melodrama), it is the story of Savage Keith Rickman, the son of a Cockney bookseller and an aspiring poet, who, after an affair with a music-hall singer, meets and falls in love with Lucia Harden, a sensitive upper-class woman who unwittingly becomes his literary muse (the "divine fire"). A primary obstacle to Keith's literary success is the influence of Lucia's cousin, Horace Jewdwine, the upper-class literary critic and journalist who "discovers" Keith and is a rival for Lucia's affections until he learns that her fortune is gone. Horace's jealousy and lack of courage keep him from promoting Keith's art and attending to Lucia's welfare, and his inaction nearly sinks the poet's career and his opportunity for love.

Written in a third-person omniscient style that relies predominantly on what Dorrit Cohn calls "psycho-narration" ("the narrator's discourse about a character's consciousness" (14))[3] to express the inner life of its characters, the novel combines aspects of romance, realism, and philosophical idealism, and it contains a number of themes which recur in Sinclair's fiction. Keith's pursuit of his artistic dreams and integrity is hampered by his financial limitations as well as the often petty realities of a literary world dominated by class consciousness, rigid critical philosophies, and commercial concern for public taste. His career is further complicated by the tensions of romantic and sexual love and their effects on his inspiration and production. Developing a scenario which becomes highly unlikely (especially for women artists) in Sinclair's later fictions, the novel records the triumph of philosophical idealism as Keith's patient self-abnegation and loyal service of his beloved's needs yield not only artistic and romantic success but also a little glimpse of heaven. Gazing into Lucia's eyes at the novel's conclusion, Keith finds that: "Love in them looked upon things invisible, incorruptible; divining, even as it revealed, the ultimate mystery. He saw that in her womanhood Nature was made holy, penetrated by the spirit and the fire of God" (*Divine* 596).

Critical and popular response to the novel was extremely positive, especially in America, and for a time it enshrined Sinclair as the foremost woman novelist in England. Viewed from a contemporary perspective, however, the novel's limitations are often painfully obvious. The third-person omniscient "psycho-narration" has a distant and static quality to it, and the novel has a general tendency to talk about rather than illustrate its themes throughout its nearly 600-page length. This is seen in a number of pages-long dialogues in which the characters parrot Sinclair's philosophical ideas on genius, love, and art. The tale of the struggling artist is presented in stereotypical "New Grub Street" terms, and descriptions of Keith's career and love life get carried away in passages of lofty prose, heavy-handed symbolism, and idealized characterization, as in Sinclair's description of the inspirational Lucia quoted above and this reaction to one of Keith's creative dry spells: "But where was that divine solitude? Where were those long days of nebulous conception? Where the days when he removed himself . . . and watched his full-orbed creations careering in the intellectual void? The days when Keith Rickman was as a god?" (368).

In spite of its artistic limitations, the novel is a good example of idealistic fiction in its presentation of the "path to individuation" of Keith, whose literary career parallels the integration of his personality. Moving away from his first stage of writing classically inspired but ethereal poetry, Keith "lets flesh and blood humanize his rhetoric and his ego-driven fantasy" (Boll 178) through his affair with Poppy, enabling him to create love poetry of greater substance and reality, but even this is inadequate. Only through the "union of intellectual, sexual, and social stimulation" (180) offered by Lucia does Keith find his niche as an author of verse drama and settle down as both husband and critically and commercially successful artist. Keith's ability to "have it all" in the end is a fitting conclusion for the hero of a novel of idealism, but such a fate becomes problematized (and is impossible for a female protagonist) in Sinclair's more realistic and deterministic novels to come.

The next phase of Sinclair's novel writing (1907–1913) is prompted, in part, by her repudiation of what she saw as the public's overly enthusiastic reception of this final novel of her idealistic period (Zegger 34). In fact, twenty years later, Sinclair says, "I dislike hearing people say . . . that they prefer *The Divine Fire* to any other book of mine" (Steell 513). Without straying too far from familiar themes, Sinclair takes on a predominantly realistic style and, influenced by the work of H. G. Wells as well as artistic discussions with him, writes novels dealing with social problems. In this "transition from the Victorian to the modern novel" (Zegger 56), Sinclair turns her attention from metaphysics to social reform, focussing especially on "the position of women in society whose progress was impeded by conventional ideas about women and by the flaws in the institution of marriage" (39). One of Sinclair's significant contributions in these novels is a more open treatment of taboo issues such as adultery, divorce, and sexual desire (especially in women).

The Creators: A Comedy (1910) is a representative novel of this period because of its primary focus on a contemporary social problem—the constraints which gender expectations, especially in marriage, place on women artists—and its realistic style, which uses the third-person "psycho-narration" of *The Divine Fire* but with far fewer symbolic and idealistic discourses and more attention to the internal life of the female characters. It is different, however, from the "marriage novels" which preceded it (*The Helpmate* and *The Judgement of Eve*, both 1907) because, as Sinclair wrote to her editor, Richard W. Gilder, in 1909, she intended it to be "'a novel of character' rather than of social problems—one that was to show the way in which the creative drive affected people" (Zegger 50). At the core of the novel is a coterie of literary artists who struggle to reconcile the demands of their creative genius and love lives, although the probability of their success is largely determined by how they conform to their sex roles, which creates extra barriers for the women. Despite the rigid conventions of gender identity which are reflected in the novel, Sinclair sometimes challenges the traditional form of the marriage novel by constructing, in the words of Janice H. Harris, "a provocative range of motifs relating to love and quest, gender symmetries and asymmetries, the pleasures and confines of heterosexual bonds, and the gagging and unmuffling of the heroine" (439).

As suggested at the opening of the chapter, a person's integration with his/her conversely sexed creative genius is represented in this novel as a more easily attainable goal for a man because there is little conflict between the demands of a literary career and his gender role as a husband and father.[4] This is seen most clearly in the experience of George Tanqueray, who writes novels of psychological realism and believes that "*the unpardonable sin in a great artist—isn't so much marrying as marrying the wrong person*" (*Creators* 476). Recognizing the incompatibility of two writers in a marriage, George resists his true but artistically problematic love for a fellow novelist named Jane Holland and finds the perfect complement to his career in the person of Rose Eldred, a self-effacing lodging house servant and nurse who has no connections with the literary world and is content to serve his needs.

Differences of class and intellect make George and Rose's married life uneventful and unstimulating, but George fills the void through his writing: "his genius was a thing of flesh and blood. . . . it was sufficient to itself. It fulfilled the functions, it enjoyed the excitements and the satisfactions of sense. It reproduced reality so infallibly, so solidly, so completely, that it took reality's place; it made him unconscious of his wife's existence" (203). In this passage, George's genius (earlier gendered as feminine) serves as a mistress supplying the passion his marriage lacks and their progeny (realism) erases the female reality in his life. In her censure of George's one-sided marriage, Sinclair also seems to be taking realism to task for ignoring women's experience. (Although set within a realistic novel itself, this critique points the way toward Sinclair's eventual move away from the patriarchal limits of realism.)[5]

Set in sharp contrast to George's relatively placid negotiation of career and manhood, and taking up a large share of the novel's attention, is the experience of three women writers, whose "powerful drive to create that they feel, and the egotistical focus of that creativity, seem to them to be the result of a masculine force which inhabits their female bodies," leaving them "feeling divided, at war with themselves" (Miller 190). Each of them illustrates a different and more difficult struggle with the artist/gender role conflict. First of all, Jane, whose genius matches and possibly surpasses that of George, does not find the resolution of her art and womanhood so easily. Continually struggling with the competing demands of her writing and social expectations concerning her domestic life, she eventually finds a workable compromise in her dual-career marriage to Hugh Broderick, a magazine publisher who seems to understand Jane's artistic needs. However, she still encounters great suffering as she is required to shift her energies between the apparently mutually exclusive spheres of authorship and wife/motherhood. It is noteworthy here that her finest novel is written before her marriage and her next best is generated in a period of sexual abstinence with Hugh. When Jane finally attempts writing while pregnant, it results in the near death and "delicate nerves" of the child when it is born, thus proving the advice of Hugh's brother, a doctor: "Either there must be no more books or no more children. You can't have both" (406).

A second tenuous combination is seen in the relationship of two writers: Laura Gunning, a writer with "a small and charming talent for short stories, little novels" (57), whose financial success provides the support for her husband, Owen Prothero, a poor, obscure, "visionary" poet whose works are unfashionable because they are "too portentously inspired" and "inaccessibly divine" (177–178). This union of role-reversed writers (with Laura as the breadwinner and Owen as the weaker party) is pervaded by an aura of doom which is fulfilled in Owen's premature death from tuberculosis. An ironic coda to this example of the untenability of a marriage of artists and its detriment to the female partner comes as Laura gives up her writing to edit Owen's poems and memoirs, "convinced that's the way his immortality will come" (523).

The third female author of the novel, Nina Lempriere, represents the final option for a woman who wishes to succeed in the literary world; in Nina's case, "virginity was the law, the indispensable condition" (313) of developing and exercising her genius. Significant to Nina's different state is her depiction as the most masculine of the three women: at one point, she proclaims that "I'm so much more like a man than a woman that the rules for women don't apply" (243). Her difference is further highlighted by the fact that her genius is not represented as the opposite sex struggling within her but is linked with the goddess Diana: it is "the genius of wild earth, an immortal of divinely pitiful virgin heart and healing hand ... a huntress of the woods and the mountains, a runner in the earth's green depths, in the secret, enchanted ways" (313). Consistent with Nina's unorthodox role, an atmosphere of lesbian desire is present in her physically affectionate friendships with Jane and Laura.[6]

Unfortunately, the novel ends with a sense of all of its central relationships disintegrating. Dissatisfied by their home life and its effect on their writing, both George and Jane require retreats in the country away from their spouses for months at a time in order to write. They flirt with the idea of going off together, but in the end, both return to their marriages of convenience, and Jane becomes a tired, middle-aged woman who considers giving up her genius before it breaks her. Laura is left with the memories and memoirs of Owen, and Nina passes by in the final scene as an unaffected observer of the tired former lovers. Perhaps the lassitude of the novel's closing is a reflection of the author's own state at the time; Sinclair "became seriously ill" while writing the novel, but the fact that it was being serialized forced her to keep meeting deadlines, thus compromising its quality (Zegger 50).

Whatever the cause of its final deflation, the novel suffers from overblown prose (although to a lesser degree than *The Divine Fire*), particularly in the passages discussing the "creators" in terms that can be offensively elitist or numbingly cliché, as in this passage on Jane's appreciation of her genius: "You had to come to it clean from all desire, naked of all possession. . . . For the divine thing fed on suffering, on poverty, solitude, frustration. It took toll of the blood and nerves and of the splendour of the passions. And to those who did not stay to count the cost or measure the ruin, it gave back immeasurable, immortal things" (*Creators* 113–114).

Also, although it is subtitled "A Comedy," *The Creators* has a tendency to take itself far too seriously, and its resolution is far from being a renewal of life through marriage.

In general, Sinclair effectively represents "the conflict between artistic aspiration and a 'feminine' subjectivity which is constructed around ideas of womanly self-sacrifice and the nurturance of others" (Pykett, "Writing" 112). She also successfully raises challenges to the state of early twentieth-century marriage, articulates the pressures faced by female artists, and stretches gender categories in some of her characters, but the novel's style causes the emotional dynamics of the story to fall flat. The almost exclusive communication of the characters' feelings indirectly through the third-person narrator's discourse (there are almost no examples in the novel of what Cohn calls "quoted" or "narrated monologue") creates a sense of distance from the characters that diffuses the sometimes intense conflicts of their inner lives, as in this flat and unconvincing presentation of Jane's reactions after her love is sacrificed for her career: "She no longer thought of Tanqueray. Or, if she did think of him, her thinking no longer roused in her the old perverse, passionate jealousy. She no longer hated her genius because he cared for it. She even foresaw that in time she might come to love it for that reason" (113). These limitations suggest that Sinclair had not yet found the best mode through which to dramatize her central emotional concerns. Although she does not openly state that the third-person omniscient narration of realism is inadequate to the task of representing the interiority of her characters, both male and female, Sinclair soon turned to experiments in narrative style which combined such narration with other elements that she hoped would better represent the conflicts generated by creative genius. This was done especially (and most effectively) in novels with female protagonists, suggesting that Sinclair felt that something different from realism was necessary to give these modern women their emotional due.

Transitions in Theory and Technique: *The Three Sisters*

By far the most significant period of Sinclair's career came during the 1910s, a time in which her horizons were broadened extensively in a number of fields. Modernist developments in psychology, philosophy, politics, and literature inspired in Sinclair her most prolific and diverse output of essays, reviews, and longer theoretical pieces. Her absorption of the momentous shifts in Western thought immediately before and during the World War I years soon made its way into Sinclair's fiction, significantly altering its form and scope and deepening the intensity of some of its characteristic themes. Noteworthy in the years leading up to 1914 are Sinclair's fascination with the science of psychology, her participation in the fiery debates of feminism, and her thorough research in the lives and work of the Brontë sisters, all of which influence the writing of *The Three Sisters*, an unconventional novel which initiates the phase of her finest "experimental" work.

Sinclair's openness and dedication to the intellectual life is aptly illustrated in her passionate engagement with the development of psychoanalysis. Translations of Freud's works were appearing for the first time in English around 1910, although Sinclair most likely had access to his ideas earlier either through her ability to read the original German or through the writings of Havelock Ellis or other English psychologists (Zegger 57–58). In any case, 1913 was a significant year because during it Sinclair became a major benefactor and member of the board of the Medico-Psychological Clinic of London, "the first clinic in England to include psychoanalysis in an eclectic array of therapeutic methods" (Boll 104). Through her reading and advocacy work, Sinclair eventually became conversant enough to write reviews of two of Jung's books that also included her own comments on the theories of psychoanalysis, which she applauded as a much-needed antidote to "Victorian Puritanism."

Of particular interest to Sinclair was the notion of sublimation, the "diversion of the Life-Force, of the Will-to-live, from ways that serve the purposes and interests of species, into ways that serve the purposes and interests of individuals" (*Defence of Idealism* 5), which she saw as a positive force that was undervalued by both Freud and Jung. She particularly admired Jung's chapters on deliverance and sacrifice in *Psychology of the Unconscious*: "The idealist will find in them the answer to his feverish questioning. He will find that throughout man's history man's goal has always been one and the same thing—Sublimation; the freedom of the Self in obedience to a higher law than preceding generations have laid upon him" ("Symbolism" 144). The theory of psychoanalysis provided Sinclair "with the means of transcending the dichotomy of her idealistic view of man as being capable of achieving his self-realization and fulfillment by his own will and her naturalistic view of man as being determined by his environment and his heredity" (Zegger 58). Novels like *The Three Sisters* and *Mary Olivier* serve as dramatizations of how the influence of psychoanalysis, "the best, if . . . not the only method of conversion" ("Symbolism" 144), can free the individual, at least to a degree, from the determinism of family and society.

Just as important to the blossoming of Sinclair's ideas and its effect on her fiction is her participation in the feminist movement of the early 1900s. Her earliest contribution came in the form of two letters sent in 1908 to the pro-suffragist periodical *Votes for Women*, the first of which is a general statement of admiration for and approval of suffragettes. The second is also an expression of sympathy, but it includes an optimistic statement of her hopes for feminism's effect on culture, which bears marked similarities to the ideas of her modernist successors: "The coming generation will, I believe, witness a finer art, a more splendid literature than has been seen since the Elizabethan Age. . . . The Nineteenth Century was an age of material cocksureness, and of spiritual doubt. The Twentieth Century will be the age of spiritual certainty . . . [which will] come through the coming revolution, by the release of long captive forces, by the breathing in among us of the Spirit of Life, the genius of enfranchised womanhood" ("Letter"). Philosophizing six years before D. H. Lawrence in *Study of Thomas Hardy*, Sinclair shares his view of the materialist Victorian age as spiritually lacking and also proclaims a much-needed renewal of the "Life-Force" (although to her it is a female rather than "phallic" force). Writing well before Virginia Woolf in *A Room of One's Own*, Sinclair communicates a similar view of the nineteenth-century age as a materialistic and patriarchal ("cocksure") one, which she believes will be superseded by a female-inspired and -inscribed era.

Sinclair enters the feminist debate with full force in the years 1912–1914, motivated largely by the volatile rhetoric and manipulative stereotypes of the anti-suffragists, especially as espoused by Sir Almroth Wright in a letter to *The Times* in 1912. Wright, taking up an essentialist position based on his sense of the physiological and psychological differences between women and men, advances the thesis that the women's movement is a "hysterical revolt" made up of mostly unmarried women who can only be brought to peace when they recognize their own "natural disabilities" (mental, physical, and moral), which render them incapable of exercising the vote wisely, and focus their energies on their womanly duties as daughters, wives, and mothers (7–8).

Sinclair's most effective response to Wright came in a pamphlet entitled *Feminism* written for The Women Writers Suffrage League. Careful to announce that she is "not an ultra-feminist" and does not see suffragism as "a war of one sex against another" (14), Sinclair takes apart Wright's argument that repression of the "Life-Force" (or sexual energy), which he sees as naturally oriented toward motherhood, usually leads to "hysteria, neurosis, and the detestable manifestations of degeneracy" in unmarried women. Drawing upon a psychologically informed version of idealism, Sinclair appeals to the power of sublimation to transform and transmute sexual reproductive energy "into still higher and subtler energies," particularly in the work of "the artist, the enthusiast, [or] the visionary" (30–31).

Despite its progressive purpose, Sinclair's defense of a woman's right to vote (and to live a healthy unmarried life, if she chooses) rests largely on an essentialist notion of womanhood which Sinclair broadens beyond marriage and motherhood to include other options for women who possess creative genius. Like her male opponent, she agrees that a woman's fundamental identity is linked to the biological process of procreation: "There is everything in that everlasting readiness to bring forth; everything in those profound and intarissable wells of instinct, in that stream of the Life-Force of which Woman is pre-eminently the reservoir" (30). As part of this privileged relationship to the Life-Force, Sinclair claims, some women periodically have intense, almost mystical, experiences of reality: "moments of heightened vision and sensation, when things seen—common things—trees in a field—a stretch of sky—became transfigured and took on I know not what divine radiance and beauty." These experiences are represented as uniquely female: "these moments are most intimately associated with adolescence and the dawn of womanhood; . . . they are incident to falling in love; . . . they are part of the pageant of sexual passion; the psychological side of the great decorative illusion by which the Life-Force lures us to its end" (31). As we shall shortly see, Sinclair's efforts to communicate these mystical moments and how women creatively respond to them led her to a new form of the novel. As Pykett notes, in Sinclair's fiction "this mysticism works in complex and contradictory ways," sometimes "to destabilize and complicate conventional gender categories" and sometimes "to re-present a mystified version of essential (spiritual) femininity, and to reinscribe conventional gender roles" ("Writing" 115–116).

Not only does Sinclair argue for certain qualities that are essential to women; in "A Defence of Men" (1912) she assigns particular "primordial" and "fundamental" qualities to men, most specifically in the area of sexual morality: "in matters of sex feeling and of sex morality man (let us admit it at once) is different from and inferior to women." Sinclair places the responsibility for this moral inferiority as well as "the superior virtue of women" to "Nature's care." The end result of such moral inequity is the "consecration of woman's womanhood to suffering" and sacrifice, which explains her greater spiritual strength than man's (559). As Sinclair puts it, "in the stern economy of Nature, woman's spirituality has been bought at the sacrifice of his" (560). Recognizing that man can prey upon woman's spiritual weakness but unwilling to blame man for his moral weakness in the modern world, Sinclair suggests that woman preys upon man "with the irresistible appeal of her weakness" and boldly asserts that "there cannot be a low standard of sexual morality on man's part without some corresponding, if more secret laxity on woman's" (562). Not content to rest with this unequal state of affairs, Sinclair sees hope in the Feminist movement and, in a clear reversal of gender roles and qualities, places the greater responsibility for change on woman: "I have more hope in that spiritual change in woman which has made a man of her, and which will inevitably inspire her with the tenderness, the courage, and the chivalry of giving man his chance" (566). Sinclair's investment of women with higher spiritual substance may point in part to why her innovations in the novel seem more fitted to the experience of her women characters than that of her men.

A final source of illumination of the ideas behind Sinclair's move toward writing a different kind of novel is found in the literary criticism she wrote around this time. In her novice years as a writer in the late 1890s, Sinclair wrote several reviews of contemporary novels, and these are generally straightforward explications of plot and appreciations of the novel's qualities and limitations. However, as Boll points out, in her reviews Sinclair also tended to "read the novelist in the novel" (Boll 173), citing for praise things like an author's "lucid perception" and "cultivated and conscious irony." Not so surprisingly, the elements of fiction which she valued explicitly in these reviews reflected her own writing style and interests at the time: for example, "uncompromising . . . realism," "sympathy for [the] characters" ("No. 5" 377), and "powerful and fascinating psychological study" ("Mormon" 373).

A more articulate and developed sense of Sinclair's critical concerns emerges in the next ten years as she writes more extensive pieces on individual authors, namely George Meredith and the Brontë sisters, in whom she finds strikingly similar qualities to admire. Her essay on Meredith (1909) presents the author as a pioneer, "the first to deliver the English novel from that degradation" faced by the Victorian novelist, who is caught "between the devil of realism and the deep sea of sentiment . . . [which] distorted his whole attitude to life and his view of the Real" (414). Intelligent and versatile, Meredith is seen by Sinclair as a jack-of-all-literary-trades: a philosopher, poet, realist, psychologist, and dramatist who "refuses to be placed" by the "preposterous labels" of literary conventionalists (413). Sinclair makes mention of Meredith's definition of fiction as "the summary of actual Life, the within and the without of us," and points out that, to achieve this goal, he steps outside of realism, tampering with "the illusion of actuality" through his "lyrical passages" in order to express "the illusion of emotion, of passion, of reality at its highest intensity" (414–415). Finally, Sinclair celebrates Meredith as a man (like Thomas Hardy) who knew "the truth about a woman," recognizing the "degradation" toward women of sentimentalism and depicting it in his often tragic tales of the modern woman "animated . . . with the fires of positive brainstuff" (416).[7] Meredith's skill at stretching literary genres by moving away from patriarchal realism to represent the interior life of the modern woman is a clear inspiration for Sinclair's development.

Beginning in 1907, Sinclair undertook her most significant critical project, an appreciation of the Brontë sisters and their work that started with a series of introductions to the Everyman's Library versions of their novels and Mrs. Gaskell's *Life of Charlotte Brontë* (all but one were written between 1907 and 1910) and culminated with her book *The Three Brontës* (1912), a summary of her research and opinions which is both biographical and critical in nature. On the biographical side, Sinclair emphasized the home life of the Brontës at Haworth as a primary influence on their work, strongly believing that unlike "great men," whose relations are only "temporary obstacles (more or less offensive) to their career" which can be suppressed, "great women . . . cannot thus get rid of their relations. Their lives are inseparable from them, their works in many cases inexplicable without them" ("Introduction," *Life* xiii).

Especially relevant for appreciating the upcoming change of style and subject in Sinclair's fiction is an understanding of the way Sinclair "reads"

Charlotte and Emily as women authors. As represented in the introductions and *The Three Brontës*, Charlotte emerges as the perfect model for a Sinclairan heroine. Like the women of *The Creators*, "hers was one of those minds, essentially feminine, that are only stirred to fruition by great suffering" (xiv). Because "her inner life was luminous with intense realisation," and her actions demonstrate her capabilities for "self-development" and "self-repression," Charlotte's experience is an idealist's dream (*Brontës* 198). Sinclair finds Emily far harder to read due to her detachment and relative obscurity in her lifetime. Living in the shadow of Charlotte's success, Emily "stands apart in an enduring silence, and guards for ever her secret and her mystery" (193). Based on a reading of *Wuthering Heights*, however, Sinclair identifies Emily as even more emotionally intense than her sister: a "mystic . . . by temperament and by ultimate vision" whose "passionate pantheism was not derived . . . [but] was established in her own soul" (198). This spiritual quality occupies a central place in Sinclair's idealistic scheme of things.

In addition to their passionate and creative characters, Sinclair is drawn to the Brontës' diverse writing style. Emily is granted pre-eminence here, possessing "a voice, a quality, an air absolutely apart and distinct, not to be approached by, or confounded with any other" (273–274). Although both sisters can be faulted for problems with form, Emily is the "greater 'realist'" because of her "instinct for the ways of human passion" and ability to let this passion run its full course (272). While less inspired than her sister's, Charlotte's style is still admired by Sinclair for its varied quality. Like George Meredith, Charlotte is praised for being "utterly and marvelously pure from sentimentalism, which was the worst vice of the Victorian age." A major source of frustration to Sinclair (previously seen as an asset in Meredith's work) is the fact that Charlotte "defies analysis. You cannot label her. What she has done is not 'Realism,' neither is it 'Romance.' She displeases both by her ambiguity and by her lack of form" (188). Yet, despite aspects of generic and structural sloppiness, the result of her work at its best, in a novel like *Jane Eyre*, is the presentation not of "a transcript of reality," but "reality itself, pressed on the senses" (123). This is as good a description as any for the kind of effect Sinclair wishes to achieve in her next several novels.

In the wake of her immersion in the world of the Brontës, it is appropriate that Sinclair turns to a Brontë-inspired setting for her next novel, *The Three Sisters* (1914). The suggestiveness of its title to *The Three Brontës* notwithstanding, the resemblances of the novel to the Brontës' lives are minimal. The date of the novel is unidentified, its setting is far to the north of Haworth, and only two of the characters share similarities with their Brontë forebears. Rather than fictionalizing the lives of the Brontës, Sinclair's primary purpose is to dramatize the troubled situation and psyche of three young women in the Victorian age (none of whom is a writer). As we shall see, Sinclair's increased concern with the psychological aspects of their lot pushes her toward new novelistic forms, through which she "continues to *reproduce* the forms and matter of the New Woman Novel as well as reworking them and developing her own modern 'pointelliste' or imagist style of crystallized symbolic scenes and moments" (Pykett, "Writing" 113).

The story is a relatively simple one. The three Cartaret sisters have recently been moved by their father to the village of Garth after an episode in which the youngest daughter, Alice, caused a scandal by pursuing a man to whom she was attracted. Reeling from his own share of disappointment in love (his first two wives died and his third "had run away from him" after four years of marriage (20)), the Vicar is extra vigilant in watching his daughters in their new home, regularly imposing prayers on his "reluctant and most hostile" daughters and trying to restrict their contact with men. Familial peace is threatened in the form of Dr. Steven Rowcliffe, probably the only desirable man in town, who becomes an object of affection for all three sisters. The majority of the novel is taken up with sorting out the intense and largely sexual passions stirred up by the interactions of these principal characters and tracing the often agonizing paths each sister takes in her quest for personal fulfillment.

On one level, the novel can taken as an extended fictional response to Wright's views on feminism (Zegger 71). In her representation of each sister, Sinclair dramatizes three very different reactions to their patriarchal environment, and each serves as a case study of the inadequate and often harmful lifestyle options available to Victorian women. Alice, the youngest daughter with the most overt sexual desires, is subject to several bouts of hysterical illness due to the repression of her libido, and inner peace comes only through an accidental pregnancy that leads to her fulfillment through marriage and motherhood. The experience of Mary, the oldest daughter, offers a sharp contrast to the sexually charged yet somewhat guileless Alice. On the surface, "sweet and good" Mary is the most obedient and placid of the sisters (74), constantly taking her father's side, but behind the scenes of her domestic docility, she manipulates events so that she marries Rowcliffe, even though his heart belongs to Gwendolyn. Gwendolyn serves as the typical Sinclair heroine. The most intelligent, independent and truly passionate of the sisters, she becomes the most wronged because of her willingness to sacrifice herself to the needs of her family. Taking a job in another village to allow the literally love-sick Alice a chance to marry Rowcliffe, Gwendolyn ends up returning home to find both sisters entering into marriage while she is left to care for her stricken father.

Sinclair's interest in psychoanalysis is skillfully incorporated into the fibre of the novel, and Sinclair's focus on "desires and motivations which exist on an unconscious level" are conveyed through "a symbolic style . . . as well as through parenthetical narrative commentary" (Miller 195). Beginning with its festering presence in the Vicar, repression is represented as the cause of much of the novel's action and despair. The lack of a healthy outlet for the Vicar's sexual desires is at the heart of the Christianity-cloaked but mean-spirited environment of the house and his railings against his daughters' potential love relationships. Repression is also at the center of each of the sisters' struggles. In Alice, it first manifests itself in her playing of the piano "with her temperament, febrile and frustrate, seeking its outlet in exultant and violent sound" (13), and it eventually takes the form of several bouts of illness tied to her frustrations in love. For Mary, sexual repression produces a double life; prim and pure in public settings, she allows herself to reflect (regretfully) on "her throbbing, sensuous womanhood" only in a scene in which she puts away barely used (for lack of suitors) summer gowns in the attic (69–70). The duplicity beneath her obedient demeanor finally erupts into actions of conniving and prevarication in her quest for Rowcliffe. Only for Gwendolyn, whose "heightened perception of beauty in nature" serves as "compensation" for her unrealized love (Boll 227), does repression become sublimation (in Sinclair's sense of the word), yielding a life of self-sacrifice that is true to the ethics of philosophical idealism but also, in Gwendolyn's case, far from happy.

Another innovative aspect of the novel derived from psychoanalysis is Sinclair's representation of the characters' unconscious thoughts and motivations. (At this point it is primarily the content rather than the narrative style of the characters' interiority that is innovative, as it is communicated primarily through psycho-narration.) For example, there are periodic references to the Vicar's projection of sexual frustration and rage onto his daughters and his unwed, pregnant servant Essy, and these diverted passions eventually bring on his stroke: "he did not know that he visited his wife's shortcomings on their heads, any more than he knew that he hated Essy and her sin because he himself was an enforced, reluctant celibate" (*Sisters* 136). Alice nearly surrenders her chance for happiness with Jim because, "without . . . being in the least aware of it," she "fabricated one enormous fear, the fear of her father's death" (294) as an obstacle to her decision to marry. Finally, in a scene in which Sinclair briefly slips into the use of "cant words" (Boll 228), Rowcliffe falls under Mary's spell by being "made subject to a sequence of relentless inhibitions and of suggestions overpowering in their nature and persistently sustained," particularly "one incongruous and irresistible association" recalling an attractive, red-haired nurse from his past (*Sisters* 242).

Sinclair's decision in this novel to dramatize feminist issues and communicate the psychological aspects of the characters in a way that departs from her previous work necessitated a shift in style and form as well, and *The Three Sisters* is very different from its predecessors on this account.[8] Instantly noticeable is the physical structure of the novel, which is segmented into brief episodes that function like snapshots of events and moods. Drawing from Abel Chevalley's definition of Sinclair's technique as "impressionism, 'pointillisme'" (206), Boll sees the novel moving "to a beat" through its organization "in short chapters, in broadly spaced sections within the chapters, in paragraphs of a single sentence, and even in the separation of the last paragraph in a chapter," and this "spacing helps to keep the musical beat going" (228).

Although the impressions provided by this "pointillist" style are written in third-person omniscient prose, usually in a "psycho-narration" mode, there are moments when the novel shows hints of Sinclair's impending move to a more complex hybrid of narrative methods that makes up her version of "stream of consciousness." At certain points, usually moments of emotional intensity, a character's consciousness is represented through a mix of techniques which creates a sense of interior conflict and the disjunction of the thought process. For example, early in the novel, as Alice is contemplating the possibility of encountering the attractive Dr. Rowcliffe, the narration moves within a few lines from psycho-narration to quoted monologue to free indirect discourse in an accurate reflection of Alice's adolescent excitement and impatience:

> . . . She was thinking another thought.
> "If Mr. Greatorex is dead, Dr. Rowcliffe won't stay long at Upthorne. He will come back soon. . . ."
> . . . he would be shown into the drawing-room.
> Would he? Would Essy have the sense? No. Not unless the lamp was lit there. Essy wouldn't show him into a dark room. And Essy was stupid. (*Sisters* 11)

Another of Sinclair's dominant techniques in her later novels, shifting from third- to second- person narration to produce a deeper connection to a character's inner life by giving the reader access to the mind's dialogue with itself, is briefly evident in Ally's contemplation of her father's reaction to her: "Ally didn't care a rap what he thought of her. . . . She was much too happy. Besides, if you once began caring what Papa thought there would be no peace for anybody" (90). Other extended instances of Sinclair's use of a narrative hybrid occur at significant romantic moments, for example, as Gwendolyn sorts out own her feelings about Rowcliffe and as Mary schemes to attract his affections. There seems to be a connection between gender and genre here because these changes in narrative mode usually occur when the author is relating the inner experience of her female subjects.

The shift in thematic and stylistic approaches signaled by this novel is best exemplified in the character of Gwendolyn, who is a forerunner of the more "modernist" heroines of Sinclair's postwar novels. Although she is not an artist, of all the female characters in the novel Gwendolyn comes the closest to possessing that creative genius which Sinclair prizes as a potential source of fulfillment for single women. This is found most clearly in her special passion for and connection with nature, which is drawn from Sinclair's impression of Emily Brontë as viewed through the lens of

Wuthering Heights. On several key occasions in the novel, Gwendolyn experiences examples of those "moments of heightened vision and sensation" which Sinclair described in *Feminism*, and these sexually charged mystical experiences are what carry Gwendolyn through her numerous disappointments: "she was apt to be carried away by the pageant of earth and sky; the solid darkness that came up from the moor. . . . She was off, Heaven knew where, at the lighting of a star in the thin blue; the movement of a cloud excited her. . . . She shared the earth's silence and the throbbing passion of the earth as the orbed moon swung free" (157). The passage's uninspiring and awkward prose ("throbbing passion," "orbed moon," etc.) shows that Sinclair has not lost her tendency toward romantic cliché but the vaguely poetic style and syntax of the passage hint at her future representation of such mystical moments through a more successful "stream of consciousness" mode.

Although Gwendolyn is gifted with a sensibility that is shared by other Sinclair heroines, the available outlets for her expression of the Life-Force are severely limited. In a sense, Gwendolyn never has the chance for a genuine love relationship with Rowcliffe because she turns her passion into "adoration" by idolizing the "god-like" Rowcliffe for his self-sacrifice as a doctor (147). Once she loses Rowcliffe to Mary, Gwendolyn is left in the role of devotee, feeding her passion through occasional walks on the moor with Rowcliffe that are marked by an "intensity" which belong to "another scale of feeling and another order of reality" (306–307). The majority of her time is spent in inadequate diversions of her mind and emotions, either slaving away for her father or escaping into intellectualism by becoming a "furious reader" of literature and philosophy, knowing that "there was nothing like Thought to keep you from thinking" (351–352). Even at the end of the novel, Gwendolyn is left at cross-purposes: "There were moments when she saw herself as two women. One had still the passion and the memory of freedom. The other was a cowed and captive creature who had forgotten; whose cramped motions guided her; whose instinct of submission she abhorred" (337). Sinclair continues to depict this split woman in her later fictions, but changes brought about by the war and certain literary developments in the 1910s give her a more adequate vehicle for representing the modern woman's divided state.

Entering the "Stream": *Mary Olivier* and *Harriet Frean*

Like her modernist peers, May Sinclair was profoundly affected by the events of World War I, but it took on greater force in her life and writing because she had direct experience of the conflict on the front in Belgium. Invited by Dr. Hector Munro to be the secretary, treasurer, and official journalist of a volunteer ambulance corps, Sinclair was anything but a detached observer; she helped evacuate the wounded and got dangerously close to the battlefield on several occasions. Her intense experience took literary form in two different ways. In 1915 she published *A Journal of Impressions in Belgium*, a record of her seventeen days of service, the title and style of which give hints of what is to come in her fiction. As the "Introduction" states, her aim was simply "to set down only what I had seen or felt, and to avoid as far as possible the second-hand": ". . . in writing out I have been careful never to go beyond the day, never to add anything, but to leave the moment as it was. I have set down the day's imperfect or absurd impression, in all its imperfection or absurdity, and the day's crude emotion in all its crudity, rather than taint its reality with the discreet reflections that came after" (*Journal*, "Introduction"). This impressionistic approach takes on a fuller form in a few of Sinclair's succeeding novels although, ironically, not in the one that is directly based on her war experience, *The Romantic* (1920), which is a work of psychological realism.

Sinclair's desire to capture impressions, sampled in both *The Three Sisters* and *A Journal of Impressions in Belgium*, emerged during these years largely because of her exposure to imagist poetry. Inspired by its "beauty of restraint and stillness and flawless clarity," she befriended and championed imagist poets like H. D., Ezra Pound, Richard Aldington, and F. S. Flint, whom she felt rid poetry of "the sentiment that passed for passion all through the nineteenth century" ("Two Notes" 88). A few of her writings on these figures reveal her understanding of the "movement" and certain characteristics which she brings into her fiction. In "Two Notes" ("On H. D." and "On Imagism"), Sinclair declares that, "Presentation not Representation is the watchword of the school. The Image . . . is form and substance." Never communicating the form of a thing (or of a passion, emotion, or mood) as an abstraction, the Image is "in no case . . . a symbol of reality (the object); it is reality (the object) itself. You cannot distinguish between the thing and its image." The imagists' return to "direct naked contact with reality" (88) is very appealing to Sinclair, especially as applied to the life of the emotions, a project which she sees is particularly important and difficult in the modern age: "The modern poet requires a greater freedom of form and movement . . . because he has a larger heritage of emotions and ideas. . . . and so far as these modern states of mind are subtler and more complex, they call for a subtler and more complex medium of expression" ("Flint" 11). In her fiction, Sinclair hoped to create a parallel to the form of imagist poetry through her adaptation of the "stream of consciousness" style, although with decidedly mixed results.

The despair of the war years did nothing to check Sinclair's enthusiasm for philosophical idealism; if anything, it increased her devotion, as evidenced in the publication of *A Defence of Idealism*, an argument against the materialism and pluralism of the "New Realists," who held sway over philosophic opinion in those days and dismissed the concepts of the spiritual self and the unity of being that were so prized by idealists. *A Defence of Idealism* is largely a negative document, in which Sinclair takes apart various realist and pragmatist positions in painstaking detail, but it ends on a positive and even uplifting note with a chapter on mysticism that is significant to understanding Sinclair's finest novels. As a way of reviving idealism, she links her philosophical theories with the Eastern tradition of mysticism to argue for the participation of finite selves in the "Infinite Spirit." The "certainty" of this communion comes through rare experiences of "such heightening of psychic intensity that we discern Reality here and now" (338). Sinclair's description of these experiences recalls the epiphanies described in her earlier work; they are "moments when things we have seen all our lives without truly seeing them . . . change to us in an instant of time, and show the secret and imperishable life they harbour; moments of danger that are moments of sure and perfect happiness, because then the adorable Reality gives itself to our very sight and touch" (339).

The twin influences of imagism and mysticism come together in Sinclair's landmark piece of literary criticism, "The Novels of Dorothy Richardson," a review of the first three volumes of *Pilgrimage*. Impressed by "the startling 'newness' of Miss Richardson's method, and her form," Sinclair begins the essay with a call to "throw off the philosophic cant of the nineteenth century" and the old categories used to speak of reality: "it is absurd to go on talking about realism or idealism, or objective and subjective art" because "[a]ll that we know of reality at first hand is given to us through contacts in which those interesting distinctions are lost" (442). Drawing upon feminine imagery which is to be echoed later by Woolf (who is indebted to this article for her work in "Modern Fiction"), Sinclair describes reality as "thick and deep, too thick and too deep, and at the same time too fluid to be cut with any convenient carving knife." In light of this depth and fluidity, "[t]he novelist who would be close to reality must confine himself to this knowledge at first hand" and, in the words of another reviewer (Mr. J. B. Beresford), "must . . . simply plunge in" (442–443).[9] While Sinclair marvels at Richardson's "performance," she notes that she is only following the lead, "independently, perhaps unconsciously" (443), of French writers like the de Goncourts and Marguerite Audoux, as well as that of James Joyce in *A Portrait of the Artist*.

The hallmark of this relatively brief article is its application of William James's phrase for the working of the mind, "stream of consciousness," to a literary style.[10] An essential quality of this method (so similar to the imagists' goal of "presentation not representation") is the invisibility of the author, who must only inhabit a position inside the protagonist's mind and psyche: ". . . she must not interfere; she must not analyse or comment or explain. . . . She must not be the wise, all-knowing author. She must be Miriam Henderson" (443). The result is an apparently formless fiction: "Nothing happens. It is just life going on and on. It is Miriam Henderson's stream of consciousness going on and on" (444). Sinclair especially admires this style's "intensity," which is "the effect of an extreme concentration on the thing seen or felt," and the way it yields novels "of an extraordinary compression" and "extenuation" (445).

Another result of this intensity is the blurring of boundaries, such as that between subject and object, that are so highly treasured by patriarchal realism. In presenting only what happens in Miriam's mind, "Richardson seizes reality alive. The intense rapidity of the seizure defies you to distinguish between what is objective and what is subjective either in the reality presented or the art that presents" (446). Sinclair is so enchanted with Richardson's accomplishment that she finds in it a reinforcement of her idealism. Using language that recalls her philosophy of female experience (and thereby suggests this is a feminine form of the novel), she calls Richardson's approach "a mysticism apart" because in the end, "What really matters is a state of mind, the interest or ecstasy with which we close with life" (446).[11] Sinclair herself turns to this intensity and ecstasy in composing her next and best novel.

In many ways, *Mary Olivier: A Life* can be seen not only as the apex of Sinclair's novel-writing career but also as a nearly comprehensive summary of her theoretical interests and characteristic themes. A female *Bildungsroman* that is largely autobiographical, the novel traces the life of an Englishwoman from the ages of two to thirty-seven and, in its course, serves as a critique of Victorian values, a psychological case study, a philosophical exploration of the developing self, and a diary of an artistic imagination. Most importantly of all, it marks a major shift in Sinclair's writing style in which she produces her own version of the "stream of consciousness" mode in order to capture the intense inner life of her protagonist as she journeys away from the restrictions of Victorian convention and toward self-awareness and self-possessed, modern womanhood.

The story line of the novel, a series of pointillist scenes that are divided into five chronological sections ("Infancy," "Childhood," "Adolescence," "Maturity," and "Middle-Age") which correspond to "the stages of the mystical way" (Zegger 107), intersects with Sinclair's own life in numerous ways.[12] Mary is born into the family of an alcoholic father, a pious and controlling mother, and three brothers: Mark, the favorite; Roddy, the sensitive one; and Dan, the black sheep of the family who follows in his father's tippling footsteps. The first three sections of the novel are taken up with Mary's home life, which is hardest on her as she competes with her father and brothers for her mother's attention and affection.

Her plight is further complicated by the fact that she is not a typical late-Victorian girl; intellectually curious and tomboyish, Mary constantly frustrates her mother's expectations of what it means to be a proper, domestic girl. This is exemplified early on in Mary's unorthodox experiences of and reflections on the nature of God, which develop into an open rebellion against her mother's Christian faith. As Mary grows toward womanhood, so do her creative imagination and independent mind, and she pursues their impulses through a course of private study and writing, which serves as a further threat to her fitting into a culturally accepted gender role. Running parallel to Mary's intellectual and artistic journey is a series of emotional relationships with men that ultimately prove to be incompatible with her self-fulfillment. In the end, Mary is portrayed as a spiritually and emotionally happy woman who has had to sacrifice love to her sense of duty and independence.

Mary Olivier might have been a standard tale of a repressed woman's struggle to come into her own but for its unusual narrative style. Obviously motivated by her recent reading and critique of Dorothy Richardson's work, Sinclair puts her own spin on the "stream of consciousness" mode. Although a great deal of the novel is written in the third person, much of it employing psycho-narration to present Mary's thoughts, this work differs from the style of both Richardson and Joyce (in *A Portrait*) in two key ways. First of all, they use a neutral omniscient narrator to represent the inner thoughts and emotions of their protagonists, while Sinclair uses Mary herself to tell the tale (mostly in the third-person) as an adult from a position of "current retrospection" with "no auctorial anticipation" (Boll 239–240). This adoption of a third person autobiographical voice allows for some aesthetic distance while remaining completely within the protagonist's consciousness.

An example of the difference is seen in the way in which Joyce and Sinclair represent their early childhood experience. In an attempt to convey a sense of immediacy and innocence in these early scenes, Joyce writes in an age-appropriate vocabulary and syntax, but Sinclair's approach is that of "re-creation through memory," so that although her scenes "have the choppy, disconnected feeling of early memories, . . . [t]hey form short sections which reveal a complete incident, an important step in the development of Mary's mind and emotions" (S. Kaplan 51–52).[13] This is evident in the very first section of the novel, which communicates a disjointed series of Mary's infant memories through a narration that periodically switches from third to second person. The effect of these shifts draws attention to the remembered quality of the story and highlights particularly intimate sensory moments, as in this glimpse of Mary being maternally comforted after a scare:

> Mamma took her into the big bed. . . . Mamma's mouth moved over her wet cheeks, nipping her tears.
>
> Her cry changed to a whimper and a soft, ebbing sob.
>
> Mamma's breast: a smooth, cool round thing that hung to your hands and slipped from them when they tried to hold it. You could feel the little ridges of the stiff nipple as your finger pushed it back into the breast.
>
> Her sobs shook in her throat and ceased suddenly. (*Mary* 4)

The second difference from the "stream" style of Joyce and Richardson is connected to the novel's dual setting within Mary's past and present points of view: the narration Sinclair employs is multi-faceted and multi-vocative. Marking a significant change from the almost exclusive use of psycho-narration in Sinclair's earlier, more realist fictions, at a number of significant moments in the novel, the focus is on Mary Olivier's secondary consciousness, which reports her "perceptions, actions, feelings, impressions, fantasies, thoughts, and dreams in 'oratio recta' and 'oratio obliqua,' in formulations of introvocative (second person), ectovocative (third person), and egovocative statements" (Boll 240). Rather than "an endless outpouring of the endless perceptions and reflections which may occur in any given interval of time" (as in the work of Joyce and Richardson), there is an overt exercise of control here, yielding "merely the *imitation* of a stream, not a stream at all" (S. Kaplan 50). In her use of different types of vocative statements, Sinclair can record direct sensation and emotion ("I"), internal dialogue ("you"), and more distant reflection ("she"), all the while remaining within the protagonist's perspective.

This shifting of person and voice can be somewhat jarring, but it produces a unique effect, as in this glimpse of Mary's thoughts on a train en route to boarding school:

> Grass banks. Telegraph wires dipping and rising like sea-waves. At Dover there would be the sea.
> Mamma's face—Think. Think harder. The world was going on before your mind started. Supposing you lived before, would that settle it? No. A white chalk cutting flashed by. God's mind is what both go on in. That settles it.
> The train dashed into a tunnel. A long tunnel. She couldn't remember what she was thinking of the second before they went in. Something that settled it. Settled what? She couldn't think any more. (Mary 137)

The periodic shifts in the narration help convey a sense of the competing voices and emotions inside Mary's head at this confusing time of transition in her life. Clipped phrases of physical description are used to communicate the external world of the rushing train which occasionally intrudes upon Mary's reflections. The use of the imperative ("Think") and introvocative ("you") in the second paragraph enable the representation of an internal conversation in which Mary reflects on her mother's good-bye and the tension underlying their relationship while at the same time engaging in one of her philosophical reflections on the connection between the mind and the material world ("God's mind is what both go on in"). Finally, the shift to the ectovocative ("she") registers the disruption of Mary's racing thoughts by the tunnel, and it captures her attempt at this remove to literally re-member her preceding reflections. At other times in the novel, the shift back to the third person shows how "the writer Mary, looking at her own life from a great distance in time or feeling, separates herself from the thoughts of the character Mary" (S. Kaplan 51).

There is nothing in Sinclair's theory to suggest that she means this narrative style to be a particularly feminine one, but in the creation of her version of the "stream," Sinclair finds a more appropriate form than that of her earlier novels to convey the complexity and tension which make up the experience of the modern creative woman. This is demonstrated in the style's suitability as a medium for embodying Sinclair's characteristic themes. The novel's depiction of Mary's situation within a patriarchal family dynamic contains what is probably Sinclair's least forced dramatization of a psychological situation. Presented through the consciousness of the passionately involved yet wisely reflective Mary, the Oliviers' failure to live up to the ideal "family romance" is seen in immediate and illuminating ways.

Particularly effective is the way in which Sinclair blends Mary's insights about the psychological motivations and Oedipal struggles among her parents and brothers with her often intense feelings of rejection and inadequacy in the family circle. This is most manifest in Mary's reading of Mark's position as the central object of the family's affection. The narration is poignant in its balancing of Mary's acute insight into the jealousy and displaced anger generated in the family by her mother's preferential treatment of Mark and her own painful experiences of the fallout from this unjust dispensation of love, as in Mary's observations upon Mark's long-awaited return from a stint in India: "Mamma and Mark were happy together; their happiness tingled, you could feel it tingling, like the happiness of lovers. They didn't want anybody but each other. You existed for them as an object in some unintelligible time and in a space outside their space" (*Mary* 241).

Directly related to this dysfunctional family drama is Mary's coming into her identity as an unconventional young woman, a process beset by conflict and insecurity that is sometimes brilliantly represented in the unfolding of Mary's consciousness. Primarily centered in the potent love-hate relationship with her mother,[14] Mary's journey toward self-possession comes up against all of the forces which Sinclair articulates as inimical to woman's equality. Constricted by her mother's expectations of her gender role ("I like to see you behaving like a little girl, instead of tearing about and trying to do what boys do" (70)) as well as the threat of inherited hysteria (embodied in the unbalanced Aunt Charlotte, who "just fell in love with every man she met" (237)), Mary's efforts to be her own person often take place covertly and come at great emotional cost.

Her primary refuge as an adolescent becomes the usually male-inhabited world of ideas, which increasingly envelops her inner life as she becomes exposed to new perspectives in philosophy, literature, and theology which challenge her narrow Victorian existence. This sets up numerous battles with her mother over her faith and fate. The constant internal division Mary experiences between what she feels called toward intellectually and what is expected of her socially is evident in the conclusion to a fight she has with her mother over using Mark's books: "She was sorry for it now, miserable, utterly beaten. Her new self seemed to her a devil that possessed her. She hated it. She hated the books. She hated everything that separated her and made her different from her mother and from Mark" (129).

Appropriate to the interior focus of the novel, glimpses of Mary's truest self emerge in moments of what she calls her "secret happiness," experiences that first arise in adolescence and are intimately linked to Mary's sexual and artistic drives. Sinclair's "stream" method is tailor-made for these moments, quintessential examples of the "heightened vision and sensation" she claims creative women experience in contact with the "stream of the Life-Force." These experiences usually begin with a sensory encounter with nature that has a transfigurative quality: "The five trees stood up, thin and black, in an archway of golden white fire. The green of their young leaves hung about them like an emanation" (93). Mary's response to these epiphanies are of an intense sexual, emotional, and spiritual or mystical quality: ". . .the sudden, secret happiness . . . more than anything was like God. When she thought of it she was hot and cold by turns and she had no words for it. She remembered the first time it had come to her, and how she had found her mother in the drawing-room and had knelt down at her knees and kissed her hands" (144).

Far from being simply a periodic "high," Mary's "secret happiness" is at root connected to her deepest and most creative self, and as in Sinclair's earlier novels, the search for its proper channeling is expressed as an irreconcilable conflict between genius and gender role. Almost from the start, Mary's encounters are accompanied by an impulse toward artistic creativity, first through intensely emotional piano playing, much like Alice in *The Three Sisters*. However, this is too public an affair and it subjects Mary to her parents' criticism, so she is drawn to the more clandestine pursuit of poetry: "She knew what she would do; she had always known. She would make poems. They couldn't hear you making poems. They couldn't see your thoughts falling into sound patterns" (184). Her literary career takes a long time to develop because of her mother's resistance and the inherent difficulties of a woman breaking into the literary world. After much struggle, and through the influence of a male literary friend, she finally gets her first poem and then a slim volume of poetry published, but her accomplishment has a contrary effect on her inner self: "Funny—it was the least real thing. . . . If you took it up and looked at it the clearness, the unique, impermanent reality would be gone, and you would never get it again" (344).[15]

Running parallel to Mary's expression of the "Life-Force" through poetry are her romantic and sexual desires, through which she is drawn into several potential love relationships, none of which proves secure and all of which interfere with her literary career.[16] Two of these experiences, one in adolescence and one in middle age, come closest to fulfilling Mary's sexual and intellectual needs. In the first, with Maurice Jourdain, Mary is swept up in passion and a sense that she has found her soul mate, as in this burst of emotion initiated by physical memories of her beloved: ". . . she was mainly aware of a surpassing tenderness and a desire to immolate herself. . . . Her self had a secret place where people couldn't get at it, where its real life went on. He was the only person she could think of as having a real life at all like her own. She had thought of him as mixed up for ever with her real life" (211).

This union of hearts and "real life" is not to be; using the excuse of financial misfortune but really threatened by the prospect of a lifetime with such an intellectual woman, Maurice breaks off their engagement. In the aftermath, Mary recognizes that her love for him was not truly of the soul and has drained some of the Life-Force from her: "If she could only go back to her real life. But she couldn't. She couldn't feel any more her secret, sudden happiness. Maurice . . . had driven it away" (226). A similar fate befalls an affair in later life with Richard Nicholson, Mary's literary mentor who offers her the chance to break away from her constricted world for a life and career in London. Mary's act of self-sacrifice in caring for her invalid mother is ostensibly the primary obstacle to their union, but Mary explains that her resistance comes from a mysterious sublimating force inside her which is "absolutely real" because it "makes you happy without the thing you care most for in the world" (366).

The conclusion of the book finds Mary alone with this particularly female mystical sense of a connection with the "real" that is the source of an "inconceivable freedom" (367). There is an increasing sense of immediacy and intensity as Mary comes to understand and make peace with her inner self. Totally alone yet freed by her mother's death and Richard's marriage to another woman, Mary's happiness becomes a more pervasive experience that she recognizes as a union with God: "She had a sense of happiness and peace suddenly there with her in the room. Not so much her own as the happiness and peace of an immense, invisible, intangible being of whose life she was thus aware. She knew somehow through It, that there was no need to get away" (375). In a paradox that is characteristic of philosophical idealism, Mary ultimately ties her personal freedom to consciousness of God and the merging of her will with God's.

It is noteworthy that after this mystical experience, and as the novel approaches the present moment (calling to mind the conclusion of *Orlando*) from which the writer Mary is narrating her story, the "stream of consciousness" moves from its customary shifts between third- and second-person narration to an exclusively first-person account in the final few sections of the novel. Once Mary has encountered the "reality" of herself and God, something no human relationship can supersede, her sense of personal integration is marked by the text's repeated use of "I": "I stripped my soul. . . . I tried to doubt away this ultimate passion, and it turned my doubt into its own exquisite sting, the very thrill of the adventure. . . . If it never came again I should remember" (379–380). This is a significant move because, although there is nothing in Sinclair's theory to indicate that this stylistic shift is meant as a feminine representation of interiority, nowhere in her other "stream" novels does she apply such an extensive use of first person narration to a male character.

Unhampered by the demands of marriage and family and "completely open to God and at one with all creation" (S. Kaplan 71), Mary is able in her mystical moments to escape the determinism of her world and briefly enter the stream of reality in the most fulfilling way possible for a woman of her creative nature. Yet there is something disturbing about the way in which Mary, although choosing her single life and the sublimation of her sexual energy through mystical reveries and writing, finally conforms to "the traditional concept of feminine receptivity: its passivity and its openness to physical reality" (67). In essence, her "feminine self . . . is only found in giving itself up" (70), a revelation that is a source of irony since the foundation of the ethic of self-sacrifice is Christianity, one of the obstacles from which Mary fights so hard to free herself. Although one might wish that Mary could combine her passive mystical self with more active pursuits in her relationships and writing career, at least she is rewarded with a sense of peace and gratification while giving up opportunities for love. As we shall see, this is not the case for the next Sinclair heroine.

Life and Death of Harriet Frean (1922) is, at least in the person of its protagonist, a negative counterpart to *Mary Olivier*. As Sinclair herself put it, the novel was an "experiment": "I wished to see what I could make out of the study of a small, arrogant creature, not selfish entirely, and not wilfully cruel, but incredibly blind and with a wizened soul. I went with her over the road I had already gone with *Mary Olivier* and put her to similar tests" (Steell 559). Like her previous work centering on female characters, the novel is an examination of the effects of repression in the Victorian era but with a twist: this time there is no positive sublimation to redeem the heroine from her burdensome existence. Written in a variation of the "stream of consciousness" style of *Mary Olivier*, the novel is structured in a way that mirrors "the particularly unimaginative and restricted consciousness" (Zegger 119) of the title character; at 184 pages it is much briefer than its predecessor and written in a "sheared" style (containing fewer "stream" passages and much more third-person psycho-narration) that sadly echoes Harriet's intellectual and emotional limitations. The sterility of its heroine notwithstanding, the novel possesses a poignancy which shows that its style can be applied, albeit in a limited way, to a woman who lacks the creative gifts of a Jane Holland or a Mary Olivier.

The plot of the novel, although set some thirty years earlier and stretching over a seventy-year lifetime, bears some parallels to *Mary Olivier*. Harriet is raised in a repressive family situation with a distant father and a pious mother who are sparing in their affection and generous in stressing the virtue of self-sacrifice. Like Mary, she has the opportunity for a love match with a young man, but she declines it in a spirit of self-sacrifice because he is engaged to her best friend, and she ends up caring for her sick mother. However, that is where the similarities end, because Harriet is no Mary Olivier. As a child she commits a few acts of rebellion but, rather than strengthening her sense of independence, the violation of her parents' expectations crushes her with guilt: "*their* unhappiness was the punishment. It hurt more than anything" (*Harriet* 23). In a switch from the earlier novel, the parents have more substance than their child; Harriet's father is a free thinker who reads Darwin and Huxley, and her mother has a mystical side: "Her mother had some secret: some happy sense of God that she gave to you and you took from her as you took food and clothing, but not quite knowing what it was, feeling that there was something more in it, some hidden gladness, some perfection that you missed" (40–41). When Harriet, like Mary, attempts to improve herself through intellectual reading, she proves a dullard and eventually takes to novels, "satisfied with anything that ended happily and had nothing in it that was unpleasant, or difficult, demanding thought" (114).

Because of Harriet's lack of depth in comparison with Mary, there is no real coming-of-age in this *Bildungsroman*, if it can be called that. Harriet's self-sacrifice soon becomes self-righteousness, and the repressive forces in her life are never transformed through sublimation into liberating creative energies. By middle-age she carries herself with an air of superiority, having constructed an exalted self-image based on rationalizations of her passive behavior, and many of her reflections serve as a court of petty judgments against her friends who have acquired the very things she sacrificed. In a pathetic contrast to Mary's blissful moments of revelation through nature, an experience of "secret, unacknowledged satisfaction" (73) for Harriet comes when she can pity her best friend who is suffering an hysterical illness brought about by the knowledge of her husband's love for Harriet. It seems appropriate that Harriet's death is due to the hereditary cancer she contracts, as if the unreleased repression in her life has finally eaten away at her being. As Stark puts it, "Harriet strives so hard to imitate her mother that dying of the same illness as her only appears to be a logical consequence" (268).

Although the story of Harriet is a depressing one which is devoid of the hope which concludes *Mary Olivier*, somehow Sinclair's "stream" method is fitting for both tales. There is a difference between the novels in the degree to which direct passages of the protagonist's thought stream are used. In *Harriet Frean* Sinclair employs third-person psycho-narration much more frequently, probably because Harriet is much less reflective than Mary and does not possess the same level of mystical and creative gifts, which lend themselves so well to the "stream" style. What few passages include second-person narration and a more free-flowing sense of Harriet's thoughts appropriately occur early in the novel when Harriet is struggling against the forces of repression, as in this moment of childish blasphemy:

> Suddenly a thought came rushing at her. There was God and there was Jesus. But even God and Jesus were not more beautiful than Mamma. They couldn't be. . . .
>
> Saying things like that made you feel good and at the same time naughty, which was more exciting than only being one or the other. But Mamma's face spoiled it. . . . what did she think God would do? (15–16)

As Harriet gets older, conforming herself to Victorian standards of female submissiveness and stifling her intellectual curiosity, the narrative style takes on a reportorial quality and access to Harriet's thoughts is presented almost totally through psycho-narration. Ironically, the only free-flowing passage toward the end of the novel occurs when Harriet is under an anesthetic for her cancer operation and many of her repressed thoughts and feelings are blurted out.

Even though Harriet is a woman of limited intellectual and creative abilities, having the tale told from inside her consciousness is revealing and moving, especially in those moments when one sees firsthand the process of rationalization this sad woman must go through to maintain a semblance of self-respect. It is a tribute to Sinclair's handling of the narration in both tales of female repression that each is capable of generating a profound emotional response in the reader. Just as the reader celebrates Mary Olivier's liberation from the forces which block her individuation through a healthy form of sublimation in her mystical reveries and writing, so too the reader sympathizes with Harriet's piteous life of resignation. It remains to be seen whether Sinclair is capable of the same level of success with a male subject.

THE "STREAM" DRIES UP: *ARNOLD WATERLOW* AND *ANTHONY WARING*

Sinclair's version of the "stream" method yields her most insightful and substantial accounts of female repression and the contrasting ways in which it can be sublimated, but she did not intend this style to be applied exclusively to women's experience. In 1924, continuing her "obsession for making these experiments," she set her sights on the repression of men in the modern world by writing *Arnold Waterlow: A Life*, which was "intended to be a male *Mary Olivier*" (Steell 559). True to Sinclair's thematic program, the novel traces the life of a protagonist who is raised by distant parents in a strict Victorian family setting and pursues his independence through the world of ideas and romance, but who is ultimately forced to sacrifice his personal needs to the demands of his loved ones. Numerous parallels can be drawn between the plot and character of the two novels, but Sinclair's attempt to transfer the success of *Mary Olivier* to a representation of male experience leads to a breakdown in literary style and emotional power. At least in practice, there seems to be something about Sinclair's innovation in the "stream" method which is more germane to her representation of female experience.

As his early life unfolds, Arnold resembles an identical twin to Mary. First of all, he grows up in the shadow of a favored older brother and is hypersensitive to his mother's partiality and his father's jealousy. Secondly, at an early age Arnold has an unorthodox experience of God that foreshadows his questioning of his family's faith. Finally, like Mary, he has a quick and intellectually thirsty mind and an intimate, almost mystical love of nature, seen in this encounter with some purple lilies: "As he looked at them and put out his hand to touch them he trembled with the shock of this unsurpassable encounter.... as if he had known them, as if they knew him and were waiting there for him" (*Arnold* 70). His similarity to his literary sister is underlined by the fact that, for possessing this mystical quality, Arnold is perceived as effeminate; his older brother Richard torments him with accusations of being "Tame" and "Domestic" because of his love for the flowers, which for Anthony are a source of "perfect, unspeakable happiness" (72–73).

As if in reaction to the charge of being unmanly, Arnold's life takes a masculinizing turn and embraces Victorian ideals when he enters the world of public school, where he becomes "good at games" and can "box and wrestle better than any other boy of his age" (123). His de-sensitizing continues when his father's financial misfortunes force Arnold to pass up a university education and enter directly into an office job at a cheese factory which "was disastrous to the inner life. His mind was no longer free. He had to pin it down to what he was doing" (163–164). The primary outlet for Arnold's emotions becomes his love life, but this too is demoralizing because he gets caught up in two romantic triangles with tragic results. His first love is a pianist, Rosalind Verney, whose career ambitions and need to be needed take her away from her marriage to Arnold and into an affair with Max Schoonhoven, a fellow musician. Arnold rebounds through an affair with a kindred spirit, Effie Warren, but his bliss is shattered by Rosalind's shameful return and his dutiful keeping of a promise to take her back at any time.

It would be fitting to be able to say that the breakdown in style of the novel matches the emotional changes in Arnold's life, but that would be to ascribe more conscious effort on Sinclair's part than I think is warranted. The childhood scenes of the novel are closer to the style of *Mary Olivier*, suggesting a certain degree of innocence and even gender neutrality in the early experiences of Mary and Arnold. As Arnold is sucked more and more into the male Victorian world of public schools and business, it stands to reason that his external experience is accompanied by a drying up of his inner life and that this is marked by a flattening-out of the narrative style. However, the novel's narration never fully takes on the sometimes lyrical quality of its female-centered predecessor.

The early sections of the novel consists of shifts between second- and third-person narration of Arnold's perspective, but he is much less reflective than Mary and there is not the same level of passion communicated in the account of his family turmoils. One reflection of this is seen in the fact that, even early on, this novel contains a great deal more dialogue, which takes over the latter half of the novel, making it seem more an account of Arnold's external world than of his inner consciousness. Sadly, the most extended "stream" passages used during Arnold's adult life are tedious ones that occur when, like Mary, he takes up what is considered the masculine pursuit of philosophy: "He thought for hours on end about the nature of knowledge and reality. How do we come to know anything? . . . Spinoza didn't prove God's existence, he simply took it for granted. You could only know God as thought and as extension" (206–207). A final indicator of Sinclair's weakening of the "stream" style in this novel is the fact that, for significant stretches, Arnold's story takes a back seat to the love troubles of Rosalind. On a couple of occasions, there are abrupt breaks in the novel's continuity as the narration slips outside of Arnold's head and into that of Rosalind or his mother.

Some critics explain the deterioration of Sinclair's "stream" style as a dissipation of her creative energies due to physical illness and literary exhaustion or to "an excess of method over matter, an over-concern with the new in both thought and style" (Taylor 116). While these may be important factors to consider, I also think the problem lies in the application of this type of narration to her vision of a modern male life. As portrayed by Sinclair, Arnold lacks a number of the qualities found in Mary's character which were so skillfully represented by means of the novel's unique narrative form. Although he possesses intellectual curiosity and a mystical sensibility during childhood, as a man Arnold never develops the same level of creativity and inner spiritual resources that Mary does. In choosing to fulfill his expected gender role in society, Arnold allows the repression which besets him on all sides to define him, rather than engaging artistic channels by which he might sublimate that repression in a healthy way.[17]

Examples of Arnold's interior limitations are found, first, in his moments of mystical revelation, which are so passionate and freeing for Mary but seem schematic and abstract in Arnold's life, as if they are included to uphold a philosophical thesis rather then flesh out a character: "The God he had found last night was more than the object of his metaphysical thinking, the Thought of thought; more than the Reality seen in the sudden flash of his mystic vision; closer than thought or seeing, he was the Self of self, the secret, mysterious Will within his will. Where It was, there could be no more grief" (*Arnold* 441–442). Arnold also lacks the psychological complexity which sets up those intense and engaging dialogues within Mary's consciousness that are an apt reflection of her divided state as an unorthodox woman in a restrictive time. This is seen especially in the lack of development in the novel of the psychological connections between Arnold's childhood family experience and his adult life, as if proving Sinclair's earlier statement in *The Three Brontës* that a man's relations are only "temporary obstacles" to his career.

In the end, Arnold's lack of inner substance in comparison to Mary's inner richness and the accompanying failure of the "stream" form in his story could be the results of lassitude on Sinclair's part, but I also think they point toward a set of contradictions in Sinclair's perception and construction of their gendered roles. On the one hand, I do not think that Sinclair is equating interiority with the feminine here; rather, there is a suggestion that, just as they repress women with genius by means of gender norms, the patriarchal world and its construction of masculinity can suffocate the inner life of creative men, which would explain Sinclair's lessening of the "stream" mode in this novel. As she says of the modern context in "A Defence of Men": "it is a day of getting, of concentration on material things. . . . And whatever spiritual ferment works in the present industrial disturbance, man, immersed in the material welter, is more than ever handicapped" ("Defence of Men" 561). However, on the other hand, this explanation cannot be completely reconciled with the ways in which Sinclair's fictional universe sometimes reflects her essentialist idea of a specifically female Life-Force and suggests that the "stream" mode is especially meant to depict the turbulent experience of a creative woman in the modern world.

Sinclair's final use of the "stream" style comes in a companion piece to *Harriet Frean* entitled *History of Anthony Waring* (1927), another condensed story of a less-than-exceptional protagonist who never overcomes the restrictions of his environment. Like *Harriet Frean*, the story is told in clipped chapters, each revealing a slice of Tony's dull life. After the premature death of his mother, Tony is raised largely by his aunt, who constantly reminds him and his father of her sacrifice in taking care of them. Tony shares Arnold Waterlow's quickness at arithmetic and passion for literature and is quite happy in his studies, but he occasionally suffers from "black fits," although their psychological import is not well developed. Too poor to go to military school, Tony works at a solicitor's office for a while, but then he meets good fortune in the form of an inheritance after his aunt's demise and is able to enter the world of publishing. Tony's forays into the world of romance leave him sorely wanting and eventually destroy him. His first relationship ends in a broken engagement; the next is a naive, short-lived affair with a prostitute; the third is an unhappy marriage to a lower-class nurse who cannot appreciate Tony's literary passion and career; and the final and truest love of his life ends in renunciation ("the one great act of his life" (*Anthony* 121)) and regret, his ironic death literally due to an overstimulated heart upon meeting his renounced lover thirty years later.

The message of *Anthony Waring* echoes *Harriet Frean* in its questioning of the virtues of self-sacrifice, whether in the life of a man or a woman, but a comparison of the two finds Anthony's tale wanting in emotional power. Perhaps because Tony is a more interesting and successful character than Harriet (and a man), his hard-luck story does not possess the degree of poignancy of her pathetic life. This is possibly also due to a lack of the psychological resonance between childhood and adult life that is so manifest in the account of Harriet's experience. Like *Arnold Waterlow*, this novel spends too much time chronicling the protagonist's melodramatic love life (often through insipid dialogue), and because his lifestyle options have been more plentiful, Tony's renunciation of love does not carry the same sense of urgency and fatalism that it does for his female counterpart. For the most part the narration stays inside Anthony's perspective, and there are a few remnants of the "stream" style: "he felt her power as a teacher and respected her. . . . Lessons held him. Over lessons he was always good. And when you were good Aunt Sarah wasn't really so bad" (24). However, much of the narration has a minimalist quality that doesn't mature as Anthony gets older, making the story read like a childish realist account that conveys little sense of reflection or inner struggle on the protagonist's part.

Does Anthony's story fail when presented in this format because it is a fundamentally different experience from that of a woman? That is an impossible question to answer but, even more than in *Arnold Waterlow*, Sinclair's treatment of this man's life conveys a sense of distance and awkwardness that makes her two female-centered triumphs even more outstanding. Reflecting a sense of the dwindling of Sinclair's art, one reviewer of the novel suggests that she "ceased, sometime since, to have . . . 'anything to say.' It is obvious, that is, she is no longer moved either by that impulse to social protest which once tinged even her work or by any less definite need to communicate an individual attitude toward life" (Krutch 481).

A coda to the parabolic success of Sinclair's novel career is perhaps best drawn from one of her last novels, *Far End* (1926), which provides a semi-autobiographical overview of her career, albeit cast in the guise of a male protagonist. The novel depicts the career and love life of Christopher Vivart, a novelist whose development mirrors that of Sinclair herself. Having achieved success in writing realistic novels of the "passion of sex," Christopher goes on to write a "philosophical novel" dealing with the "passion of truth" (*Far* 32) called *The Idealist*, the story of a professor who struggles between idealism and realism. After serving in World War I, Christopher suffers from a lack of inspiration but is finally moved to write a new kind of novel, which he describes in terms akin to Sinclair's theory in "On Imagism" and "Dorothy Richardson." He hopes to create a narrative that eliminates "God Almighty, the all-wise, all-seeing author" (80) and achieves "a unity of form" and "substance" (84), which tells the story only as it happens in the male protagonist's consciousness: "It's presentation, not representation, all the time. There's nothing but the stream of Peter's consciousness" (83). The novel garners tremendous acclaim so he attempts the same style with a female subject, which is also successful.

Despite the fact that it bears loose similarities to Sinclair's career, *Far End* contains a series of notable reversals. First, it is a realistic novel about an experimental novelist who is male. Secondly, the sexual order of the "stream of consciousness" novels he writes (male then female) is the opposite of Sinclair's own, and in what is perhaps a stroke of wishful thinking, both are critically acclaimed (contemporary reviews of *Mary Olivier* and *Arnold Waterlow* were not nearly so laudatory). It seems telling that the final novel Christopher writes is called *The Hypocrite* and, true to its name, it is a "study of hypocrisy"; the style of the novel is not made clear, but its title possibly reflects Sinclair's attitude toward the course of her own work.

Much as she might have liked to apply her literary innovation to protagonists of both sexes, Sinclair comes up short in transferring her style to her construction of a male perspective, and what results is second-rate fiction. Her version of "stream of consciousness" works best when applied to what she represents as the complex inner life and spirituality of a creative modern woman who must struggle for independence and her own place in a restrictive society. The multi-vocality and shifting perspective of Sinclair's "stream" style complements her feminist attempt to represent the conflict generated by patriarchal repression and the freedom provided through female sublimation, thereby tying form to gender in Sinclair's practice if not her theory. Reservations about the success of her execution notwithstanding, Sinclair is not alone in her literary project of envisioning more balance between the sexes. The construction of a modern fictional world in which the forces of one sex do not dominate the other is one of the primary goals of the final author we will consider, D. H. Lawrence, who was probably influenced by Sinclair's pioneering psychological work in *The Three Sisters*.

CHAPTER FOUR

From Consummation to "Remasculation"
D. H. Lawrence's Quest for the Phallic Novel

INTRODUCTION

> What we call the Truth is, in actual experience, that momentary state in living [when] the union between the male and the female is consummated. This consummation may be also physical, between the male body and the female body. But it may be only spiritual, between the male and female spirit. (*Study* 72)

> ... it seemed to him, woman was always so horrible and clutching, she had such a lust for possession, a greed of self-importance in love. (*Women in Love* 192)

> ... a permanent relation between a man and a woman isn't the last word. ... We want something broader. I believe in the additional perfect relationship between man and man. (345)

Taken as a whole, the work of D. H. Lawrence may best be described as passionately self-contradictory, as these passages illustrate in a small way. From the start, the so-called "Priest of Love" made the primary focus of his literary career an exploration of the human passions, particularly in terms of heterosexual relations, and his primary goal was to represent the consummation of male and female he envisions in *Study of Thomas Hardy*. However, as the excerpts of Rupert Birkin's feelings in *Women in Love* show, contrary forces block the path toward what Lawrence would ultimately call "phallic consciousness" (a form of sexual balance) between lovers, revealing a tension that is present in most of Lawrence's novels and essays. On the one hand, Lawrence posits a heterosexual ideal for spiritual and sexual wholeness, but on the other hand, misogynist and homosexual impulses related to his own personal struggles often undercut his formulations of this ideal.

Most readers are aware of the fact that sexual and gender conflicts are at the heart of Lawrence's novels and are primarily played out on the level of character, both in terms of the gender identity of individual characters and their sexual relationships with one another. Perhaps less familiar to readers is the fact that Lawrence's critical work also shows an intense concern with gender issues. From the first of his significant critical pieces, *Study of Thomas Hardy*, which explores how knowledge of the "Natural Law" of male and female can yield "supreme art" (*Study* 127–128), to one of his latest essays, "A Propos of *Lady Chatterley*," which states the purpose of *Lady Chatterley's Lover* as getting "men and women to be able to think sex, fully, completely, honestly and cleanly" (*Phoenix II* 489), his ruminations are immersed in the language of gender and sexuality.

One of the most striking aspects of these works is Lawrence's employment of this language as a critical weapon in ways that are both similar and diametrically opposed to Woolf's gendering of literary form and history. Although early in his career Lawrence sometimes depicts the feminine as a source of regeneration, a number of his later book reviews and other nonfiction literary pieces contain derogatory feminine metaphors to describe the modern novel and negative judgments made on the basis of an author's effeminate qualities or lack of masculine ones. Lawrence's use of the language of gender here follows the lead of Max Nordau and other critics of the degeneration of culture, who conceive of the early twentieth-century period as rendered sterile by dominant social and political forces, especially democracy, industrialization, and feminism (Pykett, *Engendering* 132–133). In direct contrast to Woolf, Lawrence represents the modern age as emasculated and/or feminized, and he finds its sterility reflected in the state of modern literature. His quest to theorize and fictionalize relationships of "phallic consciousness" takes shape as a battle to redress the gender and sexual imbalance of his time by reforming the novel and thereby recovering its vitality. However, although Lawrence sometimes depicts his goal in heterosexually equitable terms, his writings sometimes demonstrate a masculinist and/or conflicted homoerotic bent which problematizes his utopian vision.

In the 1920s Lawrence composed a series of biblically and apocalyptically flavored essays that contains his most passionate musings on the state of the novel and its hopes for the future. His central credo in these essays is that the perfect literary form for restoring vitality to the modern age is the novel, which he calls "the one bright book of life . . . a tremulation [that] can make the whole man alive tremble" (*Phoenix* 535). It is probably the most moral art form because it "is the highest example of subtle inter-relatedness that man has discovered" (528) and "a perfect medium for revealing to us the changing rainbow of our living relationships" (532). The novel's chief asset, for Lawrence, is its limited aim: it is "the highest form of human expression so far attained. Why? Because it is so incapable of the absolute" (*Phoenix II* 416). At its best, it avoids being pinned down by an author's predilection for a dominant idea or purpose and simply "demands the trembling and oscillating of the balance" of life so as to reveal "true and vivid relationships," especially "the great relationship, for humanity, . . . the relation between man and woman" (*Phoenix* 529–531).

In Lawrence's pseudo-religious sense of art, the novel is the "Book of Truth" or the new Bible, and the novelist is its prophet or savior, "superior to the saint, the scientist, the philosopher, and the poet, who are all great masters of different bits of man alive, but never get the whole hog" (535). Central to Lawrence's version of the history of salvation (of art and culture as well as humanity) are sex-gender categories, and the formation of his gospel (i.e., the novel) both reflects and influences his contradictory ideas on sex and gender roles. In other words, gender and sexuality clearly inform Lawrence's ideas and labors on the novel, yet the theory and practice of his fiction not only depict traditional gender and sex roles but also construct new and holier ones for modern times.

In this chapter I will explore how this "sacred" relationship between gender and genre is represented in Lawrence's theory and fiction. Because his most engaging and provocative literary theory focuses on sex-gender relations, I want to pay attention not so much to formal or technical innovation as to character development in Lawrence's novelistic practice, especially the ways in which the tensions of his theories of gender and sexuality are embodied in the personal conflicts enacted within and among his protagonists. Although the path of Lawrence's writing career and sexual theory is often eccentric or inconsistent,[1] there seems to be a general movement from an early optimism about male-female sexual relations, through a darker, more cynical period, to a hopeful celebration of heterosexual union toward the end of his career. Lawrence's conscious focus on man-woman love notwithstanding, the specters of misogyny and conflicted homosexuality are never far from the surface of his work, and they make their strongest appearance in the postwar years.

By way of proceeding, I will examine some of Lawrence's key essays in conjunction with the novels Lawrence was writing at the same time, showing the process of development, reversal, and contradiction in Lawrence's sexual philosophy and its relation to the theory and practice of the novel over the course of his literary career, especially as it gets embodied on the level of character. As we shall see, as with Forster, the inconsistencies in Lawrence's work and the emotional conflicts of his protagonists often reflect his own personal experiences of gender ambiguity and sexual confusion.[2] Because of the massive quantity of Lawrence's writings and the broad scope of this study, my references to the essays and novels will be necessarily selective and brief, with a primary focus on gender issues.

In *Fantasia of the Unconscious*, Lawrence himself raises the issue of the logical priority of the ideas generated in his fiction and essays: "This pseudo-philosophy of mine . . . is deduced from the novels and poems, not the reverse. The novels and poems come unwatched out of one's pen. And then the absolute need which one has for some sort of satisfactory mental attitude towards oneself and things in general makes one try to abstract some definite conclusions from one's experiences as a writer and a man" (15). Lawrence suggests here that his literature is produced in an unconscious, free-flowing way (suggesting a "divinely inspired" quality to the composition of his "Book[s] of Truth") and that his theoretical work is developed through conscious, mental activity and is secondary to the fictional material. While critics might applaud Lawrence's elevation of his poetic and fictional work over his critical and philosophical pieces, his suggestion that literary practice is prior to theory does not always stand up to closer scrutiny. As I shall soon show in greater detail, Lawrence's novels are not produced in an intellectual vacuum: his fictional ideas and themes emerge in part from his own philosophical work as well as that of other thinkers, and each successive novel he undertakes is influenced in significant ways by the critical and theoretical work which has preceded it. That being said, I will hold Lawrence to his word and give priority to his novels as the most important or "purest" expressions of his thought.

In my treatment of this matter, I will follow a chronology suggested by Cornelia Nixon,[3] which divides Lawrence's career and ideology into three periods. The first period covers the years leading up to and including the completion of *The Rainbow* in 1915, during which Lawrence, influenced by the sexual theory of Ellis and Carpenter, posited what seems to be his most balanced sense of the relationship between the sexes as a goal to be achieved in his novels, and his expressions of misogyny and homosexuality are only intermittent. The second period goes from the World War I-scarred years after 1915 (during the writing of *Women in Love*) up to 1925, in which Lawrence's approach becomes much more pessimistic and misogynist and is primarily concerned with homoerotic and homosocial bonds between men, as seen in novels like *Kangaroo* and *The Plumed Serpent*. The final period encompasses Lawrence's thought and writing from 1925–30, in which he returns to a focus on male-female relations in his hope of writing a novel of "phallic consciousness," of which *Lady Chatterley's Lover* is his most successful effort although it, too, has strong strains of man-loving and woman-hating.

CONSUMMATION OF MALE AND FEMALE: EARLY VIEWS ON THE NOVEL

Although there was often a powerful negative thrust to his assessment of other writers' efforts, Lawrence was a creator as well as a critic and was never one to shy from positively pursuing the literary ideals that he felt so many writers failed to meet. In diverse genres of literature and discursive prose, Lawrence set out to articulate and embody his theory of art, a theory which, even in its earliest expressions, was intimately tied to human relationships, especially the dynamic between male and female. From an early age, Lawrence had a clear sense of his literary goal, and it was always connected with the idea of interpersonal union. In his first essay, "Art and the Individual" (1908), the 23 year-old Lawrence answers the momentous question, "What is the mission of Art?" with great optimism: "To bring us into sympathy with as many men, as many objects, as many phenomena as possible.... The passion of human beings to be brought into sympathetic understanding of one another is stupendous" (*Phoenix II* 226). Lawrence's primary literary means of eliciting this sympathy is his fiction, but his non-fiction writings on the novel and human relationships in general also help him approach his goal. In this section, I will look at how Lawrence's efforts at representing heterosexual union in the period before World War I, in both his essays on sexual relations and the two key novels of this period (*Sons and Lovers* and *The Rainbow*), repeatedly reveal gender conflict within the individual and sexual conflict between potential lovers.

Sons and Lovers (1913), a largely autobiographical work, is a quintessential Lawrentian novel of gender conflict both within its protagonist, Paul Morel, and between him and several characters toward whom he directs his love. The novel plays out two of Lawrence's central gender-related themes: the assertion of manhood and the achievement of physical and spiritual union between the sexes. Paul is the classic product of a distant father and smothering mother and, as a result, suffers intense gender confusion from an early age. Inordinately bonded with his mother from the womb, Paul is a "delicate and quiet" child who "was so conscious of what other people felt, particularly his mother. When she fretted he understood, and could have no peace. His soul seemed always attentive to her" (*Sons* 48 & 57).

Although Paul appears to be solely his mother's child and, indeed, over-identifies with her in an unhealthy way, he actually has a love/hate relationship with both parents. On the one hand, Paul follows his mother "like her shadow" and directs all his emotional energy toward her to the point where "the two shared lives" (114), but, on the other hand, he is intensely observant of and attracted to his manly, working-class father. (The narrator's physical descriptions of Walter Morel point toward Lawrence's more overt homoeroticism in later novels.) Most of Paul's future struggles follow from the fact that he is overly associated with the feminine, represented here in his absorption in his mother's affairs, from gossipy talk to shopping trips, and in his preference for intellectual and artistic pursuits because of his delicate constitution: "he was not strong enough for heavy manual work" (88).

In adulthood Paul plays out his unresolved childhood gender and sexual conflicts through his dichotomous love relationships with the virginal and spiritual Miriam and the experienced and physical Clara. His inability to integrate the emotional and carnal aspects of love stems from his incestuous attachment to his mother, toward whom Paul moves from veneration to loathing as he becomes more aware of her suffocating influence and resistance to his two amours: "sometimes he hated her, and pulled at her bondage. His life wanted to free itself of her. It was like a circle where life turned back on itself, and got no farther" (345). Latent feelings for his father emerge in his infatuation with Baxter Dawes which climaxes in a homoerotic fight scene that is a precursor to the famous "Gladiatorial" chapter of *Women in Love*. Freedom and hope for his artistic career only come for Paul once he escapes all three of his female entanglements, which he achieves through hastening his mother's death, reconciling Clara with her husband, and rejecting a union with Miriam. Deep ironies abound as the novel simultaneously adores and abhors the feminine, suggesting by novel's end that Lawrence has come nowhere near to his goals of reconciling the masculine and feminine in himself or balancing the sexes in a love relationship.

Lawrence's nonfiction work in this pre-war period takes up and attempts to develop the gender-related issues enacted in *Sons and Lovers*. Although none of these early essays discusses the theory of the novel in an extended way, Lawrence puts forth in them, in the words of Mark Kinkead-Weekes, "an enormous effort of systematic analysis." During this time, Lawrence accomplished "the working out in the unpublished 'Foreword' to *Sons and Lovers*, the *Study of Thomas Hardy*, and 'The Crown,' of a comprehensive 'theory' of sexual relationship," ("Eros" 113) which he called his "metaphysic," an understanding of which is crucial to comprehending Lawrence's idea and practice of the novel. The "Foreword" (which is really an unpublished afterward written in 1913) is a curious blend of personal experience, theological speculation, and sexual psychologizing that is "a first attempt to find a formulation for Lawrence's deepest convictions, by rewriting Christian theology in terms of the relation between man and woman" (Kinkead-Weekes, "Marble" 374). This essay follows directly from the writing of *Sons and Lovers*, providing an analysis of Paul's relationship with his possessive and strong-willed mother (whom Lawrence describes as a "Magna Mater") and an insight into one of the driving forces behind Lawrence's theory.

The "Foreword" spins out some unorthodox theological ideas from Lawrence's concept of the "Magna Mater," performing some significant gender shifts and revealing an underlying misogyny (that will lurk beneath much of his work) in the process. Drawing from the traditional patriarchal Christian theology of the relationship between God the Father and Jesus the Son as one of begetting, and the concept of Jesus as the "Word made Flesh," Lawrence upends both notions in order to proclaim a gyno-centric theology of human sexual relations. In direct opposition to the Christian doctrine of God's Word proceeding into flesh, Lawrence reverses the direction of the process and says that, because "women simply go on bearing talkative sons. . . . 'The Flesh was made Word,'" which makes God the Flesh and "the Son is the mouth." ("Foreword" 96). With God as a fleshly but not spiritual source, then "the Father . . . were more properly, the

Mother," and we only know this God "in the Flesh, in Woman. She is the door for our in-going and our out-coming" (100).

In terms of human relations, this new theology which appreciates the divinity of woman's body would appear to be a feminist's dream but, in an vein similar to that of the courtly love tradition, Lawrence turns this divinization of woman to man's ends. By coming home from work to a sexual relationship with a woman, a man experiences "the exclamation of joy and astonishment at new self-revelation . . . of that which is Woman to a man. . . . [H]e shall then while he is with her, be re-born of her . . . [and] shall go forth with his new strength" (101–102). Relations between man and woman are complicated, however, by the man's bond to his mother. Reflecting the confusion of Lawrence's own life as well as the overwhelming maternal force in *Sons and Lovers*, the "Foreword" ends with harsh words about the destructive and self-perpetuating powers of the Oedipal relationship: ". . . the man who is the go-between from Woman to Production is the lover of that woman. And if that Woman be his mother, then is he her lover in part only. . . . And if a son-lover take a wife, then is she not his wife, she is only his bed. And his life will be torn in twain, and his wife in her despair shall hope for sons, that she may have her lover in her hour" (102).

Volatile sexual feelings also find their way into Lawrence's literary criticism during this period, and one of the most striking aspects of his assessment of novelists is the way he judges them from the perspective of gender. In the case of male authors, Lawrence condemns what he sees as the feminine or sentimental tendencies of their prose and extols its masculine qualities. His reading of the most renowned nineteenth-century realist writers sometimes seems more an indictment of their failure to live up to the Lawrentian male ideal than an evaluation of their literary merits. For example, in a 1913 review Lawrence portrays Thomas Mann in sickly terms as "delicate in constitution" and suffering from a "soul-ailment" out of which "he makes his particular art." He is also proclaimed "the last sick sufferer from the complaint of Flaubert . . . [who] stood away from life as from a leprosy," fighting against the "disordered corruption" of physical life with "his fine aesthetic sense, his feeling for beauty" (*Phoenix* 309 & 312). Describing Flaubert and Mann as frail aesthetes suggests that they suffer from a kind of literary neurasthenia, conjuring up Victorian images of illness and impotence; in doing so, Lawrence dismisses their brand of realism as no better than the cries of weak men and hysterical women.

Lawrence did not condemn nineteenth-century realism out of hand, however; there were a few male authors whose novels he not only admired but also saw as forerunners of the "phallic" novel he eventually hoped to write. For example, in an early letter (1908), Lawrence considers Balzac's *Eugenie Grandet* "as perfect a novel as I have ever read" and extols it as an example of "level-headed, fair unrelenting realism," without "a grain of sentimentality . . . a touch of melodrama, or caricature, or flippancy." Not only does Balzac avoid in his work what Lawrence represents elsewhere as a feminine temptation toward sentiment; as a novelist Balzac resembles either a thorough anatomist or a manly denuder (or even a rapist) of his subject, depending upon how one reads Lawrence's imagery: "Balzac can lay bare the living body of the great Life better than anybody in the world. He doesn't hesitate at the last covering. . . . [H]e goes straight to the flesh" (*Letters 1*: 91).

Edwardian male novelists come under Lawrence's gender-sensitive critical lens, usually in an unfavorable light. He repeatedly uses the language of impotence and passivity to describe their novels and images of physical revulsion and illness to describe their effect, once again suggesting a draining of masculinity from the modern novel as well as from its writers and readers. Arnold Bennett's *Anna of the Five Towns*, Lawrence says in a 1912 letter, "makes me feel fearfully queer . . . makes me feel quite ill. . . . I hate Bennett's resignation. Tragedy ought really to be a great kick at misery. But *Anna* . . . seems like an acceptance—so does all the modern stuff since Flaubert. I hate it" (459). A year later Lawrence writes with admiration for H. G. Wells's work, but he finds that it "depresses me . . . he hurts me" (543), and he ultimately dismisses Wells's importance as a novelist in domestic terms: "He is really a writer of books of manners. . . . His folks have no personality—no passion. The feeling in the book wanders loose" (*Letters 2*: 74).

Although Lawrence rarely writes of female authors, he also measures them in gendered terms. He shows some admiration for the Brontë sisters and George Eliot, but, like many of their male peers, they too fall short of his phallocentric novelistic ideals. In a 1908 letter, Lawrence speaks of *Shirley* and *Jane Eyre* as "two of my favourite English books" but goes on to disparage the construction of their heroes (as well as that of Eliot in *Adam Bede* and *Mill on the Floss*) as lacking true manliness, something apparently only male authors can provide: "Strong stern men bore and irritate me; their strength lies in their insusceptibility to half the influences that deflect morality. . . . Pah—I hate women's heroes. At the bottom men love the brute in man best" (*Letters 1*: 88). Lawrence also criticizes Eliot for her scholarly quality: "Folks *will* want things intellectually done, so they take refuge in George Eliot. I am very fond of her, but I wish she'd take her specs off, and come down off the public platform" (101). In a curious way, Lawrence denigrates these women's novels for possessing emotional distance and didactic content, which might be considered masculine qualities, while failing to capture the life of the feelings, traditionally seen as a feminine sphere, in their characters.

Ironies abound in Lawrence's lack of appreciation of the women novelists who went before him. According to F. R. Leavis, Lawrence belongs in the "great tradition" of the English novel which begins with Jane Austen, one of his "unmistakable" influences, and his "innovations and experiments are dictated by the most serious and urgent kind of interest in life . . .

a spirit that, for all the unlikeness, relates Lawrence closely to George Eliot" (*Great* 24–25). In particular, Leavis feels *The Rainbow* demonstrates that "Lawrence belongs to the same ethical and religious tradition as George Eliot" and that "[a]s a recorder of essential English history," he is a "great successor" to her (*DHL: Novelist* 120 & 123).

Carol Siegel also shows how Lawrence was much more connected and indebted to the work of the Brontës and George Eliot than his few references to them suggest. Lawrence's depiction (at least in his earlier works) of "the natural female state as furious rebellion" (16) owes a great deal of debt to his Victorian female predecessors' representations of women in novels like *Jane Eyre*, *Mill on the Floss*, and especially *Wuthering Heights*. Siegel compares Lawrence's work to a palimpsest because his "gendering of voices is always profoundly intertextual," and one layer of this gendering comes from the way "Lawrence quotes and responds to prior texts by women." However, paralleling in many ways the troubled mother-son dynamic in Lawrence's life and *Sons and Lovers*, the influence of female literary forebears on him is conflictual and anxiety-producing. Although Lawrence claimed that he believed in "the primacy of the female" and wished to represent women with a strong voice in his fiction, he was intimidated by the authority of his female precursors and insecure about the similarity of his themes to theirs, and this manifests itself in his dominant tone of anger toward them (53–54). Examples of his debt to such work can be seen in his "reconstruction of the major themes of *Wuthering Heights*" in the writing of *The White Peacock* and in his rewriting of Bertha Mason from *Jane Eyre* as Bertha Coutts in the second and third versions of *Lady Chatterley's Lover* (56 & 85).

Lawrence's primary critical work of the pre-war period, *Study of Thomas Hardy* (begun in 1914) further complicates the relationship between the sexes and directly relates it to the production of art. *Study of Thomas Hardy* is an exploratory work (as Lawrence describes it, "a little book on Hardy's people" which is "mostly philosophicalish, slightly about Hardy" (*Letters* 2: 198 & 292)) that was unpublished in his lifetime and is, in the words of Frank Kermode, a "mixture of art history, heterodox trinitarian theology, and literary criticism" (39). Because it is in the nature of Lawrence's early nonfiction writings to advance in the manner of "a poetic 'procede,' of moving from point to point not by the logic of argument but by the logic of association" (Black 8), and to progress by means of shifting metaphors, it will be helpful for our purposes to look at several of these clusters of ideas and metaphors which relate to male-female relations and the creation of art. What we will find is a conflicting picture: Lawrence further develops his ideals of androgyny in art and union without dissolution of the sexes, but his theory is also marked by an essentialism toward sex roles and misogynist and homoerotic impulses under the surface.[4]

When speaking of male-female relations, Lawrence proceeds from a central essentialist tenet: "except in infinity, everything of life is male or female, distinct . . . [e]very single impulse, is either male or female" (*Study* 55). Lawrence allows for only one exception to this belief in universal single-sexed entities, and that is human consciousness, which he believes is made up of both sexes like his central image in *Study of Thomas Hardy*, the poppy, which has both male and female elements of stamen and pistil. This idea of an androgynous or bisexual human consciousness (which shares similarities to the ideas of Woolf, Forster, and Sinclair) is further developed and even extended to the body later in the essay when Lawrence explicates his gendered sense of the history of religious worship and art. Lawrence sees various phases as identified with one sex or the other, e.g., Greek art as based on male stimulus, medieval Christian worship and art as driven by a female impulse toward the male Christ and, although it is not mentioned here, Victorian and Edwardian literature as tamed by a feminizing influence and "the modern age as one in which the male is in the ascendant" (Pykett, *Engendering* 131). Of particular interest is his representation of Renaissance art as forging "the Union and fusion of the male and female spirits, creating a perfect expression for the time being" (*Study* 66).

Lawrence uses the figure of Michelangelo to represent a position vis-à-vis art that is bisexual in body as well as spirit. Linking the creation of art with bodily desire, Lawrence states that Michelangelo "must react upon himself to produce his own bodily satisfaction, aware that he can never obtain it through woman. . . . For his own body is both male and female" (70), and this mixture is readily seen in his voluptuous, androgynous figures. (Of course, the homoerotic aspects of Michelangelo's art possibly played a role in Lawrence's admiration, even if he was unaware of this fact.) The case of Michelangelo is a rarity, however, for Lawrence goes on to state that "[a] man who is well balanced between male and female, in his own nature, is, as a rule, happy," but he has difficulty being an artist because "It is only a disproportion, or a dissatisfaction, which makes the man struggle into articulation . . . [which is] the cry of desire or the cry of realization" (71). There is something double-edged about Lawrence's theory here: from one perspective, androgyny can be of personal benefit because it provides happiness; from another perspective, however, except in rare cases like that of Michelangelo, such self-satisfaction does not lead to artistic creativity because it is only "disproportion" or "dissatisfaction" that yields "articulation" (i.e., art or writing). At this stage Lawrence seems confused about the advantages of an androgynous consciousness, at least for an artist or a writer.

Despite his talk of androgynous bodies and spirits, Lawrence's notion of the ideal union of the male and female is primarily filtered through the image of heterosexual intercourse. To illustrate this relationship, he draws upon unusual images of male-female union that sometimes lack a sense of equilibrium. In one chapter, Lawrence speaks of love and procreation in balanced aquatic terms: "when there comes the flood-tide, then the dual stream of woman and man, as the whole two waves meet and break to foam, bursting into the unknown, these wells and fountain heads [of the womb] are filled" (53). Shortly after this even-handed characterization, however, he moves into a paradoxical and disproportionate mechanical metaphor, initially suggesting a turn to the feminine as the source for regeneration: "The supreme effort each man makes is . . . the effort to clasp as a hub the woman who shall be his axle, compelling him to true motion." Notice here that traditional sexual images are reversed (woman is phallic axle and man is womb-like hub/hole), and that woman is even, apparently, the initiator; she is, in fact, described as "the begetter of his whole life. . . . ideally, the soul of the woman possesses the soul of the man, procreates it and makes it big with new idea, motion, in the sexual act" (56–57).

Procreative powers notwithstanding, woman's activity in a sexual relationship is only a preface to man's ultimately dominant active role in the world and in creating art. Lawrence represents his sense of woman's essential passivity in numerous ways: references to the love partners as "the woman of his body" and "the man of her spirit" (56–57) equate the female with the physical and the male with the spiritual, but the labeling of the male spirit as the "Will-to-Motion" and the female spirit as the "Will-to-Inertia" (59) seems a reversal of the dualism and is used to assign the function of activity to men and passivity to women. Further reinforcing this duality of role and energy, later on Lawrence speaks again in bisexual terms, only to take them back in the next breath, thereby throwing into question his earlier ideas about the possibility and desirability of a truly androgynous identity:

> For every man comprises male and female in his being, the male always struggling for predominance. A woman likewise consists in male and female, with female predominant. . . . The male exists in doing, the female in being. The male lives in the satisfaction of some purpose achieved, the female in the satisfaction of some purpose contained (94).

The image of heterosexual relations also drives his notions of art and the novel, as quoted earlier: "What we call the Truth is, in actual experience, the momentary state in living [when] the union between the male and female is consummated. This consummation may be also physical. . . . But it may be only spiritual" (72). As the "Book of Truth," the novel is intimately tied to representing the union of man and woman, and, in fact, that is what Lawrence praises outright in his assessment of Hardy's novels, of which "the first and chiefest factor is the struggle into love and the struggle with love: . . . of a man for a woman and a woman for a man" (20).

In his analysis of Hardy's characters, Lawrence shows how such theories take form in the novel; in doing so, he draws upon the categories outlined above and seems to advocate an androgynous emotional existence for the characters he admires. For example, Lawrence sees Tess of the d'Urbervilles as initially typical of Hardy's female characters: "not Female in any real sense . . . [but] passive subjects to the male. . . . Tess sets out, not as any positive thing, . . . but as the acquiescent complement to the male. The female in her has become inert" (95). In her attempt to overcome her limits and express her female side through integration with a man, Tess becomes caught between two polar opposites: one man (Alec d'Urberville) who is "only physically male" and seeks to know Tess in the flesh because, for him, "the female in himself is the only part of himself that he will acknowledge: the body, the senses"; and another (Angel Clare) to whom "the female in himself is detestable" and who can see Tess only as "the Female Principle" because what he "wants really is to receive the female impulse other than through the body" (483–484). Tess's quest is doomed since neither of her lovers can help her to wholeness because each refuses to integrate his own androgyny. Lawrence sees *Jude the Obscure* as the mirror image of *Tess*: "Jude is only Tess turned round about. Instead of the heroine containing the two principles, male and female, at strife within her one being, it is Jude who contains them both, whilst the two women with him [Arabella and Sue] take the place of the two men to Tess" (101).

Lawrence may recognize androgynous or bisexual forces within Hardy's main characters and put forth an ideal of integration as the aim of their (and the novel's) development, but he still clings to notions of overarching essential dualities that condition the roles of men and women and the novelist's depiction of them. The final chapter of *Study of Thomas Hardy* sums up human history as a struggle between "Two Complimentary Absolutes, the Absolute of the Father, of the Law, of Nature, and the Absolute of the Son, of Love, of Knowledge. What remains is to reconcile the two" (123). Like so many other dualities in his philosophical thinking, Lawrence assigns each of these forces a gendered identity: "the principle of the Law is found strongest in Woman, the principle of Love in Man." This duality appears to reverse the traditional idea that the categories of law and love are gendered, respectively, as male and female, yet Lawrence also links "mobility" and "change" to the male and "stability" and "conservatism" to the female (127), once again assigning woman a passive role. Lawrence sees the role of the artist, who, in the past, has created a "wrong" or "forced" conclusion, "to seek the true balance, to give each party . . . his due, and so to seek the Reconciler" and create a "pure utterance" (126–127). This task of balance is carried out by the artist (configured as male in the essay) in a process by which he must "submit to the law of himself" and "the law of the woman" and "know that they two together are one within the Great Law. Out of this final knowledge shall come his supreme art" (128). The good news here is that "supreme art" involves a conjoining of the male and female, but these qualities and forces are rigidly defined and only united, it seems, by a male artist.

The idiosyncratic ideas on the forces of male and female and sexual relations between men and women formulated in *Study of Thomas Hardy* were not conceived in a vacuum. Lawrence was working on the novel now known as *The Rainbow* (1914–1915) when he wrote the essay, and his study of Hardy's art and people helped him find "a language in which to conceive the impersonal forces he saw operating within and between human beings" (Kinkead-Weekes, "Marble" 380). Having struggled through versions of a novel variously titled *The Sisters* and *The Wedding Ring*, Lawrence finally settled upon writing what became *The Rainbow*, the saga of three generations of one family, the Brangwens, in their struggles to achieve balanced married relationships. For the most part, the forces at work in the to-and-fro of these erotically charged relationships divide along gender lines, in a way that suggests the opposite of Sinclair's identification of natural connection with the female and intellectual consciousness with the male. In this novel, on one side is the "[b]lood-intimacy of the man" and on the other is the "conscious awareness and education of the woman," although these are not offered "as essentially male and female characteristics . . . but as complementary to one another in a really satisfying human way of life" (Draper 59), generally achieved through sexual union. Of particular note here is the fact that, in all three generations, the woman has the most power in the relationship. The novel is not only a continuation of Lawrence's exploration of the "Magna Mater" or matriarchy but also (serving as yet another example of Lawrence's debt to his female predecessors) a representation of "the familiar New Woman story" (Pykett, *Engendering* 124) of a "woman becoming individual, self-responsible, taking her own initiative" (*Letters* 2: 165).

The sexual struggle is played out with limited success in the first two generations of the novel. Tom Brangwen, like Paul Morel, is a "sensitive" and "delicate" child and "his mother's favorite" (*Rainbow* 15–16) who has trouble reconciling emotional love and physical lust in his relations with women. He finally finds "transfiguration" and a "new birth" in his relationship with the mysterious Polish widow, Lydia Lensky, a union which is characterized by means of a typical Lawrentian paradox, a fluctuation between "such intimacy of embrace, and such utter foreignness of contact" (49). (This contradictory attraction-repulsion movement is a foreshadowing of the conflict between desires for heterosexual union and homosocial/sexual bonding in the fractured narratives of *Women in Love* and the later "male leader" novels.) Recalling the language and imagery of *Study of Thomas Hardy*, Lawrence generally describes Tom and Lydia's sexual relations (and those of the other couples in the novel) in exalted essentialist ("She was beyond him, the unattainable") and religious terms ("it was the baptism to another life, it was the complete confirmation" (95)).

The next generation carries on the sexual conflict through the relationship of Anna Brangwen, Tom's stepdaughter, and her cousin Will, another sensitive man who is an artist with a particular interest in church architecture and carving, but who is represented as "inarticulate and stupid in thought. But to some things he clung passionately" (171). Lawrence presents their story in biblical terms through numerous allusions to both Old and New Testaments, including the stories of Adam and Eve, Noah and the flood, and the Annunciation to the Virgin Mary. A good example of the gendered opposition in Anna and Will's relationship emerges in their visit to a church during which Will is drawn to the physicality of the structure which takes him out of himself ("He did not want things to be intelligible") to the point where "his real being lay in his dark emotional experience of the Infinite." Anna, on the other hand, can only connect with the church service and cannot escape her self-consciousness: "the thought of her soul was intimately mixed up with the thought of her own self" (158–159). As do the first generation of lovers, Will and Anna experience the stereotypical Lawrentian attraction-repulsion dynamic of heterosexual relations: "it went on continually, the recurrence of love and conflict between them" (167). However, there are occasionally moments of genuine union, in which Will is given "a new, deeper freedom" and comes "into his own existence" (190) through relations with Anna. There is a definite inequity of relations here, as Anna becomes "Anna Victrix" through motherhood, establishing "a little matriarchy" that makes her feel "all the future was in her hands" (207–208).

The novel's strongest threat to heterosexual union occurs in the third generation of the family through Ursula Brangwen's on-and-off relationship with Anton Skrebenski. From childhood Ursula has a turbulent connection with the "unknown, dark, potent" powers (211) of the men in her life, beginning with her attraction to her father (the "all-powerful . . . tower of strength" (215)) and the development of a "curious taunting intimacy" (226) between them. Her quest to comprehend and merge herself with this male force continues in her love union with Anton, but this devolves into destructiveness. Ursula's female sexual power, which is repeatedly linked to the moon, is too threatening to Anton, and she continually overpowers him. For example, at one point, she feels drawn "to lay hold of him and tear him," with hands "like blades, . . . to dissipate, destroy as the moonlight destroys a darkness, annihilate, have done with" (321). His abandonment of her to go to Europe causes Ursula's sexual life to flame "into a kind of disease" and leaves her "overwrought and sensitive" (333).

At this vulnerable point, Lawrence moves Ursula into the realm of lesbian desire and, in the process, unleashes misogynist impulses that complicate Ursula's path to sexual fulfillment. Ursula's brief relationship with her Diana-like drawing teacher, Winifred Inger, includes a few passionate moments in feminine-coded aquatic settings. However, the bond is short-lived, as Ursula is overcome by a sense of "sort of nausea" at the thought of Winifred's "ugly, clayey" body and "would consent no more to mingle with the perverted life of the older woman" (343–344). Lawrence's abhorrence of lesbianism[5] becomes a more general anti-feminism in his representation of Winifred as a free-thinker who is "interested in the Women's Movement" and his linking of Ursula's personal setbacks to a desire for increased intellectualism. In the novel's cruelest moment, which stands as a partial repudiation of his New Woman novel influences, Lawrence disposes of Winifred through a convenient but passionless marriage to Ursula's Uncle Tom, which is justified by the narrator because both are worshippers of the "monstrous mechanism that held all matter" (350) and therefore devoid of human feeling.

An interesting shift occurs in the novel at this point as its goal seems to move from integration with another to integration within oneself, represented in Ursula's attempt "to recover the lost blood-intimacy, to save herself from the overdeveloped consciousness that atrophies the old intuitive life" (Draper 59–60). The failure of her relationships with Anton and Winifred leaves "the body of love . . . killed" in Ursula, and she takes up a teaching position in a boys' school in order to experience and thereby free herself of "the world of work and man's convention" (*Rainbow* 406). Ursula's struggle against the forces of maleness leads to acts of violence against her students, but somehow her "real, individual self drew together and became more coherent" (407) during her two years of teaching. Continuing her quest for increased intellectual consciousness by going to college, Ursula's encounter with science leaves her "in dread of the material world" and anxious to return to Anton. She comes close to marrying him, but her power to possess him rather than be possessed by him scares Anton off and Ursula is once again left on her own, yet this time with a difference.

At novel's end, having realized that she cannot "create her man according to her own desire" but must recognize one "created by God" (494), Ursula stands gazing at the rainbow, filled with potential and confident that she will find a balanced sexual relationship to complement her newfound sense of self. Ironically, in a novel that shows signs of anti-feminism, the ending serves as "a renovatory vision which portends an alliance (in this case, a fragile and tenuous one) between the New Woman and the working class" (Pykett, *Engendering* 124). It is also ironic, however, that shortly after the creation of this stunning tableau of female independence, Lawrence's ideas about sex relations and his fiction underwent a radical redirection.

Man-Loving and Woman-Hating: Postwar Views of the Novel

"The Crown" is a perfect transition piece for illustrating the transformation during World War I of Lawrence's philosophy of relationships and its embodiment in his criticism and fiction. Lawrence published only the first half of its six original sections in 1915, and by the time the whole work appeared in *Reflections on the Death of a Porcupine* in 1925, he had substantially altered the text. Uncovering some of the sexual subject matter that was excised in the later version reveals a significant change from the experience and thought of Lawrence's pre-war days, a change that is reflected in the writing of *Women in Love*. "The Crown" is largely a metaphorical reflection on the forces behind the war and an ambiguous call for a response to its threat, but for our purposes, its significance lies in a couple of images used to convey the dissolution or "reduction" which he believes has brought about the war, a disintegration that, in Lawrence's mind, is the product of the previous century's feminine culture.

In Section 4, "Within the Sepulchre," Lawrence uses an image of the constricted delivery of a baby to represent the coming into being of the "false absolute self" which reigns in the modern era and is the ultimate cause of the war. The corruption of modern culture is caused by the "withered loins" of "the womb of the established past," i.e., the feminized, overly self-conscious era of the nineteenth century. Because modern man's unborn self is "shut in" at the hour of labor due to "the dry walls of the womb which cannot relax," his "reaction can only take the form of self-consciousness" in which it "conceives itself as the whole universe." This "triumph of the ego," in which "dissolution and corruption set in before birth," results in the fact that "[t]here is no more fight to be fought, there is no more to be sought and embraced" (*Reflections* 278–280).

In this passage, the maternal womb (representing the influence of the previous era's history and culture)[6] serves as a prison, the paradoxical source of man's destruction before his birth and the negator of that which is most manly about him (i.e., his fighting spirit) before he enters the world's fray. Lawrence uses the language and imagery of emasculation to explain the impotence of modern man in a feminized, self-conscious society. Another example of the female destruction of the male spirit and ego occurs in a later section which tells of a maimed soldier at the seaside who is set upon by a group of women who are "fascinated" by him, desiring "his perfect completeness in horror and death" and seeking "to devour him . . . greedy voracious people, like birds seeking the death in him, pecking at the death in him" (291–292). In a perfect example of the instability of the gendered discourse of degeneration in the modern age, Lawrence, who had earlier in *Study of Thomas Hardy* seen "the war as one of the problems caused by an exhausted, masculinized, routinized, mechanized and anti-individualistic society" (Pykett, *Engendering* 132), transforms the horrible destruction of this war created and fought by men into the sinister scavenging of sex-starved women.

According to Lawrence, the emasculation of modern man has adversely affected sexual relations between men and women. Whereas the healthy goal of a man's seeking a woman in love is "union," in the past century hyper self-consciousness has led to a state in which "within the glassy, null envelope of the enclosure [of the ego], no union is sought, no union is possible; after a certain point only reduction." In this age of reduction, sexual union is merely mechanical: "He seeks to plunge his compound flesh into the cold acid that will reduce him, in supreme sensual experience, down to his parts" (*Reflections* 283–284). As we shall now see, Lawrence believed that the decline in genuine heterosexual union had an adverse effect on modern cultural production and encouraged homosexuality, which was for him a dead-ended response.

Translating his critique of modern sexuality into the sphere of literary criticism (a practice which increasingly occurs in his writings), Lawrence uses the character of Myshkin from Dostoyevsky's *The Brothers Karamazov* to describe how "men of finer sensibility and finer development" cannot accept merely reduction in their sexual relations with women, so the process shifts to their mental life, as evidenced in Myshkin's "monologue of self-analysis, self-dissolution . . . where he falls into a fit" (284). The end result of such intellectual reduction is "alluring sentimentalism . . . the garment of our vice." In Lawrence's view, this sentimentality has overtaken literature and the arts and has led to a pedophilic desire to return to "the *corruptive* state of childishness," such as in the movies where "[o]ur heroines become younger and younger . . . and touched with infantile idiocy." For Lawrence, this "slimily, pornographically reaching out for child-gratifications is disgusting," and this state of affairs, also manifest in "the prevalent love of boys" (285), shares his scorn.

Lawrence's tirade on the degradation of male-female relations and its link to the sentimentalism of modern culture originally included another key element in the 1915 version of "The Crown": as Michael Herbert points out in the notes to *Reflections on the Death of a Porcupine*, a long excursus on homosexuality was cut in 1925. In the earlier version, following the treatment of Myshkin's mental reduction, Lawrence went on to speak of another route taken by the man of "finer sensibility" in this age of reduction: "In physical contact he seeks another outlet. He loves men, really. This is the inevitable part of the activity of reduction, of the flux of dissolution, analysis, disintegration, this homosexuality." Lawrence sees the shift to homosexuality as a movement away from the desecration he believes takes place in a purely physical and reductive sexual relation with a woman, which is only possible for "coarse, insensitive men": "A sensitive man is too subtle, he cannot come like a perverse animal, straight to the reduction of the self in the sex. . . . So that a woman becomes repulsive to him, in the thought of connection with her. It is too gross, almost horrible."[7] In reaction to this repulsion, such a man chooses to love either a boy or "a man who is to a certain degree less developed than himself," his desire being "to get back to a state which he has long suppressed," but in either case, "[h]e is given up to the flux of reduction, his mouth is upon the mouth of corruption" (472).[8]

From all appearances, Lawrence's ideas on homosexuality at this stage were highly critical of the practice, and there are three experiences in this period which serve as potential causes of his homophobic attacks. First of all, in March 1915, Lawrence was invited to Trinity College, Cambridge, to see Bertrand Russell and meet his intellectual circle of friends. In a letter to David Garnett describing the visit, particularly his shock at finding J. M. Keynes (whom Lawrence knew to be actively homosexual) lounging sybaritically in his pajamas, Lawrence says that the encounter was "one of the crises in my life. It sent me mad with misery and hostility and rage," and he encourages Garnett to "stop this blasphemy against love" and "try to love a woman" (*Letters 2*: 321). (As we saw earlier, he believed that the same advice would help E. M. Forster get over his personal difficulties.) The deep depression which followed this experience initiated a new train of thought and imagery for Lawrence in which "the association of homosexuality, black beetles, and corruption dominated Lawrence's letters and became linked in his mind with the war" (Nixon 11).[9] This bizarre series of connections appeared in his dreams and writings of the period, as in this letter to Lady Ottoline Morrell: "I like sensual lust—but insectwise, no—it is obscene. I like men to be beasts—but insects—one insect mounted on another—oh God!" (*Letters 2*: 331).

The second experience which possibly affected Lawrence's writings on homosexuality in this period was his cultivation of a friendship with Katherine and Middleton Murry, two writers with whom he shared many political and philosophical ideals; in fact, they were part of the core group in Lawrence's attempt at forming a utopian community called Rananim. Their relationship was a rocky one and it eventually exploded, partly because of tensions created by Lawrence's attraction to Middleton, with whom he tried but failed to forge an intimate friendship.[10] Ironically, one thing which united them was their discussion of their sexual limitations with their wives (Meyers, *DHL* 143). A third influence on Lawrence's ideas is the fact that, in 1916 or 1917, Lawrence finally found a potential outlet for his homosexual leanings in his relationship with William Henry Hocking, a Cornish farmer alongside of whom Lawrence worked in the fields for two summers. Lawrence saw in Hocking a physical and intellectual counterpart: he is described as "manly and independent" and "strangely beautiful and fair in spirit" (*Letters 2*: 664), but he "hasn't enough mental development, mental continuity" (Lacy, Letter #1113). Although proof of the relationship's physical consummation is sketchy and Kinkead-Weekes concludes that it was "unlikely," since "there is no evidence whatever of homosexual preference" in Hocking (*DHL* 379), Frieda acknowledged the relationship in her letters but also took credit for returning Lawrence to the heterosexual fold: "I think the homosexuality in him was a short phase out of misery—I fought him and won" (F. Lawrence 360).

The dual threats to manhood of female smothering and homosexual love, so conflictually portrayed in "The Crown," are given graphic literary treatment in *Women in Love*. The novel also reflects Lawrence's personal sexual conflict in this period, a time of marital tensions with his wife

Frieda as well as struggles with same-sex attraction toward men like Murry and Hocking. Kinkead-Weekes sees both "The Crown" and *Women in Love* as written "with a terribly heightened sense of polarization, the universal opposition of creation and destruction" ("Marble" 395). Lawrence represents this polarization in just about all of the relationships in the novel, beginning with the friendship between Birkin and Gerald, which was inspired by Lawrence's relationship with Murry and was originally set in an overtly homosexual context. The "Prologue to *Women in Love*" (written in 1916 but never published as part of the novel), which bears "a very close resemblance to the confessional case studies of 'inverts' and homosexuals found in the sex-psychology literature" (Pykett, *Engendering* 19), presents a classic male-male match-up. Gerald is the "butch" figure, "hard in his muscles and full of energy as a machine . . . [and] always active," while Birkin is his "femme" counterpart, "quiet and unobtrusive . . . almost weak, passive, insignificant . . . [and] delicate in health." The bond between the men is carefully repressed, however: "the knowledge that . . . they loved each other, that each would die for the other . . . was kept submerged in the soul of the two men" (*Phoenix II* 93).

Like the plots of so many romantic novels, the "Prologue" depicts an erotic triangle in which the body of a woman serves as the site for a man's acting out of his conflicted sexual desires. In another example of Sedgwick's thesis on the distorted enactment of male homosocial and homosexual desire through a heterosexual love triangle, Birkin's passions are cruelly displaced onto his relations with Hermione since he cannot freely pursue his feelings for Gerald for fear of societal disapproval. In language reminiscent of the excised portion of "The Crown," Lawrence relates Birkin's plight: "He was consumed by sexual desire, and he wanted to be fulfilled. Yet he did not desire Hermione. She repelled him rather. Yet he *would* have this physical fulfillment, he would have the sexual activity. So he forced himself towards her" (99–100).

While the "inverted" scripting of the Birkin-Gerald relationship in the "Prologue" is consistent with the dynamic of the wrestling scene in the final version of the novel, what is truly striking in the "Prologue" is that Lawrence goes on to describe Birkin's conscious struggle with physical homosexual desire, "the one and only secret he kept to himself" (107), an awareness which is almost totally absent from the published novel. Set off against his experience with Hermione and other women is Birkin's insight that "it was for men that he felt the hot, flushing, roused attraction which a man is supposed to feel for the other sex . . . the male physique had a fascination for him." His friendships take on a passionate and promiscuous quality, and (like Forster and Lawrence himself in his feeling for Hocking) Birkin is attracted to men of a different station than he: "men of no very great intelligence, but of pleasant appearance: ruddy, well-nourished fellows" (103–104). Of particular significance is the way Birkin's taste in men follows the lines of the two basic elemental forces in the novel: he is drawn to "white-skinned, keen-limbed men . . . the northmen, . . . and then the men with dark eyes . . . dark-skinned, supple, night-smelling men, who are the living substance of the viscous, universal heavy darkness" (105).

The man-loving which is so central to the "Prologue" becomes the undercurrent of the male-female relationships in *Women in Love* (1916–1917), all of which include the danger of female smothering and reveal intense levels of woman-hating. The epitome of the misogyny in the text is Lawrence's representation of Hermione, his most developed embodiment of the destructive feminine force of modern self-consciousness. Described as "a *Kulturträger*, a medium for the culture of ideas" who has "a lack of robust self . . . no natural sufficiency, [and for whom] there was a terrible void," Hermione is presented as a shrewish pursuer of Birkin, drawn to his (phallic) ability "to close up this deficiency" (*Women* 16). The deadly power of Hermione's threat to Birkin's manhood comes to the fore when, after numerous rebuffs from Birkin, she experiences a "voluptuous consummation" (105) as she smashes his head with a paperweight.

This destructive female force enters into both of the novel's central heterosexual relationships. Birkin and Gerald are attracted to women who they fear will destroy them by virtue of their heightened self-consciousness, and this temptation produces constant conflict as both men attempt to balance their needs for male self-sufficiency and friendship with the demands of the women in their lives. One of the relationships, that of Gerald and Gudrun, illustrates the consequences of a male-female coupling which is dominated by reduction, or Northern "ice-destructive knowledge" (254), as Lawrence calls it in the novel, which in Gerald's case is tied to his family's industrialist legacy. In this pairing, the self-gratification of each lover threatens the well-being of the other, and Lawrence graphically depicts the resulting perils in his representation of Gerald's attempted choking of Gudrun and his ultimate demise in the frigid Alps.

The coupling of Birkin and Ursula has storms of its own, particularly due to Birkin's conflicting desires. On one hand, Birkin feels drawn into a "strange conjunction" with Ursula, "not meeting and mingling . . . but an equilibrium, a pure balance of two single beings:- as the stars balance each other" (148). On the other hand, Birkin has an intense fear of being smothered by Ursula's female power, which in one passage is clearly linked to Lawrence's dreaded "Magna Mater": "it seemed to him, woman was always so horrible and clutching. . . . She wanted to have, to own, to control, to be dominant. Everything must be referred back to her, to Woman, the Great Mother of everything" (200). His fear of the feminine feeds his desire to bond with Gerald in order to fulfill "a necessity inside him all his life—to love a man purely and fully" (206), a quest most powerfully represented in the chapter called "Gladiatorial."

As the novel progresses, Lawrence presents Birkin's ideal of star "equilibrium" with Ursula as a more constructive path for heterosexual relations than that of Northern "ice-destructive knowledge," but the physical consummation of their union carries homosexual undertones, as it comes through an act of anal intercourse in which Ursula achieves release by worshipping Birkin's "flanks" (313). This scene is symbolic of the fact that, even up to the end of the novel, Birkin hangs on to the conflicted hope of having "two kinds of love" (481), sexual bonding with a woman and friendship with a man. For all of Lawrence's talk of achieving equilibrium in a heterosexual relationship, the preferred woman's position in *Women in Love* is decidedly submissive, and according to Jeffrey Meyers, Birkin "never actually abandons homosexuality. By substituting anal marriage for inversion, he sublimates and satisfies his desires in an alternative . . . way" (*Homosexuality* 149).

In this period Lawrence continues his practice of gendered literary criticism. For example, he repudiates the fussiness of realism in a 1916 letter that describes Ivan Turgenev as: "so very critical, like Katherine Mansfield, and also a sort of male old maid" (*Letters 3*: 41). At this time he also showered rare praise on a female contemporary, Catherine Carswell, with whom Lawrence enjoyed an extended friendship and frequent correspondence. In one encouraging letter, Lawrence states: "I think you are the only woman I have met who is so intrinsically detached, so essentially separated and isolated, as to be a real writer or artist or recorder. . . . to want children, and common human fulfilments, is rather a falsity for you, I think. You were never made to 'meet and mingle,' but to remain intact, *essentially*, whatever your experiences may be. Therefore I believe your book will be a real book, and a woman's book: one of the very few" (*Letters 2*: 595). Numerous contradictions emerge from this assessment of Carswell's qualifications for authorship. First of all, she is praised for her detachment, a quality which Lawrence found undesirable in writers like Austen and Eliot. Secondly, it is significant that Lawrence believes that Carswell's capacity to write a "real . . . woman's book" depends upon remaining "intact" (a Diana image), which means foregoing motherhood and other "common human fulfillments" (i.e., love relationships) from which other women authors often draw material for their writing. In other words, Lawrence appears to feel that Carswell can write most like a woman when she lives least as a woman is expected to live. This could be read as a feminist position on Lawrence's part, but (much like the characters in Sinclair's *The Creators*) he seems to see motherhood and love (from a woman's perspective) as obstacles to literary "truth." Lawrence's generous support hides the fear of a threat that a woman's experience might pose to novel writing, although it is that very experience which provides the subject for much of his own work.

In the nonfiction work of this period, Lawrence's practice of using gender as a literary measure is perhaps most obvious in *Studies in Classic American Literature* (1917–1918), which offers Lawrence's idiosyncratic and reactionary perspective on a number of nineteenth-century American male authors. His free-flowing essays on the three novelists of the book (Cooper, Hawthorne, and Melville) are a mixture of admiration and castigation because of the basic split Lawrence finds in their writing, which he sees as a reflection of the general division in the American psyche and the American author between emotion and ideal, or "blood-consciousness" and "mind-consciousness." Although these dualities are not always explicitly gendered as opposites as they are in *The Rainbow* and *Women in Love*, and Lawrence usually advocates a balance of the two, his sympathies often lie with the physical, primal and passional pole of the dualism in the work of these writers. The language and imagery he uses in *Studies* to describe "blood-consciousness" suggest that it is a masculine force Lawrence wishes to support in contrast to the more ideal, abstract, and lifeless feminine force which he believes has dominated society for too long.

Studies in Classic American Literature is full of Lawrence's characteristic masculinist judgments about American novelists. For example, Lawrence censures Cooper for unconsciously illustrating in his "Anglo-American novels" the falsehood of American democracy. Influenced by Wyndham Lewis, who represented democracy as one of the "symptoms of cultural decline and ... feminine characteristics" (Pykett, *Engendering* 51), Lawrence describes it as an emasculating force, "something anti-life" (*Studies* 59), whose effects are evident in Cooper's depiction of people who "are all pinned down by some social pin [of democratic equality], and buzzing away in social importance or friction" (49). However, Lawrence also lauds Cooper for the way in which, in his manly "Leatherstocking novels," he "had a nice dream of something beyond democracy," creating "[a] stark, stripped human relationship of two men, deeper than the deeps of sex" (59). In a similar way, Lawrence represents Herman Melville's personality as going in two directions, split between his primal and domestic desires:

> Melville writhed for eighty years.
> In his soul he was proud and savage.
> But in his mind and will he wanted the perfect fulfillment of love . . .
> the lovey-doveyness of perfect mutual understanding (150).

This division between Melville's primitive, manly drives and his sentimental, feminine desires is reflected in the manner of his writing, which shifts between the influences of materialism and idealism, as in the style of *Moby Dick*, which Lawrence describes as a "curious lurid style, almost spurious, almost journalism, and yet not spurious: on the verge of falsity, still real" (*Symbolic* 236).

In his assessment of the nineteenth-century American literary tradition, Lawrence resorts to two overtly sexual strains of rhetoric to support his cause of recovering manly "blood-consciousness" to revivify modern society. The first is a misogynistic one that is most evident in his reading of

Nathaniel Hawthorne's *The Scarlet Letter*, which Lawrence sees as "a sort of parable, an earthly story" rather than a "romance" (*Studies* 89), and which he proceeds to treat, in the words of Lydia Blanchard, as "a satire of strong women, of the way in which men allow women to make fools of them" ("Reader" 170). The relationship between Arthur Dimmesdale and Hester Prynne is an example for Lawrence of "mind-consciousness" or understanding run wild, a relationship in which Hester is the classic American woman, for whom the "greatest triumph" is that "of seducing a man: especially if he is pure" (*Studies* 94). Dimmesdale's downfall comes, not by means of his sin of adultery, but because his belief system fails to incorporate his passion for Hester and, thus, Hester's power is unleashed: "let a woman loose from the bounds and restraints of man's fierce belief, in his gods and in himself, and she becomes a gentle devil. . . . The colossal evil of the united spirit of Woman" (98–99).

In a curious digression from the matter of the novel, Lawrence links Hester's destructiveness with the deceptive spirit of modern woman, dating from the "last war." This anti-feminist diatribe, stemming from his fear of the "Magna Mater," calls to mind his fictional representation of strong-willed, intellectual women like Hermione in *Women in Love*: "The very women who are most busy saving the bodies of men, and saving the children: these women-doctors, these nurses, these educationalists, these public-spirited women, these female saviors: they are all, from the inside, sending out waves of destructive malevolence which eat out the inner life of man, like a cancer. It is so, it will be so, till men realize it and react to save themselves" (99).

Lawrence's invective against the strong-willed Hester and women of her ilk has a vicious real-life parallel in a tirade he directed at Mary Cannan, one of his female literary acquaintances, and the plan she has for a novel of sexual seduction based on her own experience of getting a short haircut. A 1920 letter reveals Lawrence's rage as he describes his reaction to her new look: "I can't bear the sights [sic] of her. It brings out all the pseudo-mannish-street-arab aggressive selfish insolence, which affects me nowadays, as a male . . . I plainly hate her." His anger is taken out through his power as an established author to destroy her work: "I set my foot on that nasty worm of a novel, and killed it.—Conceit, hideous, elderly, megalomaniac sexual conceit, that's what ails these elderly scavenging bitches" (*Letters 3*: 551–552). Cannan's haircut and its use as source material are perceived by Lawrence as her attempt to take on a mannish role and usurp the power of the male pen in order to write what he considers to be an abomination of a novel because of its blatantly female-centered sexual content. Lawrence's characterization of Cannan is both homo- and gynophobic in its construction of her appearance as a lesbian-coded mannishness and description of her novel as reflecting doglike sexual desires. In *Studies in Classic American Literature* Lawrence proposes a solution to the threat of devilish women like Hester and Mary Cannan that will become the subject of his last novels: a manful conquering of their spirit that releases what Hawthorne calls the "voluptuous, oriental characteristic" of women and, by their choice, introduces what Lawrence sees as a "new era, with a whole new submissiveness to the dark, phallic principle" (*Studies* 101).

This harshness toward his female peers to the point of "slandering them in essays" reflects yet another irony in Lawrence's conflicted literary life and reveals one of the "strategies" that modernist men and women of letters use "for defusing anxiety about the literary combat in which they often felt engaged" (Gilbert and Gubar 149). Lawrence was largely dependent on women in the production and editing of his novels, especially his earlier, more successful works like *Sons and Lovers*, *The Rainbow*, and *Women in Love*. Significant layers of Lawrence's palimpsest-like novels emerge from the fact that "(w)omen participated in Lawrence's work as models for characters and as contributors of verbal and written source materials, but their major role in relation to his work seems to have been as critics" (Siegel 41). On one level, Lawrence engaged in "the usurpation of women's words" (Gilbert and Gubar 152) by "borrowing" from the personal experiences (as described to him or recorded in diaries and memoirs) of women like Lydia, his mother; Jessie Chambers, his first true love; and, of course, Frieda, his wife. On another level, he relied on the critical talents of women such as Louisa Burrows, Helen Corke, and Mabel Luhan, as well as Jessie and Frieda. The most overt example of Lawrence's connection to a woman in a writing endeavor is his co-authoring of *The Boy in the Bush* (1923) with Mollie Skinner, but his role was more که of a novel-doctor than a close collaborator in the effort, and the results yielded tepid reviews.

Lawrence's fearful raging against the strength of the modern woman is accompanied by a homoerotic gospel of male bonding, which peeks through some sections of *Studies* and takes a more deliberate shape in Lawrence's fiction and philosophical writings of the early 1920s. He finds one of the most commendable aspects of Cooper's Leatherstocking tales to be the relationship between Natty Bumppo and his Native American brothers, especially Chingachgook. Although Lawrence claims that the "perpetual blood-brother theme" of the novels is "sheer myth" because there is "a feeling of oppression" between the two races ("the red life flows in a different direction from the white life" (*Studies* 56–57)), Cooper's myth or "dream beyond democracy" still impresses Lawrence because in it he finds "the nucleus of a new society," which is homosocially based: Cooper "dreamed a new human relationship. A stark stripped human relationship of two men, deeper than the deeps of sex. . . . The stark, loveless, wordless unison of two men who have come to the bottom of themselves" (59–60). Also in line with Cooper's myth is Walt Whitman's vision of "manly love" or "the love of comrades," which is praised in the last chapter of *Studies* and is seen as directly linked to the discarding of women in the "progression of merging": "Woman is inadequate for the last merging. So the next step is the merging of man-for-man love" (177–178).

Written shortly after *Studies*, the essay "Education of the People" is full of "attacks on democracy . . . and the feminization of society which he was to develop in his male romances" (Pykett, *Engendering* 133), and it includes "curses . . . upon the women, the self-conscious provokers of infinite sensations, of which man is the instrument" simply for the purpose of "soul-thrills and sexual thrills" (*Phoenix* 631). As a way of combating such co-opting of male potency, Lawrence "erects the icon of the questing male . . . in place of the rejected icon of the mother" (Pykett, *Engendering* 134) by issuing a Cooperesque call to his brothers to regain their pioneer spirit (and masculinity): "let the men scout ahead. Let them go always ahead of their women. . . . Let there be again the old passion of deathless friendship between man and man. . . . Men who can only hark back to woman become automatic, static" (*Phoenix* 664–665). Some critics see the revision of Lawrence's conflicted focus on homosexual desires to an apparently more chaste concern for male-male friendships as a running away from his own sexual ambiguity and experience, and this movement ultimately takes the form of a political solution. Cornelia Nixon pointedly sums up the connections between Lawrence's politics, homosexuality, and misogyny:[11] "He also began to formulate a political scheme that would channel his apparent desire for bonding with other men and render it acceptable to himself as a force for rebuilding the world once the war had destroyed the old political order. And he began to denounce women, blaming them, and their self-conscious sexuality in particular, for the state of the world" (Nixon 15).

These words serve as an appropriate thematic description of the progression of two of Lawrence's novels in this period which, like a number of the "male romances" of the early twentieth-century, revolve around the twin forces of subjugating women and exalting men, beginning on the level of individual friendships between men and moving to attempts at political fraternity. In 1917, while Lawrence was composing the essays of *Studies in Classic American Literature*, he wrote *Aaron's Rod*, the story of a man who abandons a suffocating life with his wife and children to go off in search of his identity as a flute or "rod" player. After he gets violently ill due to an adulterous affair with a woman, Aaron begins a homoerotically charged friendship with a writer, Lilly, who nurses him to health (most effectively by means of massage) and counsels him against a life of love and self-sacrifice for any woman. Through Lilly's help, Aaron moves along the path of regaining "mastery" of his own isolated soul by moving beyond the "love-urge" and toward accepting the "power motive" in his life, which, in Lilly's philosophy, requires the submission of the woman to the "deep power-soul" of the man and the submission of the man to "the heroic soul in a greater man" (*Aaron's* 297–299).

The move away from the mutual heterosexuality of *The Rainbow* and through the sexual antagonism and homosexual undercurrents of the relationships in *Women in Love* and *Aaron's Rod* leads Lawrence to explore the politics and sexual energy of male leadership in *Kangaroo*, a partially autobiographical novel written in 1922. Once again Lawrence presents the story of an artist, this time a poet named Richard Somers who, having been rejected for service in the army, escapes his dreary homeland in postwar England (along with his wife) in search of a new world in Australia and a new source of inspiration for his work. The apolitical Somers, in the hope of achieving the ideal of male friendship that is the subject of some of his own writings, bonds with a local Socialist named Jack who leads him to the charismatic and powerful "Kangaroo," the half-Jewish leader of the Diggers, a revolutionary group which hopes to overthrow British dominance of the country.

A strange physical and spiritual bond springs up between Kangaroo and Somers, adding to tensions in Somers's marriage that have arisen from male-female struggles to assume authority in the relationship and intensifying his confusion about how best to realize his need for "the new passional bond in the new society. The trusting love of a man for his mate" (*Kangaroo* 197). Attempts to draw Somers into the political brotherhood of the Diggers fail when he rejects Kangaroo's party as being too authoritarian and his principle of "[t]he perfect love that men may have for one another, passing the love of women" (324) as being willful and manipulative. However, the emotional response of Somers's repudiation of Kangaroo seems as much based on homophobia and anti-Semitism as it is on philosophical and political differences. Somers finally abandons his quest in Australia and heads to America, withdrawn into his "isolate" self and seeking "the true majesty of the single soul" (303) and believing only in the "deep, self-responsible consciousness in man" (348).

"Comrade love" had proved a failure, both in Lawrence's life and his fiction, but he still felt an intense need to redress the wrongs of what he felt was a sexually overturned society. His next important theoretical work takes a psychological approach to the problem, in the essays "Psychoanalysis and the Unconscious" (1920) and "Fantasia of the Unconscious" (1921), in the latter of which Lawrence "rejects the [earlier] version of the theory of bisexuality or sexual indeterminacy" and transvalues "the sex-gender categories he had elaborated in the 'Study of Thomas Hardy'" (Pykett, *Engendering* 136).[12] In an attempt to revise Freud's psychoanalytic theory, which Lawrence found to be too focussed on the activity of sex, he proposes a new psycho-biological theory of the body's relation to consciousness which identifies specific physical poles of consciousness that are determined by biological sex and by which sex roles should properly function. The primary problem, in Lawrence's eyes, is that these roles have been reversed in modern society: "Man [whose 'positivity' is in the 'volitional centres' in the upper body] has assumed the gentle, all-sympathetic role, and woman [whose 'positivity' is in the 'sympathetic' centres in the lower body] has become the energetic party, with the authority in her hands" (*Fantasia* 97). This reversal has led to what Lawrence called "the hermaphrodite fallacy," in which "Man begins to have all the feelings of woman—or all the feelings which he attributed to woman. . . . He begins to imagine he really is half female. And certainly woman seems very male" (99–100). It seems that Lawrence's goal in his final years of writing was to remedy this imbalance by finding a way to put man back "on top" of the sexual scale and put woman back into her rightful submissive place. In both his essays and fiction, as we shall now see, this became a quest for what he called "the phallic."

QUICKENING THE NOVEL: LAWRENCE'S LATER THEORY

Lawrence's hope for a renaissance in sex and gender roles was paralleled by a similar desire for a rebirth of the novel, and his passion for the latter project emerged quite strongly in the first of what was to be a series of essays on the state of the modern novel. Strikingly titled "Surgery for the Novel—or a Bomb," this 1923 essay threw down the gauntlet in the debate on early twentieth-century fiction, heaping disdain on both serious and popular novels alike. In Lawrence's mind, the unmanning and feminizing qualities of the nineteenth-century novel and its conventions persist in their influence on English fiction up to his present day.

Often employing negative gender imagery, the essay speaks of the modern epoch as ruled by a "democratic-industrial-lovey-dovey-darling-take-me-to-mamma state of things," and it sees the "modern novel" as a "monster with many faces . . . , almost dual, like Siamese twins," divided into two types: "the pale-faced, high-browed, earnest novel, which you have to take seriously . . . [and] that smirking, rather plausible hussy, the popular novel" (*Phoenix* 517 & 520). Although the "earnest" type (works by authors like Joyce and Richardson) seems masculine and mature in its seriousness, Lawrence presents it in terms that are similar to aspects of the feminine self-consciousness he deplores: the "earnest" novel is "childish," reflective of "arrested development," and "(a)bsorbedly, childishly concerned with *what I am*." Such writing gets the "audience . . . frenziedly absorbed in the application of the author's discoveries to their own reactions," which suggests a self-centered, masturbatory action on the part of both author and reader and is a sign that the "novel has never fully become adult" (518). "Hussy"-like popular novels (books like *The Sheik*, *Babbitt*, and Zane Grey novels) are also "childish" and reflect an "[a]dolescence which *can't* grow up" because they are "just as self-conscious, only they do have more illusions about themselves" (519).

In his age of the "dismal, long drawn-out comedy of the death-bed of the serious novel" (518) and the perpetual "adolescence" of the popular novel, Lawrence's major disappointment is the fact that "philosophy and fiction got split," rendering philosophical discourse "abstract-dry" and the novel "sloppy." His hope is that the two can "come together again—in the novel," whose future lies in "the courage to tackle new propositions without using abstractions" and "to present us with new, really new feelings" (520). What is perhaps most interesting in this general call for revitalization, however, is Lawrence's use of jarring, all-or-nothing imagery to make his case. At one point Lawrence articulates the hoped-for change in apocalyptic language: "Some convulsion or cataclysm will have to get this serious novel out of its self-consciousness," and at another point, he talks of the need for "some sort of surgical operation" (518) to rectify matters. Although Lawrence wrote well before the days of transsexuals, it is as if he were calling for a sex-change operation for the novel, which had become too feminized. Certainly the imagery used in some of his other essays on the novel links the revival of the novel to a successful reorientation of sex and gender roles, aspects of which are explored in *The Plumed Serpent*, which was begun shortly after "Surgery for the Novel."

The Plumed Serpent (1926) qualifies as an attempt to bring the ideas of philosophy and the emotion of the novel together, as it is about a romantic triangle set against the political and religious backdrop of postrevolutionary Mexico, but its literary success, according to Lawrence's own criteria, is questionable. Intensifying his anti-feminist and homoerotic thrust, Lawrence returns in this novel to a *Rainbow*-like focus on women's sexual and spiritual experience, but the results are notably different, amounting to a definitive putting of women in their place. Kate is the epitome of the modern woman. Recently widowed and tired of the European men she has known and independently travelling in a strange land, she is seeking escape from her homeland and searching for a new identity that is not based on love. She soon falls under the spell of two "dark and lustrous and fascinating" (*Plumed* 387) Mexican men, Don Ramon and Don Cipriano, aspiring saviors of the common people who attempt to draw Kate into their planned utopia, which is a combination of indigenous religion, "natural" aristocratic government, and male-dominant sexuality, all represented in the figure of Quetzalcoatl ("the Plumed Serpent"), a phoenix-like god which reconciles many contradictory forces.

Kate wavers between attraction to and repulsion from the phallic vision of the two men and initially resists their invitation for her to become the goddess of the Quetzalcoatl pantheon for fear of losing her hard-won independence and sense of having a separate soul. After a series of struggles, she is drawn in by their power and sexuality and agrees to marry Cipriano in a native rite because she comes to an awareness that "Alone, she was nothing. Only as the pure female corresponding to the pure male, did she signify" (388). Kate hopes to realize a newly articulated ideal of mutual love, "the vivid blood-relation between man and woman" (399), but her union with Cipriano requires submission to "the old, supreme phallic mystery" in "supreme passivity" (341–342) and comes at the cost of her independent will and sexual fulfillment.

The sacrifice of Kate's autonomous womanhood is best exemplified in the notorious "Aphrodite of the foam" scene, which occurs shortly after her civil marriage to Cipriano. In the tradition of patriarchal marriage, Kate's husband largely ignores her and her needs, and he makes her aware that her old love emerged from "her own old desire for frictional, irritant sensation" (421). This mode of loving is purged through Cipriano's recoil at those moments when Kate experiences the "seething electric female ecstasy" of clitoral orgasm and his subsequent training of her in "the new, soft, heavy, hot flow" of vaginal orgasm (422). (Lawrence's dualistic morality of female sexual experience is further played out in *Lady Chatterley's Lover*.)

Kate feels caught between the two worlds of her modern European existence as an independent ego and her primal Mexican marriage with its "wonderful sex" that is "powerful and sacred" (436). Lawrence represents her future as a choice between a sexually fulfilling acquiescence to male power and a gradually decaying life as an "old maid" (if she remains a feminist), a choice which is finally and tellingly given over to Ramon and Cipriano to make for her. Lawrence's attempt to meld philosophy and feeling in his representation of love in the novel yields, at times, preachy passages of psycho-spirituality and dialogue that seem more rational than passional, as in this odd theorizing about male-female relations by Ramon's second wife, Teresa, which paradoxically suggests reciprocity while upholding patriarchy: "I know where my soul is. It is in Ramon's womb, the womb of a man, just as his seed is in my womb, the womb of a woman. He is a man, and a column of blood. I am a woman, and a valley of blood. I shall not contradict him. How can I? My soul is inside him" (451). Ultimately, Kate's easy abdication of her will at the end of the novel seems to compromise Lawrence's goal of achieving balance in male-female sexual relationships. However, exhibiting what Wexler considers an a proper reading of the novel's symbolism, Janet Barron provides a more sympathetic view of Kate's choice: "Lawrence's creed of 'phallus worship' is 'counterrevolutionary' in the role he assigns to women; yet we may privately respond to the idea of the male erection *as a symbol* of desire: the problem lies not in the fantasy but in its misogynistic interpretations" (21).

Lawrence's taming of the shrewish Kate in *The Plumed Serpent* is a classic example of what Kate Millett calls "sexual politics in its most overpowering form," accomplished most subtly by Lawrence, "for it is through a feminine consciousness that his masculine message is conveyed." His project is a deceptive one, for rather than: ". . . freeing sexual behavior of perverse inhibition, [and] purging the fiction which describes it of prurient or prudish euphemism, Lawrence is really the evangelist of quite another cause—'phallic consciousness.' This is less a matter of 'the resurrection of the body' [or] 'natural love,' . . . than the transformation of masculine ascendancy into a mystical religion, international, possibly institutionalized (238). Through the exploits of Ramon and Cipriano, Lawrence succeeds in "inventing a religion, even a liturgy of male supremacy," a "phallic cult" in which "the penis alone is responsible for generating all the vital forces in the world" (283).

"The Proper Study," an essay on the novel which Lawrence wrote in September of 1923 as he was working on *The Plumed Serpent*, reiterates Lawrence's move away from his almost exclusive concern with male bonding in the postwar period toward a new understanding of human relations. Like the Mexican men in the novel, the essay employs religious language and imagery to fortify its call to transform sex roles. Lawrence rejects the reigning "literature of perversity" and "literature of little playboys and playgirls" and casts off the traditional subject matter of the novel: "You can't get any more literature out of man in his relation to man. Which, of course, should be writ large, to mean man in his relation to woman, to other men, and to the whole environment of men." In its place, Lawrence envisions a novel that will be a "new stride" toward "the first and greatest relation of every man and woman . . . to the Ocean itself, the great God of the End, who is the All-Father of all sources" (*Phoenix* 722–723). Significant to Lawrence's vision of a return to the primal sources of human experience is his representation of the ocean as a masculine principle of divinity, overturning traditional representations of the sea as a feminine force and bolstering the novel's re-masculinization with a sense of transcendental sanction. This notion of the fathering-forth of the new novel by a flexible yet male force is picked up in later essays and aligned with Lawrence's use of phallic imagery to epitomize and revitalize the novel's potential.

Supplementing Lawrence's call to reshape the novel are a couple of complementary essays written in October of 1923, "On Human Destiny" and "On Being a Man," which explore the role of man as a "thought-adventurer" and make clear that such activity is a primarily male (or phallic) experience. The first essay describes man as now "house-bound" but "destined to seek God and form some conception of Life" by struggling "down to the heart of things" and making "another bitter adventure in pulsating thought, far, far to the one central pole of energy" so as to plant new seeds of "God-knowledge, or Life-knowledge" (*Phoenix II*: 628–629). The second essay bemoans man's inability to live from the body and blood because of a limited and largely mental self-consciousness. It sharply separates the ways man ("the son of the old red-earth Adam") and woman ("the strange serpent-communing Eve") come to self-knowledge through sexual relations. Men are exhorted to "Take the risk, make the adventure. Suffer and enjoy the change in the blood" and "slowly make the great experience of . . . [f]ully conscious realization," while women are encouraged to enjoy their "strange, slumbrous serpentine realization, which knows without thinking" (620).

This erotically charged entreaty makes clear Lawrence's sense of the primal connection between sexuality and human self-knowledge, but its language once again assigns a largely passive (and even diabolic) role to woman in her "slumbrous serpentine realization," while it represents man's experience of realization (suggestive of the tumescence of erection) in much more active and sexually fulfilling terms. Such oppositely gendered experiences of human self-awareness cannot but have parallels in Lawrence's theory of the novel since it depends so heavily upon a "proper" sense of sexual relations. Given the different ways in which men and women "know" themselves and each other, one wonders whether, in Lawrence's mind, women can translate their experience into art in the same way or as well as men, a question which becomes even more pertinent in a consideration of the essays which follow.

Shortly after completing the final version of *The Plumed Serpent*, Lawrence undertook his most concerted and concentrated theorizing about the novel. In June and July of 1925, he became interested in delving into "the deeper implication in a novel" and hoped to review novels "from the standpoint of what I call morality." During this time he wrote a handful of essays on the topic "to pave the way—and have some stones to pull up and throw at the reader's head" (*Letters 5*: 275). Taken as a whole, these essays serve three functions. First, like some of his earlier criticism, they present a critique of contemporary society and its literature, often in disparaging and feminine and/or emasculating terms. Secondly, they position the novel as a unique medium by which, if it is written properly, the emptiness of culture can be challenged and the spirit of humanity can be revivified through the revelation of "true and vivid relationships." Finally, some of the essays present positive qualities which Lawrence hopes this "new novel" will have. As with so much of Lawrence's theoretical writing, his recipe for the novel of the future is presented in gendered terms which exalt the potentially masculine qualities of the novel and steer it away from feminine influences.

This 1925 series of essays is a further development of Lawrence's gendered account of the novel in which he draws a firm distinction between the feminized conventions which have strangled the modern novel and the masculinized shape it must assume in order to recapture its vitality. In "Morality and the Novel" Lawrence fashions his critique in feminine terms: the novel "dishes up a *réchauffé* of old relationships" and "does nothing more than dress [them] up in gorgeous new dresses," an action which "gives a gluttonous kind of pleasure to the mass: a voluptuousness, a wallowing" (*Phoenix* 530). "The Novel" calls into question the manliness of men who write this way, claiming that the "modern novelist is possessed, hag-ridden, by such a stale old 'purpose', or idea-of-himself, that his inspiration succumbs" (*Phoenix II* 418).

When considered along with references to the novel as a "hussy" in "Surgery for the Novel," these sexually charged images of the popular novel suggest that Lawrence sees its function as a combination of prostitution, exhibitionism and voyeurism, and he assigns denigrating feminized roles to all the participants: the novel itself is seen as a wanton and the novelist is her dresser (perhaps a madame or an effeminate man) while the reader is a lazy and lustful consumer who both revels in and takes on the qualities of the object of his/her gaze. However these curious metaphors are read, they clearly reflect Lawrence's antagonism and conflict over what he feels should be the more vital, adult pursuit of genuine novel-writing, which he equates with masculinity and male virility. Set in contrast to such feminized work is Lawrence's assessment of Tolstoy, who is admired for his "phallic splendour" and "passional inspiration" (417), and the way in which he "was true to his characters" and "worshipped the human male, man as a column of rapacious and living blood" (423).

As demonstrated earlier, the 1925 essays on the novel were written in a spirit of crisis, with Lawrence decrying the impotence of his age and its lack of genuine humanity. His general essay on the present state of art, "Art and Morality," speaks of the mechanization of human perception that has come about through the "very curious habit that civilized man has been forming down the whole course of civilization . . . [that] of seeing just as the photographic camera sees" in an attempt to capture "the little objective reality" of things. The result is that, in his general perception as well as in his artistic representation, man "*is* what he sees. He makes himself in his own image" (*Phoenix* 521–523).

In "The Novel and the Feelings" Lawrence shifts to animal imagery when he speaks of his generation as a "tamed" one (*Phoenix* 757) in which education is a mixture of knowledge ranging from the academic to the trivial ("[i]n politics, in geography, in history, in machinery, in soft drinks and in hard, in social economy and social extravagance"). Despite this "frightful universality of knowings," the image of society he presents is one of ignorance, but it is also depicted as both domesticated and feminized: "we know nothing, or next to nothing, about ourselves. After hundreds of thousands of years we have learned how to wash our faces and bob our hair, and that is about all we *have* learned, *individually*" (755). The missing link in the contemporary human experience is the "feelings," which involve the passional self and are generally denied or repressed, as opposed to the "emotions," which lie on the surface and are easily recognized and manipulated. The latter dominate modern society and culture because they can be used for one's convenience like "domesticated animals" (756–757).

To Lawrence's mind, society's obsession with the culture of emotions (and the feminine literature of sentimentalism) has led to a dead end which can only be remedied through a reorientation of humanity toward the life of the feelings, a project that Lawrence portrays in strikingly male terms. Invoking the present moment as a time to "sow wild seed again" in order "to cultivate our feelings," he calls for a rediscovery of "the very darkest continent" (typically seen as feminine) of those feelings by returning to the spirit of "the old Adam" and find "inner meaning" by "listening-in to the voices of the honorable beasts that call in the dark paths of the veins in our body, from the God in the heart" (758–759).

In these essays, Lawrence not only exalts in a general way the role of novels and novelists in helping bring about cultural and literary renewal; he also gives more specific guidelines for the renaissance of the novel, using language which seems primarily aimed at a male audience and sounds a lot like the discourse of the late twentieth-century "men's movement." "The Novel" puts forth its subject's essential qualities: it "inherently is and must be: 1. Quick. 2. Interrelated in all its parts, vitally, organically. 3. Honourable" (*Phoenix II* 422–423). As opposed to the "hag-ridden" and "sickening little personal novels" of the contemporary period, the "great" novel should not be taken up with dull heroes and "pure" heroines; rather, its "hero" should be "[n]ot any of the characters, but some unnamed and nameless flame behind them all . . . [the] God-flame in everything" (418–419). Although Lawrence advocates the quality of quickness in all protagonists regardless of their sex, his instructions on developing characters focus largely on the male ones, as in this directive: "The man in the novel must . . . have a quick relatedness to all of the other things in the novel: snow, bed-bugs, sunshine, the phallus, trains" (420).

"Why the Novel Matters" extols the novel as the "guide" to which the reader should turn to "see wherein you are man alive, and wherein you are dead man in life." A point of difficulty arises here (as in many of Lawrence's essays) in trying to determine when Lawrence uses "man" to refer to humanity in general and when he uses it to refer only to males, since the examples given of the novel's potential to instruct are primarily male activities: "making love to a woman," eating dinner "as man alive," and "firing bombs into men." Only at the end of a passage like this does Lawrence see fit to include a reference to women: "only in the novel are *all* things given full play" out of which "emerges the only thing that is anything, the wholeness of a man, the wholeness of a woman, man alive, and live woman" (*Phoenix* 537–538). (Even the subtle change of language from "man alive" to "live woman" suggests a difference beyond simple linguistic variation; perhaps Lawrence is once again signaling the "natural" passivity of woman through the shift in adjective and word order.)

Finally, Lawrence's admonitions concerning the role of the novelist seem exclusively addressed to his male peers. "The Novel" describes all "great novelists" like Tolstoy as "phallic worshippers" in their "passional inspiration" (*Phoenix II* 417), and Lawrence calls upon the writer to follow his own "character" by looking "into the flame of his own belly" and writing from that inspiration (423). Lawrence expects characters and novelists alike to be "true to the flame [of manhood] that leaps" in them, especially the flame of sex, a "life-flame" and a "deep reserve in a man" which burns "against every absolute, even against the phallic" because it is even "deeper than functional desire" and reaches toward God, "the flame-life in all the universe." The virtue of the novel is to make sure that the sex contained within it is not played with by the novelist (who is usually "a dribbling liar") and thereby made "cheap and nasty" but is, instead, revered as one of the "core flames of manhood" (425–426). Given his dismissive critique of women novelists, it is clear whom Lawrence considers his peers: the vocation of writing is the rightful purview, in his mind, of a manly company. Lawrence fictionalizes the quest for renewed vitality in love and the novel in *Lady Chatterley's Lover*, to which we now turn.

THE FEMINIZATION OF FICTION AND ITS ANTIDOTE

George Levine calls *Lady Chatterley's Lover* a novel that "is importantly about novel writing." Although his study concludes that Lawrence's work basically remains within the realist tradition, a thesis with which I take issue,[13] Levine is on target in his assessment that two of the novel's central characters, Lord Clifford Chatterley and Mrs. Bolton, his nurse, are "Victorian realists" (324). Lawrence's representation of these characters reflects his gendered ideas about the state of the modern novel: in the interaction between Clifford and his housekeeper, Lawrence fictionalizes his concern that the reigning literary tradition is primarily a feminizing and emasculating, and therefore unhealthy, force. Set in contrast to this lifeless pair are the characters of Lady Connie Chatterley and the gamekeeper Arthur Mellors, whose attempt to forge a sexual relationship based on what Lawrence calls "phallic consciousness" provides the kind of material he feels is necessary for the rebirth of the novel.

To begin with, Lawrence is far from subtle in his depiction of Clifford, the representative fiction-writer of the novel, as a disappointing member of his class and sex. He is "more provincial and more timid" than his wife Connie, as well as "just a bit frightened of the vast hordes of middle and lower-class humanity," while she is "so much more mistress of herself in that outer world of chaos, than he was master of himself" (*Lady* 10). Clifford fails to represent male authority in the sexual realm as well; he brings to his marriage a capacity for intimacy but lacks Connie's prior sexual experience: "He had been virgin when he married: and the sex part did not mean much to him" (12). Added to his social and emotional weakness is the physical injury Clifford suffered in World War I, which rendered him paralyzed from the waist down as well as impotent, thereby canceling the possibility of siring an heir to the Chatterley estate.[14]

Clifford's impotence and lack of manliness extend to his career as an author. He writes stories that are "clever, rather spiteful, and yet in some mysterious way, meaningless. The observation was extraordinary and peculiar. But there was no touch, no actual contact. It was as if the whole thing took place on an artificial earth" (16). His particular talent is that he is "really clever at that slightly humorous analysis of people and motives which leaves everything in bits at the end," but "it was all nothing, a wonderful display of nothingness' (50).[15] Behind his career is a willingness "to prostitute himself to the bitch-goddess Success . . . , if only she would have him" (21). This ugly but revealing feminine metaphor of prosperity is ironically constructed since Clifford's prostitution (i.e., his writing for a mass audience) involves a reversal of traditional sexual roles. By means of his popular writing, which caters to "the demands of a mass market which was coded 'feminine'" (Pykett, *Engendering* 55), Clifford serves as a gigolo to a female client possessing the power to bestow money and fame, and in this way Lawrence derisively transfers Clifford's impotent sexual energies to the sphere of the literary market.

Clifford's simultaneously emasculated and feminized state and its relation to his writing are most evident in Lawrence's representation of the influence of Mrs. Bolton, who plays the dual role of deferential servant and manipulative mother-figure as Clifford shifts between assertive master and needy child. The most significant aspect of their association with regard to Clifford's writing is Lawrence's characterization of "long conversations going on between the two. Or rather, it was mostly Mrs. Bolton talking." Described as a "stream of her gossip" (possibly intended as a slight on stream of consciousness novels), these chats resemble the writing of "Mrs. Gaskell and George Eliot and Miss Mitford all rolled into one, with a great deal more, that these women left out." The narrator even depicts Mrs. Bolton as a kind of Victorian novelist in her own right: her monologues are "better than any book" and could have "run to dozens of volumes," and she becomes a source for Clifford, who "was listening for 'material,' and he found it in plenty" (*Lady* 100–101).

Lawrence uses these *Kaffeeklatsch*-like discussions as the locus for a discourse on the novel, which appears in the form of "a very Victorian 'intrusion'" (Levine 326) by the narrator. In the passage, the novel, when it is not "properly handled," is like "gossip" because it can "excite spurious sympathies and recoils, mechanical and deadening to the psyche . . . [and] can glorify the most corrupt feelings, so long as they are *conventionally* 'pure.'" This kind of novel "becomes at last vicious . . . because it is always ostensibly on the side of the angels" (i.e., the "*nice*" women of Mrs. Bolton's tales), and, as gossip is humiliating, "most novels, especially popular ones, are humiliating too," serving a public that "responds . . . only to an appeal to its vices" (*Lady* 101).

In a number of ways, this scene reveals Lawrence's hostile attitude toward what he sees as the emasculating and feminizing power of the novel in his day.[16] First of all, Lawrence's representation of these conversations as akin to women's gossip casts even more aspersions on Clifford's masculinity, and the placement of a discourse on the novel in the midst of this tattletale scene suggests that Clifford's fiction is not much more than secondhand scandalmongering. Secondly, the dialogues with Mrs. Bolton align Clifford with the largely female middle-class readership of fiction, especially popular novels and stories like the ones that Clifford (and Lawrence, to a degree) wrote. Abhorring their gossipy alliance, Lawrence dismisses authors and readers of sentimental fiction as participants in a "spurious" and "corrupt" emotional life which is as "mechanical and deadening to the psyche" (101) as the more concrete forces of industrialization which have sapped the energies of Lawrence's beloved Midlands.

Finally, the only authors to whom Lawrence compares Mrs. Bolton's gossip (and, by implication, Clifford's writing) are nineteenth-century women. Mrs. Gaskell and George Eliot, of course, were both Victorian Age authors who wrote popular yet socially conscious novels, and Miss Mary Russell Mitford was a contemporary of the Romantics who wrote poetry and romantic historical tragedies, and pioneered a new genre, "village fiction," that became a dominant nineteenth-century women's literary tradition. What unites these women is their writing in a realistic vein with a careful attention to detail. By failing to mention any famous male authors in this comparison, Lawrence places what is wrong with popular fiction on the shoulders of nineteenth-century female authors and their followers, in this case feminized contemporary male authors like Clifford (and Lawrence himself) who are viewed as writing only to pander to the vulgar tastes of the female reading public. Lawrence indicates the depths to which Clifford has been feminized by his fiction-writing, which wins for him "mere publicity, amid a whole sapping of energy and malice," through the depiction of Clifford's subsequent escape from the gossipy world of story production into the mechanized world of coal production (which Lawrence also abhorred) as a step up and out toward "a sense of power" and "a man's victory" (108).

There is no mention of a literary career for Clifford in the first two versions of the novel, *The First Lady Chatterley* and *John Thomas and Lady Jane*, which suggests that something significant happened to Lawrence between the completion of the second version in February 1927 and the beginning of the third ten months later in December to prompt his addition of a savage attack on popular fiction and a thematic exploration of "the novel, properly handled." Lawrence's savage tone in his final portrayal of Clifford may have been prompted by one of the personal problems Lawrence encountered at this time. First, the cumulative physical and sexual effects of his tuberculosis affected his psychological state, as evidenced in this letter Lawrence wrote about a kind of male menopause he was feeling: "You and I are at the *age dangereuse* for men: when the whole rhythm of the psyche changes: when one no longer has an easy flow outwards: and when one rebels at a good many things" and "[o]ne is swindled out of one's proper sex life, a great deal" (*Letters* 5: 648). In the midst of his physical and psychological frustration, Lawrence's play *David* (on the friendship of the biblical David and Jonathan) opened but the reviews were negative, inciting him to this excoriation: "those reviewers should be made waitresses in Lyons' Cafes. It's about all they've got the spunk for," and "I say they are eunuchs, and have no balls" (*Letters* 6: 71 & 72). Finally, Lawrence was weighed down by the lack of financial success of his writing, as he stated in one letter: "it's God help us, when it comes to earning money by sincere work. I manage still to scramble through, but no more. The world is beastly, and gets beastlier" (90).

Scott Sanders sees numerous parallels between Lawrence's professional career and his characterization of Clifford, who is used as a means for "Lawrence's questioning of his vocation as a writer." Although Lawrence was strongly concerned in *The First Lady Chatterley* with the unjust conditions of the working class of the Midlands as a result of his visit there in 1926, his depiction of Clifford evolves by the third version to the portrait of a wealthy writer living amid "hungry and desperate villages of working people" (Sanders 188) yet "catering with his stories for the populace of pleasure . . . and 'getting on' in the world." (*Lady* 106–107). In Clifford, "Lawrence beheld a distorted image of himself" (Sanders 189), and his depiction of Clifford's ineffectual life as an author in the final version of the novel reflects the anxiety Lawrence felt about the possible triviality of his own work in relation to the social problems of his homeland. If Clifford does indeed serve in some ways as a surrogate for Lawrence (and many critics see Mellors as his other, more "masculine" half), then the feminizing tone of the scene with Mrs. Bolton is particularly significant to Lawrence's own self-projection as both a man and an artist.

The discourse on the novel in this scene is not only a negative critique of the gossipy popular novels Clifford Chatterley writes. Before attacking such "vicious" novels, the narrator speaks of "the vast importance of the novel, properly handled. It can inform and lead into new places the flow of our sympathetic consciousness, and it can lead our sympathy away in recoil from things gone dead." Its goal is to reveal "the *passional* secret places of life" where "the tide of sensitive awareness needs to ebb and flow, cleansing and freshening" (*Lady* 101). Lawrence hopes to achieve this goal in his portrayal of the bond between Connie and Mellors, whose love provides the material for a "living" novel of "sympathetic consciousness." Unfortunately, Lawrence's account of the lovers' passional relations resembles his theory of the novel in the 1925 essays: seemingly balanced in terms of male-female relations but ultimately male-centered.

As his sexual philosophy and literary theory take flesh in the relationship of Connie and Mellors, Lawrence tries to create an equitable connection. The story, originally to be titled *Tenderness*, is an account of the awakening of Connie's sexuality and the rekindling of Mellors's passion. It is emblematic of Lawrence's new form of novel, an attempt to "rewrite the literary body" (Williams 90), as its feminized author, Clifford, is replaced by a non-writer separated from the emasculating modern spirit, Mellors, who offers a new sense of meaning through the "touch of bodily awareness between human beings" (*Lady* 279).[17] In his depiction of Connie's liberation from her upper-class repression and Mellors's introduction into loving tenderness, Lawrence genuinely seems to move the cause of women's sexuality forward. However, as has been obvious in the volatile critical debate of the last thirty years, many critics have seen troubling signs of patriarchy and misogyny in the text (often settling on merely selective quotes) which, they feel, negate Lawrence's more altruistic and even feminist purposes. To give Lawrence his due, supporters of his work strongly encourage, one must read the entire Connie-Mellors relationship in context. Doing so allows one to see the series of encounters between Connie and Mellors as progressing away from what Lawrence represents as willful, egotistical sexual behavior on Connie's part and an angry, sometimes misogynistic fear of intimacy on Mellors's part to mutual, tender lovemaking founded upon simultaneous orgasm without a sense of individual ego.

On the positive side, Lawrence's project to create a new language of the body with which to combat the spirit of the "machine" is effective on a number of counts. Connie and Mellors' relationship shows a clear development in tenderness as it moves from their initial encounters, in which Mellors takes the initiative and Connie is either passive or caught up in her egocentric mindset, to marathon sex sessions that seem to defy human physiology,[18] in which both partners take active roles and have their sexual needs met.[19] In these scenes of lovemaking, Lawrence opens up the language of sexuality in important ways. As Michael Bell puts it, in the novel Lawrence achieves a "reconciliation with a language of conscious articulacy as a possible medium of feeling" (217).[20] Although considered graphic and vulgar in its day, Lawrence's concern for and detailed description of female sexual pleasure is evident in his accounts of female orgasm (e.g., "new strange thrills rippling inside her" (*Lady* 133), and "the deeps parted and rolled asunder, in long, far-travelling billows" (174)) and Mellors concepts of mutuality in love-making (including terms like "warm-hearted . . . fucking" and "tenderness" (206–207), and "cunt-awareness" (277)). According to Balbert, in their lovemaking, Mellors comes to an "uncompromising, basic recognition of her [Connie's] sexual 'otherness' as a woman" ("he was kind to the female in her" (*Lady* 121)) and an "eminently 'male' appreciation of her womb," which is the source of Connie's "instinctual passions" (Balbert 166–168). Anaïs Nin claims that Lawrence's facility in appreciating both sides of (hetero)sexual union in his fiction in explained by his "complete realization of the feelings of women." This leads to a literary style that, despite its radical differences from Woolf's prose, Nin describes in terms suggestive of Woolf's ideal: "a curious power in his writing which might be described as androgynous" (57).

Critics who find misogyny rather than mutual liberation in these sex scenes generally focus on two areas of complaint. The first is the claim that Lawrence's representation of Connie and Mellors' sexual experience and identity are ultimately dependent on Mellors's male member and perspective. Setting aside the early sex scenes that are clearly and intentionally one-sided, they point to the fact that when Connie and Mellors first achieve mutual orgasm, her experience is described in phallocentric terms as a realization of "depth of the other thing in her" leads her to the feeling that she "adored him until her knees were weak as she walked" (*Lady* 135). Later scenes also appear to place Connie in a subordinate position, none more so than the infamous euphemistically described account of anal intercourse in chapter sixteen. In undergoing this experience of sodomy,[21] which Nixon notes "is not intended for female satisfaction" (128), Connie comes "to the real bed-rock of her nature," as she is "roused up and routed by the phallic hunt of the man," which she "hated" but also "needed" and "secretly wanted" (*Lady* 247). Perhaps the most significant result of her sexual "union" with Mellors in this scene is the self-knowledge she acquires, but it seems to come through the male gaze: "She saw her own nakedness in his eyes, immediate knowledge of her. And the fluid, male knowledge of herself seemed to flow to her from his eyes and wrap her voluptuously" (248).

Many critics see in these sexual interchanges a one-sided process of realization that culminates in the sodomy scene, claiming that there is not really a reciprocal set of terms or experiences in the text through which Mellors grows in his male identity as a result of Connie's female actions and perspective. For example, Simpson points out that, despite his awareness of ancient Etruscan worship of the "arx" (a womb-symbol), Lawrence generally fails to have a vaginal equivalent to the phallus for adoration in these scenes (131–132). And John Bayley claims that, despite Lawrence's efforts to acknowledge female sexuality, "[h]is sexual imagination fantasised about men, never about women—there are no physical descriptions of women in his work in any way comparable in vividness to those of the men—and he tried to graft his fantasy of a man's world . . . on to a willed presentation of tenderness and love in a heterosexual situation" (23).

Both of these claims are rebutted by critics like Mark Spilka who point to signs of male reciprocity in Mellors's paean to Connie's vagina in chapter twelve before any mention of phallic worship on Connie's part (*Lady* 177–178), and his kissing of Connie's womb at her request in the final sex scene of the book, a moment when Mellors enters her "softly" in a "stream of tenderness" (302) that transpires while Connie is pregnant (Spilka 189–190).[22] Also, contrary to the stereotypical readings of Connie's passive adoration of the penis, Williams argues that "Connie's claim on it for her pleasure, and for theirs as a pair, suggests that the organ acts in a way which is not entirely body-specific, which makes it as much a part of the woman's sexual anatomy as the man's" (94). As for the sodomy scene, Lawrence's few defenders on this matter explain it as an unfortunate and excessive consequence of Mellors's anger from his volatile exchange with Hilda and/or as a necessary "purging of Mellors's hostility and self-doubt and of Connie's social shame" (Spilka 169).

The other primary critique leveled at Lawrence's sexual theory in the novel as being phallocentric concerns the ways that he characterizes female sexuality outside of the relationship of Connie and Mellors. This is especially harsh in the representation of Mellors's attitudes toward his wife, Bertha, who abandoned him for another man. In a conversation with Connie, Mellors vents his hatred of his wife's habit of not being able to "come-off" when he did but bringing herself to orgasm afterwards, and he uses cruel, predatory imagery to describe it: "she'd sort of tear at me down there, as if it was a beak tearing at me . . . [l]ike an old trull" (*Lady* 201–202). He goes on to claim that "the mass of women are like this" (one thinks of Lawrence's similar treatment of Hermione in *Women in Love* and Kate in *The Plumed Serpent*), calling them "mostly the Lesbian sort," and he says that when he is with one, "I fairly howl in my soul, wanting to kill her" (203). Sympathetic critics try to explain these violent male sentiments as an understandable explosion of hurt and anger on Mellors's part at his being rejected or as a reflection of Lawrence's general denunciation of the "onanism that is the dominant mode of modern love" (Balbert 171). Mellors's disgust of clitoral orgasm and lesbianism (a revulsion shared by Lawrence in some of his essays) may simply indicate his opting for vaginal orgasm as the norm for mutual phallic sexuality or reflect his ignorance of female sexual physiology (Spilka 186–188). However, read from a contemporary perspective, his attitudes denigrate and dismiss alternative sexual experiences for women, thereby reiterating their sexual dependence on men. This seems particularly hypocritical in light of Mellors's celebration of "that natural physical tenderness, which is the best, even between men" (*Lady* 277).

In the end, Lawrence's most pronounced novelistic effort to lead "the flow of our sympathetic consciousness" into "the passional secret places of life" is set in a restrictive and heterosexist context. Like it or not, Lawrence's recipe for vital sexual relations is a culturally conservative one —there is no room for sexual relationship and pleasure outside of a heterosexual union. As Williams puts it, Lawrence "cannot conceive of 'otherness' existing within and between the same sex—there is something about the mix of male and female which produces sparks, and which needs the conjunction of men's and women's bodies" (94).

The same conflict between a desire for equitable sexual relationships and a phallocentrism tending toward misogyny extends to Lawrence's final critical output. Just after he finished *Lady Chatterley's Lover* in 1928, Lawrence wrote a number of short essays on the state of male-female relations in society that sported such titles as, "Women Are So Cocksure," "Do Women Change?," "Matriarchy," and "Is England Still a Man's Country?" As might be guessed, these brief attempts at social analysis continue Lawrence's lifelong cry against the weakness of "the modern young man" and "the monstrous rule of women" (*Phoenix II* 550). His solutions to this gender instability echo statements made earlier in his career: in "Give Her a Pattern," Lawrence argues that men can and should construct a new gender identity that will "give women a decent, satisfying idea of womanhood" (538), and in "Matriarchy" he issues a call for men to become "master" again (549) and find a "new foregathering ground, where they can meet and satisfy their deep social needs, profound social cravings which can only be satisfied apart from women" (552).

Lawrence fires his final critical salvos at the conventions of the novel in two 1929 essays that register the bitterness of his battles with tuberculosis and the censors of *Lady Chatterley's Lover*. The first is entitled "Pornography and Obscenity," and it repeats a number of his gender-laden judgments about the English novel tradition. In contrast to Woolf's representation of the Victorian Age as a patriarchal "garish erection," Lawrence conceives of the nineteenth century as "the eunuch century, the century of the mealy-mouthed lie, the century that has tried to destroy humanity" (*Phoenix* 183). In his view, a primary metaphor for the previous age is "the real masturbation of Englishmen," which he claims "began only in the nineteenth century," involving an "emptying of the real vitality and real *being* of men," and manifesting itself in the literary world "in a vicious circle of analysis and impotent criticism, or else a vicious circle of false and easy sympathy, sentimentalities" (180). His language of inadequate and/or misspent masculinity once again brands the realist tradition of the novel as either powerless or merely self-gratifying. Echoing his characterization of Clifford in *Lady Chatterley's Lover*, Lawrence's estimation of the period and its literature incorporates the language of both emasculation ("impotent criticism," "eunuch century") and feminization ("easy sympathy, sentimentalities").

In the second essay, "A Propos of *Lady Chatterley's Lover*," Lawrence attempts to answer some of the uproar generated by the publication of the novel and articulates his theory of "phallic consciousness" and its connection to heterosexual relations. As in earlier essays, he tries to represent such consciousness as a dualism of male and female elements, but there is clearly more distance between them: "The blood of man and the blood of woman are two eternally different streams, that can never be mingled . . . that encircle the whole of life, . . . and in sex the two rivers touch and renew one another, without ever commingling or confusing" (*Phoenix II* 505). Despite the suggestion of equity in this duality of the sexes, it is the male organ that is responsible for the harmony of the relationship: "the phallus is the connecting link between the two rivers, that establishes the two streams in a oneness. . . . [T]he bridge to the future is the phallus, and there's the end of it" (506 & 508).

H. M. Daleski notes that Lawrence coins the term "phallic consciousness" in the late 1920s, and it refers to the physical or sensual pole of his dualistic thinking that had earlier been called the "primal" or "blood consciousness," which was usually characterized as a male force and represented in the male characters of novels like *The Rainbow*. Daleski calls this new term "a subterfuge" that enables Lawrence "to identify himself with 'female' qualities [e.g., spontaneity and tenderness] while preserving a 'male' turn of phrase" (259–260). This contradiction in terminology is symbolic of the conflict in Lawrence's theory as a whole. On one hand, Lawrence himself saw his phallic terms as inclusive (and even transcendent) of both male and female experience: for example, he calls the "phallus" a "symbol of the eternal desire" (*Phoenix II* 456) and believes that "real phallic feeling and consciousness" is "more than mere sex": it is "another reality" open to anyone (*Letters* 6 319–320). Ed Jewinski claims that Lawrence uses the term "phallus" much like Jacques Lacan does as a "central signifier of every human's utter and inescapable distinctness, singularity, and individuality" (9). On the other hand, feminists like Marion Shaw raise the problem of "how to tell a phallus from a penis," recognizing that, as *Lady Chatterley's Lover* bears out, "the God-like status of the phallus confers on its bearer an inevitable supremacy, particularly so when, as in Lawrence, the corresponding female parts and activities do not 'signify' anything very much at all but are viewed often enough with an all too literal aversion" (26). Once again, a Lawrentian gesture toward inclusivity and equality leaves women coming up short.

"A Propos" also marks a shift in his critical writing back to religious language and imagery, as Lawrence enlists an unusual ally, the Catholic Church in his defense of sexual openness. Lawrence contrasts the puritan climate and "hush! hush!" attitude (which he calls the real "obscenity") of northern Europe and America (*Phoenix II* 490–491), which has rejected his attempt to enable men and women "to think sex, fully, completely, honestly, and cleanly" (489), with the warm embrace of sex by southern Europe as found in the way the Church "recognizes sex, and makes of marriage a sacrament based on the sexual communion" (498). His spiritualization of sex takes fictional shape in *The Man Who Died* (1929), originally and provocatively entitled "The Escaped Cock," which is an account of how Jesus Christ wakes from death and wanders the earth but does not truly come back to life until he finds sexual fulfillment and leaves behind an heir ("I have sowed the seed of my life and my resurrection" (*St. Mawr* 211)) at the temple of Isis.

In this rewriting of Christian and Egyptian sacred tradition, Lawrence applies his gendered sexual theory to the genre of myth as Jesus the teacher is superseded by Jesus the lover and sex becomes the new religion. This final fictional epistle from the "Priest of Love" presents the "properly handled" modern novel as the new testament of phallic consciousness and love relations. However, the final scene is hardly a picture of idyllic heterosexual union, as Jesus, having had his temporary fling with Isis which left her pregnant, declares "I have . . . put my touch forever upon the choice woman of this day. . . . She is dear to me in the middle of my being" and moves on, for "To-morrow is another day" (211). Once again woman is the vessel for man's fulfillment and the phallic consciousness is his alone. Even to his deathbed, Lawrence's inclusive vision is undermined by a one-sided phallic reality.

In many ways, Lawrence's "Book of Truth" could really be called the Book of Gender (or Sex) since his novels are so intensely focussed on sex-gender identities and relationships, but, as I think I have shown, he is not alone among his peers. For Woolf, Forster, and Sinclair gender and sex were also very much "in the air." As thinkers and writers in early twentieth-century England, they were necessarily immersed in the volatile and contradictory discourses of gender and sexuality, and gendered theorizing and writing was a key component in their efforts to critique their culture and renovate its literary traditions. Although they are neither the only nor, perhaps, the determinate factor in the remarkable innovations in the theory and practice of the novel achieved by these four authors, matters of gender and sexuality did indeed matter in these writers' literary performance and success. Their common project of regenerating the novel seems to have meant regendering it in some form as well, and what was engendered in the process may sometimes be maddeningly contradictory or inconsistent, but it is more often creatively complex and generically rich.

Notes

Chapter One Notes

[1] Contemporary feminist critics are generally effusive in their praise of Woolf's achievement of this goal. For example, Rachel Blau DuPlessis considers her a founding mother in the process of "writing beyond the ending" through her novels' formal strategies of "breaking the sentence," which "severs dominant authority and ideology," and "breaking the sequence," which "is a critique of narrative, restructuring its orders and priorities precisely by attention to specific issues of female identity and its characteristic oscillations" (x). Sydney Janet Kaplan notes Woolf's success at creating what Liisa Dahl calls a "rounded impressionistic sentence" (Dahl 443) that Kaplan believes was "capable of handling the complexity of the feminine consciousness." This is done through a "chain of separate modifiers [that] is bound up with some part that connects the sentence to its starting point" and conveys "the movement from perception to reflection and back again" (Kaplan 81–82).

[2] *Orlando* as family history is treated in Philipson 237–248.

[3] See Woolf, "The Narrow Bridge of Art," *Essays 2*: 218–229, for her musings on what future literature which attends to emotions and "the moment" will be like.

[4] This praise of the male Georgians is tempered by Woolf's later claim in "The Leaning Tower" that these modern writers are "tower dwellers" who cannot come down because they are "trapped by their education [and] pinned down by their capital," and their work is "full of discord and bitterness, full of confusion and of compromise" (*Essays 2*: 170–172).

[5] For a developed discussion of the thorny issue of Woolf's theory of androgyny, see Bazin, Ch. I "A Quest for Equilibrium"; Bowlby, Ch. 3 "Orlando's Vacillation"; Farwell 433–451; Minow-Pinkney 8–12; Poresky 156–159; and Showalter, Chapter X "Virginia Woolf and the Flight into Androgyny."

[6] Scott provides a dizzying map of such connections among a much larger group of modernists, 10.

[7] David Ellis documents the interactions between Lawrence and Forster in 1915 and the way in which "the growing intimacy of the two writers was brought to an abrupt halt by a disagreement over sexual matters" ("Forster" 1).

[8] Jeffrey Meyers, in his biography of Lawrence, see this attack as overtly ignoring the fact that Forster was homosexual and "criticizing not only Forster's homosexual tendencies but also his own" (*DHL* 164).

CHAPTER TWO NOTES

[1] My use of the term "queer" in this chapter often plays on its dual meaning as "homoerotic," in reference to sexual desire, and "bizarre" or "strange," in reference to unusual or unconventional literary effects.

[2] According to John Beer, Forster, like other authors of his time, "had become fascinated with the dynamic element in earlier mythologies, looking to the possibility that they reflected powers which might still survive more positively in human beings" (250).

[3] Forster himself acknowledged this tension in a letter to Bertrand Russell in 1917: "Though of course there is a connection between civilisation and our private desires and impulses and actions, it is a connection as meaningless as that between a word and the letters that make it up" (qtd. in Watt 312).

[4] As Robert K. Martin and George Piggford note, although Forster was aware of his homosexual desires and status as a "minority" (Forster's own word), he "wrote his first five novels as, in effect, a 'virgin' who had never proceeded beyond kisses and hugs" ("Introduction" 11–13).

[5] Parminder Kaur Bakshi describes Forster's novels as "the battleground for the opposing claims of the respectable and the homosexual" (4), in which he "tries to adapt homoerotic desire to heterosexual themes and genres, but the hidden theme of homosexual desire inevitably explodes the values of heterosexual life," especially marriage (36).

[6] Bakshi sees a progressive development in Forster's use of the double-plot: "Each of Forster's novels is a fresh experiment in duplicity until in *A Passage to India* the demarcation between the heterosexual and the homosexual aspects of the narrative can be barely detected" (78).

[7] One explanation for the triangles could be what Thomas L. Jeffers describes as Forster's sense that he "managed to represent only three types of character: the person he thought he was, the people who irritated him, and the people he would have liked to be" (192).

[8] Glen Cavaliero notes that because Forster's sensibility "is aroused by the notion of the masculine as such, and by the male in love," in these triangles he generally "identifies himself with the woman concerned or . . . with a man who is given womanly characteristics" (133). Martin posits that in Forster's use of such triads, he is working "toward a reorganized vision of human relations in order to allow continuance without physical conception, to provide continuity without heterosex and without nuclear family parenting" ("Umbrella" 256).

Notes

[9] Joseph Bristow sees the struggle in Forster's fictions as primarily enacted between an intellectually appealing Arnoldian cultural ideal that tends toward effeminacy and a physically alluring imperialist ethos that is tied to masculine brutality. Forster's love triangles turn "inside out" the "system of social and sexual relations" that are usually represented in such conflicts: "Instead of fending off . . . homoeroticism . . . , his plots seek to exploit it." The woman (or womanly male) in the triangle is called upon to unite the "aesthete" and the "athlete," but "Forster's lifelong narrative problem . . . is how to discover a public and plausible form in which male homoeroticism could benefit from feminine authority without becoming effeminate" (58–59).

[10] Forster is generally resistant to the use of "[p]rinciples and systems" as a means by which "to attack the novel" but, in a revealing choice of words that suggests a homoerotics of reading, he acknowledges that if they are to be applied, "their results must be subjected to re-examination" by "the human heart . . . this man-to-man business" (*Aspects* 23).

[11] In another sign of the queerness of Forster's theory, Daniel Schwarz makes the point that as *Aspects* progresses from describing the first group of aspects to the second, "Forster moves further away from the doctrine of nineteenth-century realism that novels must be imitations of life and begins to introduce categories that his classically trained lecture audience would have found innovative and exciting, if at times provocatively idiosyncratic, whimsical, and even bizarre" ("Importance" 200–201).

[12] Daniel Schwarz notes that fantasy "includes the kinds of extraordinary events that [Henry] James called 'romance,' but it also includes very different kinds of speculative, tonal, and stylistic departures from realism" ("Importance" 201).

[13] A way of testing these theses could be a consideration of *A Passage to India*, considered by many critics to be Forster's most different and "prophetic" work. On the one hand, the novel seems to merit this categorization both in its emotional sobriety and in its engagement of the three official religions of India; however, although it appears to take up the style and mythology of "prophecy," the novel deconstructs the rituals and deities of organized religion, and in line with this, its form is no more realist—and in fact somewhat more "modernist"—than Forster's other novels.

[14] Alan Wilde claims that, for Forster, "Pan is . . . above all an *idea*—the abstraction of desire, an urgency made conformable to the demands of consciousness." As a result, Forster's "Pan figures . . . intimate sexuality (largely, though by no means exclusively, homosexuality) and at the same time to desexualise it" ("Naturalisation" 196–197).

[15] For an account of Edward Garnett's opinion of Forster's "sublimations or symbolisations of sex" through Pan figures, see David Garnett 33.

[16] Furbank concludes that Forster was intellectually aware of his homosexual desires by about 1900 when he was a member of the "Apostles," a conversation society of students at Cambridge who spoke openly (and largely theoretically) on the topic of homosexuality (1: 78). Heine traces his awareness to 1902, a time of "two great discoveries" (as recorded in Forster's diary), one of which, Heine posits, was "his realization that he was homosexual [which] came about through H. O. Meredith" (xxvi). Although he was sexually inhibited for a number of years (until 1916),

Forster experienced a couple of significant attractions in the years preceding and during the writing of his first five novels: one, a requited and affectionate but chaste friendship with Meredith, and the other, an unrequited infatuation with a heterosexual Indian, Syed Ross Masood. The conflicted combination of Forster's experience of homosexual desire and inexperience in the physical expression of that desire makes his choice to write in the mode of fantasy an appropriate one

[17] Forster's use of characters to represent the gods of fantasy in these early novels is sketchy in comparison to that of similar figures in *The Longest Journey* and later novels. If there is a Demeter figure in *Where Angels Fear to Tread*, Caroline would be the likeliest candidate by virtue of her gradual acceptance of the events in Italy and her serving as a go-between for Philip and Gino's reconciliation, but this is complicated by her presence in the love triangle.

[18] Bakshi suggests that Forster's "solution" to incorporating homosexual desire in the novel "was to posit the real [heterosexual] world against the imaginary [homosexual] one, connecting the two by means of journey, so that both realms reflect and counter-reflect each other" (77).

[19] Forster even wrote in his "Personal Memorandum" in 1935, "I want to love a strong young man of the lower classes and be loved by him and even hurt by him. That is my ticket, and then I have wanted to write respectable novels." (See Stallybrass, "Introduction" xiv).

[20] Caroline's role here illustrates what Bakshi sees as Forster's subversive use of "women characters to promote the theme of homoerotic love" (93) through initiating "the communion of friendship and brotherhood between Philip and Gino" (95), thereby decentering marriage and heterosexual relations in the novel (98).

[21] See Sedgwick, "Chapter One: Gender Asymmetry and Erotic Triangles" for a full explanation of this dynamic.

[22] This scene is the primary site of the underdeveloped homoerotic charge between George and Freddy, whom Goscilo describes as a "Philip-like Gino," who is "Gino's British counterpart as a child of nature even as he structurally resembles Philip in being a 'boy' who discovers a male rapport that can be couched in terms of brotherhood(-in-law)" (209).

[23] Mr. Beebe's antipathy toward marriage and attraction toward George was intensified in an earlier draft of the novel, in which "Mr. Beebe rebukes him [George] when he is unwilling to renounce Lucy" (Bakshi 142). As the text states, employing the Edwardian medical discourse of homosexuality: "So long as he could think of George as diseased Mr. Beebe had been pitiful and even sympathetic. He was ready to soothe and comfort his hopeless passion, to bind up his broken heart, to nurse him back to daily life. But the suggestion of vigour infuriated him. He became personally hostile" (Forster, *Lucy* 110).

[24] Heine suggests that by "anti-literature" Forster "may have meant the reality of his own personal desire for an ideal homosexual love" (lvi).

[25] Illustrating the conflict of opinion, Wilfred Stone claims that "the book does not succeed" because "it tries to do too many things at once and struggles vainly, as Rickie does, to achieve an identity" (215), while Carola Kaplan finds that "the book is fascinating, vivid, and strange: it has far greater vitality and psychological depth than Forster's more apparently finished novels of this early period" (197).

[26] Bakshi links Rickie's journey "from Cambridge through Sawston to Wiltshire . . . to the themes of friendship, marriage and brotherhood respectively" (124).

[27] Furbank locates the origin of Rickie's clubfoot in Forster's encounter with a lame shepherd in the Figsbury Rings, which combined "in one symbol so many elements with meaning for him: the ideal English landscape, heroic human quality in a working-class guise, and an inherited handicap (as it might be, homosexuality) courageously overcome" (1: 119). Meyers views both "the lameness of the 'effeminate' Rickie" and "the bastardy of Stephen" as "symbols of their homosexuality" (*Homosexuality* 105). Heine points out that, at the time of writing the book, Forster "knew of the contemporary scientific view [of Carpenter, Ellis and others] that some homosexuality was congenital," and believed this to be true of himself, which "militates against any thought that Forster believed his own paternal inheritance to be abnormal" (xxi & xxiv).

[28] Echoes of Pan also appear in Forster's characterization of Mrs. Elliot's lover, Robert.

[29] Entitled "Panic" and beginning with "an invocation to the woodland deities to guard Stephen" (Colmer, *EMF* 74), the chapter sees Stephen bathing in a river, wandering naked in the woods, and cracking his head against a beech tree, after which, "[w]hen he comes to himself he is no longer himself but daft, fey, part of the woods, and the animals recognize him" (Forster, "Aspect" 1230). Elizabeth Wood Ellem claims that included among "the rejected material is a description [reminiscent of *A Room with a View*] of Rickie and Harold Wonham [the Stephen figure] . . . bathing together in a woodland pool" (Ellem 92).

[30] Cavaliero describes Wiltshire as "a place of masculine companionship and ancient memories, the place where Rickie is first offered the gift of a brother" (82).

[31] The shift to English landscapes as fantastic sites in Forster's fiction suggests that they are somehow more conducive to the attainment of homosexual love than those in Italy, which seems to be primarily a place for pursuing heterosexual love (or perhaps this is just an example of wishful thinking on Forster's part).

[32] As Meyers sums it up: "This accident removes Rickie's abnormality (the lame foot) just before he dies, completes his symbolic castration by Agnes, and most importantly, severs the homosexual (and incestuous) relationship which Forster takes up again in *Maurice*" (*Homosexuality* 106).

[33] Crews suggests that "the thinness of Rickie's stories" may be "an implicit critique of the symbolic habit of mind and hence a statement of dissatisfaction with Forster's own overt dependence on symbolism" (68). This is further suggested by Forster's insecurity in writing the novel, as seen in this diary entry of March 23, 1906: "Doubt whether novel's any good: all ingenious symbols: little flesh and blood," (qtd. in Heine xiv).

[34] Heine draws attention to a diary entry of 1904, written after a trip to Greece and shortly before Forster outlined the plot of the novel, that reflects his sense that Greece "was a civilization in which he could imagine his homosexuality being accepted simply as part of the spectrum of human realities" (xxxix).

[35] Recently, critical attention has been paid to some aspects of the novel that reflect Forster's queerness in less overt ways. For example, Paul B. Armstrong's study

of *Howards End* finds the narrator to be reflective of "the epistemology of the closet" in that the ways he "invokes the powers of narrative authority even as he undercuts them" manifest "Forster's doubleness 'as a queer artist' . . . even as he tries to avoid being exposed" (305–306).

[36] The period surrounding the writing and publication of the novel was a particularly troubling time in Forster's personal life. Although it began with a statement in Forster's diary that: "However gross my desires, I find I shall never satisfy them for the fear of annoying others" (Furbank 1: 183), the year 1910 marked a number of sexual watersheds. It was during that year that Forster was unsuccessfully "made love to" by Meredith, got drawn more deeply into the sexually adventurous Bloomsbury Group, and finally revealed his passion to a quietly understanding Masood.

[37] Bakshi notes that Margaret's later reference to Six Hills as a place where "soldiers of the best kind lay buried" (*Howards* 198) is an allusion to A. E. Houseman's poem, *A Shropshire Lad* that has "homoerotic connections" (Bakshi 174–175).

[38] McDowell follows the lead of John Edward Hardy (46–50), in seeing the final chapter "as a fertility ritual over which the absent spirit of Ruth Wilcox presides and as a victory for the transcendent powers [such as 'the energies of nature' and 'spiritual modes of apprehension'] which she had embodied throughout" (McDowell 84).

[39] Operating as a kind of reversal of the coding of brotherhood in *The Longest Journey*, the word "sister," according to Bakshi "provided Forster with a convenient middle term in that it denotes neither women nor homosexuals, but offers a paradigm for love between men" (153).

[40] In a weak attempt to rescue the novel's inclusive vision, Finkelstein answers "antifeminist" critics like Lionel Trilling (who accuses Forster of gelding or humiliating Henry in the service of the "Eternal Feminine" that is taking "complete control of England") by underlining the way in which Margaret draws Helen and Henry together and "settles them down," thus showing that "sisterhood" or "sororibus" is "necessary to make the comradeship of marriage work," and leaving a final vision that is "androgynous," in which "no one, and no one sex, 'controls' anything" (92).

[41] Meyers calls *Maurice*'s plot "too simple" and its "portrayal of the emotions of love at the most significant moments in the novel disastrously false and hysterical" (*Homosexuality* 100). Herz claims that "when Forster allowed himself the luxury of writing the novel hidden beneath the surface of his other fiction," he wound up with "a novel that lacks interior life, that lacks sub-surface in direct proportion as it lacks a containing fiction." She also faults the novel's "chronicle form" as not being "a congenial mode for Forster" and prefers his "usual . . . circular or spherical" structure to *Maurice*'s "paratactic mode" ("Double" 92).

[42] As Forster ruefully told a friend three years later in the wake of his first significant experiences of homosexual love-making: "Wish I was writing the latter half of *Maurice*. I now know so much more" (Furbank 2: 40).

[43] Stephen da Silva sees Forster writing against his society's and his critics' equation of homosexuality and immaturity (i.e., "inversion" as "passing through a phase") here. By representing "the realization of homosexual fulfillment as the recovery of a lost childhood object of desire," Forster "affirms the connection be-

tween homosexuality and youthfulness but attempts to transvalue the implications of youthfulness in order to celebrate male homosexual desire" (250).

[44] Instrumental in Clive's "conversion" to heterosexuality is his ironic journey to the fantastic (and homosexual) land of Greece undertaken as a cure for an illness which seems to occur as his relationship with Maurice intensifies. After a visit to the "theatre of Dionysius" on a pilgrimage to the shrine of the "virgin" Pallas Athene, Clive writes to Maurice: "Against my will I have become normal. I cannot help it" (*Maurice* 116).

[45] On the positive side, for all her disappointment with the novel's lack of complexity, Herz appreciates the ending as a sounding of "the sure notes of the pan pipes, celebrating a love that will not hide in evasions," and finds it "absurd" to "attack" it because "[i]n terms of the novel's premises, assumptions and formal strategies, the ending is absolutely consonant" ("Double" 93). Jon Harned deems the conclusion "satisfying" because the retreat into the greenwood "bespeaks in its very indefiniteness Maurice's hard-won recognition that he has no pre-ordained identity as a homosexual, that he must create one for himself out of the discoveries that he has made about himself and those around him as members of oppressed classes" (65). Matthew Curr reads *Maurice* as "a revelatory and revolutionary intertext" to the other novels, highlighting the fact that unlike their scenes of departure abroad, Alec's decision not to emigrate to Argentina marks a moment of "triumphant *return*" to an England redeemed by homosexual love: "Here Pan is heard to pipe his rural song, and Alec repatriates the England that Forster loved from his heart. Here there will be life and truth" (60–61). On a negative note, however, Schwarz finds the ending "not idyllic but inconclusive," and asks, "how much of a victory is it if these single men are forced by convention to become 'outlaws'?" ("Originality" 635).

[46] Gregory W. Bredbeck sees Forster employing "a Nietzschean motif" in that the choice presented by the text's end is "not between knowable options *within* British culture, but between the culture and something else altogether; it is a choice between meaning and difference, not between different meanings" (54).

[47] Bluntly summing up Forster's depression upon returning to England, Virginia Woolf wrote: "to come back to an ugly house a mile from the station, an old, fussy, exacting mother, to come back having lost your Rajah, without a novel, and with no power to write one—this is dismal, I expect, at the age of 43. The middle age of buggers is not to be contemplated without horror" (qtd. in Furbank 2: 105).

[48] Yonatan Touval explores the predominance of "*Things queer*" in the text, listing numerous examples of the word "queer" and suggesting: "Queerness seems to spring everywhere and therefore nowhere, although it usually (if not always) springs in order to qualify some relation (*the* relation?) between Englishness and Indianness" (242).

[49] A third such figure may be found in the punkah wallah from the rape trial scene, who is described as an "[a]lmost naked . . . god . . . [who] stood out as divine" (*Passage* 241) and serves as "a site for homoerotic desire" through whom "Forster not only questions the dominant discourse that appropriated his own sexuality but also shows its complicity with colonial power" (Malik 224).

[50] A sign of Forster's move into prophetic writing is marked by the shift from the sexual tolerance of *Howards End* and *Maurice* to the religious tolerance displayed here.

[51] John Marx complicates Mau's status as an idyllic fantasy site by historicizing it as "the sort of Princely State whose borders were mapped by the Indian Survey . . . and whose legitimacy was preserved by the colonial policy of Indirect Rule" (70).

[52] Freedgood points out that "the 'mastery of fantasy' in this text requires that the presence of the homoerotic be limited to flickers of meaning that are intelligible only to the knowing reader," i.e., "Forster's queer contemporaries, who had to be expert at reading through the veils that (almost) occluded the homoerotic in published, and therefore public, works" (136).

[53] Recent critics read this final scene in much stronger political terms. Freedgood sees the final breach between Aziz and Fielding as "precipitated by the two men gaining both a solid sense of national identity and an active reinvolvement with heterosexuality" (139). This moment illustrates that "Forster does not wish, as Carpenter did, to overthrow the existing political order" (138), and it discredits Forster's "dream of an intercultural homoerotic community" (or "queer nation") because "the fact of empire, the security and privilege it offered to men like Forster (and Fielding), was precisely what made it possible to enjoy the fantasy of transcending it" (123). Marx posits that the "picturesque landscape" of the scene, which is constructed like a nineteenth-century travel narrative and thus "represent[s] a cultural authenticity authorized by Britain" (70), "pays testimony to the queer bond between them [Aziz and Fielding], [but] it also thematizes the difficulties ahead in their relationship" (69).

CHAPTER THREE NOTES

[1] By applying the influence and concerns of New Woman Writers of the 1880s and 1890s, especially their "use of the central female character(s) as the novel's centre of consciousness," to Sinclair's entire career, Lyn Pykett challenges the traditional tendency "to apply too developmental a model to Sinclair's career and present her pre-war fiction as simply a preparation for the thorough-going modernism of her . . . stream-of-consciousness novels" ("Writing" 113), a tendency in which I am, in part, indulging here. I am supported by Miller's claim that, throughout her career, "Sinclair sought new fictional forms with which to tell the stories of women's lives;" and "in so doing, she moved from a content-driven modernism to the modernism of form" (202).

[2] See "Green" 387–389 and "Idealism" 110–118, as well as Zegger 18–20.

[3] Cohn identifies two other techniques for communicating a character's inner life within third-person narration: "quoted monologue: a character's mental discourse," and "narrated monologue [or 'free indirect discourse']: a character's mental discourse in the guise of the narrator's discourse" (14). Sinclair rarely (and then only briefly) uses these latter two techniques, especially "free indirect discourse," in her realist fiction.

[4] This is true despite the fact that, as Miller notes, "[t]he 'genius' of all the writers in the novel, male and female, affects them in exactly the same way: when they

are writing they are determined and self-absorbed, and crave isolation and freedom from interruption" (190).

[5] Further suggesting Sinclair's dissatisfaction with realism, Miller sees the novel as marking "the beginning of a shift in Sinclair's work, as she turned her attention from external social circumstances to psychology and sexuality in order to portray what she felt was the truth of women's experience" (194).

[6] Janice H. Harris sees a number of scenes between these characters as demonstrating Sinclair's "willingness . . . to explore non-heterosexual erotic desires, particularly in her female characters" (438). Penelope Fitzgerald raises the question of Sinclair's own sexual orientation, concluding that while Sinclair was the apparently fiercely unwilling object of "an uncontrolled physical confession of furious longing, desiring and touching" on the poet Charlotte Mew's part "which terrified May" (134), the evidence points to the idea that "Sinclair is best understood as one who, after an early life of misery, practised a kind of celibacy respecting all intimate relationships" (Harris 439, footnote 3).

[7] As we shall later see, Lawrence sees the "sentimentalism" of popular realist fiction as an emasculating force, and thus of most harm to men.

[8] This shift is indicated in an introduction to *The Judgment of Eve and Other Stories* (London: Hutchinson, 1914), in which Sinclair claims that two of the works in the collection are not really short stories but "examples of a form of the novel that results from the novelist's boiling down his materials to their simplest possible expression," and she announces that she is "considering the employment of a sheared narrative style and form" (Boll 105 & 268–269).

[9] Given the way in which Sinclair represents reality as feminine and the act of writing as phallic or masculine here, it is interesting to note that, in an apparent throwback to her attitudes in *The Creators*, when Sinclair writes a novel (*Far End*) about a successful "experimental" novelist, the protagonist is male

[10] See Gillespie, "May Sinclair," for a detailed study of Sinclair's use of the "stream" metaphor, which Gillespie believes is meant to connote reality's "multiplicity and change," the keynote of the new realists, and its "unity and continuity," the emphasis of the new idealists (134).

[11] Two years later, in an interview on the future of the novel, Sinclair steers away from the stream metaphor and speaks approvingly of the "synthetic psychological novel," in which the modern novelist does not "dissect" or "probe" or "write about the emotions and thoughts of his characters. The words he uses must be the thoughts—be the emotions" ("Future" 477–478).

[12] Boll reports that "Sinclair once told a friend, Florence Bartrop, that *Mary Olivier* was substantially her life story, excepting only the love episodes; the brothers were true" (244).

[13] Pykett points to a gendered way of describing the difference: "As befits a male modernist protagonist, Joyce's hero comes to consciousness in and of language. The emergence of Sinclair's heroine into consciousness, on the other hand, is relational; it is an awareness of people and feelings as well as objects and words" ("Writing" 114).

[14] Terry Phillips notes that *Mary Olivier* and *Harriet Frean* "narrate the experience of being mothered as crippling and destructive" and that their "representation

of these daughters' unhappy experiences . . . can be traced to the gap between idealisations of motherhood and the lived experiences of women" (129).

[15] There are two noteworthy parallels to *Orlando* here: first, the chosen medium for the protagonist's creative energies is poetry, suggesting that poetic language and/or form is the most prized genre in which to write; and secondly, the success which publication brings in a male-dominated field is ultimately unfulfilling.

[16] Phillips links Mary's failure in such relationships to the "double bind" of repression she and her mother suffer under in not being able to acknowledge and therefore talk about their sexuality: "while Mary's sexuality is repressed, that which society has constructed as its opposite and which must prevent its ultimate manifestation, the pursuit of learning, is also to be repressed" (132).

[17] Boll represents the novel as a "converse" to *Mary Olivier* because Arnold "reaches the bottom, not the top of the pyramid whose summit is success in either art or intellectual achievement," as he "sacrifices his ambition to lead the intellectually realized life in order to realize a vision of the reality of God" (282).

Chapter Four Notes

[1] As Anne Fernihough puts it, "critics today seem to thrive on the sense of disjunction and disorientation produced by Lawrence's writing. . . . What *was* distinctive about Lawrence was perhaps less the particular views he expressed in his letters and essays than the unashamed, even naïve, openness with which he articulated them, not to mention his inconsistency" (2 & 6). She also suggests that "Lawrence's love of role-play from an early age . . . can be linked to the *provisionality* of his writing . . . and to the 'risk-taking polarizations and extremes' [Eggert 174] which typify much of his work" (9).

[2] Drew Milne rightly cautions that Lawrence's "fiction is both personal and a negotiation of the representative qualities of the novel. This suggests why it is not sufficient to read Lawrence's fictions as symptoms of his personal psychology, as if his writing could be psychoanalysed" (199–200).

[3] Nixon's schema is outlined in her "Introduction: Enemy of Mankind," 1–18.

[4] Drawing from the linguistic theory of Roman Jakobson, Gerald Doherty offers a compelling treatment of the ways Lawrence uses metaphor and metonymy in his sexual theory to locate the female "within a specific male plot of appropriation": "While in theory Lawrence sometimes celebrates the perfect polarization (or balance) of sexual roles, his narratives in fact project the male as the source of the erotic power that transfigures the female" ("Art" 290).

[5] According to Justin D. Edwards, Lawrence's "simultaneous admiration and repudiation of Winifred point to Lawrence's ambiguous understanding of female homosexuality" (67). He thus participated in both the rise of "a more sexualized depiction of the bonds between women" and "the development of homophobic discourses that disrupted romantic friendship between women" (60).

[6] Fiona Becket sees a kind of "nostalgia" operating in the ways "Lawrence theorizes conception, fetal development, and birth" which is connected to "his preoccupation with the origins of the unconscious" ("Being" 255).

Notes

[7] In a letter written at about the same time, Lawrence suggested that E. M. Forster fit into this category of "sensitive" men turning away from purely physical relations with women (*Letters* 2: 282–286).

[8] Lawrence's impassioned concern with homosexuality did not end here, however. In 1916, he wrote an essay on his "philosophy" entitled "Goats and Compasses" (not currently in print), which was described by Cecil Gray as "Lawrence at his very worst: a bombastic, pseudo-mystical, psycho-philosophical treatise dealing largely with homosexuality" (114n).

[9] Hugh Stevens connects these homophobic ideas with "Lawrence's experience of abuse at the hands of state authority" (52) during a medical examination by military doctors in 1916 when they "'pawed', scrutinised and mocked his naked body, a body not fit for military service" (49).

[10] While acknowledging that Lawrence "had himself been engaged with the question of his bisexuality" (*DHL* 377), Kinkead-Weekes doubts that Lawrence had "a homosexual attraction to Murry" since he was "neither of his [Lawrence's] 'types'" (330).

[11] Joyce Wexler provides a counterpoint to indictments of Lawrence such as that of Nixon by arguing that contemporary critics are guilty of "[r]eading modernist symbolism as if it were realism" and thus "they object not only to particular symbols but to the use of extreme acts and foreign cultures as raw material for Western fantasies" (60).

[12] Becket underlines "the determined and unequivocal misogyny of the bulk of *Fantasia*" ("Lawrence" 227) and calls attention to the personal contexts underpinning these ideas: Lawrence's experience of "a level of conflict in his married relationship" and feeling himself "emasculated, feminised, by his illnesses" (228–229).

[13] Levine sees Lawrence as participating in "that great struggle of the realists both to use and to reject literature and language, for the sake of a reality beyond language" and sharing "the ideals and achievements of the Victorians . . . [i]n the intensity of his moral engagement" (327). In contrast, I agree with Tony Pinkney and others who represent Lawrence as a modernist in writing this novel, particularly in his use of the "mythical method" (see Pinkney 123–147), and in his "search for authentic language against corrupted traditional public rhetoric" (Widmer 72). Pinkney also makes a strong claim for Lawrence as a "meta-modernist" who wrote "texts which interrogated to their roots some of the major modernist modes that his contemporaries busily and less self-reflexively exploited" (168).

[14] Clifford's impotence mirrors Lawrence's own inability to sire a child and the fact that when he began writing the novel, despite prior "healthy physical relations with Frieda . . . his sexual capacity suffered as a result of tuberculosis" (Meyers, *DHL* 331). When asked if this impotence was intentionally symbolic, Lawrence said it reflected "the paralysis, the deeper emotional or passional paralysis, of most men of his [Clifford's] sort and class today" (*Phoenix II* 514).

[15] In many ways, this description of Clifford's work could have come right out of one of Virginia Woolf's essays on the "materialist" novelists of the Edwardian period, the only difference being that Lawrence sees this empty kind of writing as produced by a feminized rather than patriarchal author, which once again illustrates the contradictory nature of gendered literary discourse at this time.

[16] This is particularly ironic in light of Hilary Simpson's claim that *Lady Chatterley's Lover* possesses similarities to some of the very literature he is decrying here, i.e., "the sensationalist romances of the twenties such as *The Sheik*" (17).

[17] Two critics represent the structure of the novel as exemplifying this theoretical goal. Joan D. Peters sees the novel divided between the "dead" novel of Clifford's world and the alternative "living" novel of Mellors, separated by Lawrence's treatise on "the novel, properly handled" (5–7). Charles Burack posits a shift in narration from a "modern" critical narrator to a "body-centered" narrator whereby Lawrence achieves a partial subversion of "logocentrism and ocularcentrism" of Western consciousness ("Mortifying" 491, 494 & 507).

[18] Noting that Connie and Mellors make love at least four times in Chapter 14, David Holbrook claims that such a feat is "just possible . . . for a young man, but doubtful with a man of thirty-seven who has been damaged by pneumonia" (346), suggesting that, in his impotence, Lawrence is indulging in some wishful thinking. See also Widmer 79–81 for a discussion of Lawrence's probable impotence at this time and its relation to his sexual theory.

[19] Burack presents a comprehensive treatment of the sex scenes in the novel that shows how the text's "initial attempt to revitalize readers eventually gives way to a deconstructive impulse that prevents readers from forming new erotic dogmas and encourages first-hand exploration" ("Revitalizing" 102). Doherty shows how the "sequence of orgasmic encounters between Connie Chatterley and Oliver Mellors" is contrasted with the "'backward' declension" or "Freudian path of perversion") in Clifford Chatterley and Mrs. Bolton's affair, a "regression from genital to anal and oral sexual pleasures" ("Chatterley" 372 & 374)

[20] Coming from a poststructuralist perspective, Lydia Blanchard sees Lawrence "creating a language for the feelings through the passages of lovemaking" and "also using these passages to parody not only traditional forms but also his own earlier works" ("Foucault" 26).

[21] The intensity of this scene, like that of the "Gladiatorial" chapter in *Women in Love*, raises questions for numerous critics about what they see as Lawrence's repressed homosexuality. For example, see Widmer 77, Spilka 166–167, and Nixon 10–18.

[22] David Ellis points to the scene "where Mellors and Connie decorate their naked bodies with flowers" that "begins with the gamekeeper threading flowers through Connie's pubic hair" ("Female" 148) as illustrating one of Lawrence's principal aims in the novel: "to exorcise fear of the female body" (147).

Bibliography

Abel, Elizabeth. *Virginia Woolf and the Fictions of Psychoanalysis.* Chicago: U of Chicago P, 1989.

Allen, Walter. Introduction. *Pilgrimage.* By Dorothy Richardson. New York: Popular Library, 1976.

Armstrong, Nancy. *Desire and Domestic Fiction: A Political History of the Novel.* New York: Oxford UP, 1987.

Armstrong, Paul B. "The Narrator in the Closet: The Ambiguous Narrative Voice in *Howards End.*" *Modern Fiction Studies* 47 (2001): 306–328.

Bakshi, Parminder Kaur. *Distant Desire: Homoerotic Codes and the Subversion of the English Novel in E. M. Forster's Fiction.* New York: Peter Lang, 1996.

Balbert, Peter. *D. H. Lawrence and the Phallic Imagination: Essays on Sexual Identity and Feminist Misreading.* New York: St. Martin's, 1989.

Battersby, Christine. *Gender and Genius: Towards a Feminist Aesthetics.* Bloomington: Indiana UP, 1989.

Bayley, John. "Lawrence and the Modern English Novel." *The Legacy of D. H. Lawrence.* Ed. Jeffrey Meyers. New York: St. Martin's, 1987. 14–29.

Bazin, Nancy Topping. *Virginia Woolf and the Androgynous Vision.* New Brunswick: Rutgers UP, 1973.

Becket, Fiona. "Being There: Nostalgia and the Masculine Maternal in D. H. Lawrence." *The D. H. Lawrence Review* 27 (1997–1998): 255–268.

———. "Lawrence and Psychoanalysis." Fernihough. 217–233.

Beer, Gillian. "The Body of the People in Virginia Woolf." *Women's Reading Women's Writing.* Ed. Sue Roe. New York: St. Martin's, 1987. 83–114.

Beer, John. "'The Last Englishman': Lawrence's Appreciation of Forster." Das and Beer. 245–268.

Bell, Michael. *D. H. Lawrence: Language and Being.* Cambridge: Cambridge UP, 1992.

Black, Michael. *D. H. Lawrence: The Early Philosophical Works.* Cambridge: Cambridge UP, 1992.

Blanchard, Lydia. "Lawrence as Reader of Classic American Literature." *The Challenge of D. H. Lawrence.* Ed. Michael Squires and Keith Cushman. Madison: U Wisconsin P, 1990. 159–175.

———. "Lawrence, Foucault, and the Language of Sexuality." *D. H. Lawrence's "Lady": A New Look at "Lady Chatterley's Lover."* Ed. Michael Squires and Dennis Jackson. Athens: U Georgia P, 1985.

Boehm, Beth A. "Fact, Fiction, and Metafiction: Blurred Gen(d)res in *Orlando* and *A Room of One's Own*." *The Journal Of Narrative Technique* 22 (1992): 191–204.

Boll, Theophilus E. M. *Miss May Sinclair: Novelist.* Rutherford: Fairleigh Dickinson UP, 1973.

Bowlby, Rachel. *Virginia Woolf: Feminist Destinations.* Oxford: Blackwell, 1988.

Bredbeck, Gregory W. "'Queer Superstitions': Forster, Carpenter, and the Illusion of (Sexual) Identity." Martin and Piggford. 29–58.

Bristow, Joseph. *Effeminate England: Homoerotic Writing after 1885.* New York: Columbia UP, 1995.

Brown, Gillian. *Domestic Individualism: Imagining Self in Nineteenth-Century America.* Berkeley: U California P, 1990.

Burack, Charles M. "Mortifying the Reader: The Assault on Verbal and Visual Consciousness in D. H. Lawrence's *Lady Chatterley's Lover*." *Studies in the Novel* 29 (1997): 491–511.

———. "Revitalizing the Reader: Literary Technique and the Language of Sacred Experience in D. H. Lawrence's *Lady Chatterley's Lover*." *Style* 32 (1998): 102–126.

Butler, Judith. *Gender Trouble: Feminism and the Subversion of Identity.* New York: Routledge, 1990.

Cavaliero, Glen. *A Reading of E. M. Forster.* London: Macmillan, 1979.

Chevalley, Abel. *The Modern English Novel.* Trans. Ben Ray Redman. New York: Knopf, 1930.

Cohn, Dorrit. *Transparent Minds: Narrative Modes for Presenting Consciousness in Fiction.* Princeton: Princeton UP, 1978.

Colmer, John. *E. M. Forster: The Personal Voice.* London: Routledge, 1975.

———. "Marriage and Personal Relations." Herz and Martin. 113–123.

Crews, Frederick C. *E. M. Forster: The Perils of Humanism.* Princeton: Princeton UP, 1962.

Bibliography

Curr, Matthew. "Recuperating E. M. Forster's *Maurice.*" *Modern Language Quarterly* 62 (2001): 53–69.

Dahl, Liisa. "The Attributive Sentence Structure in the Stream-of-Consciousness-Technique. With Special Reference to the Interior Monologue Used by Virginia Woolf, James Joyce, and Eugene O'Neill." *Neuphilologische Mitteilungen* 68 (1967).

Daleski, H. M. *The Forked Flame: A Study of D. H. Lawrence.* Evanston: Northwestern UP, 1965.

Das, G. K., and John Beer. *E. M. Forster: A Human Exploration.* New York: NYU P, 1979.

Da Silva, Stephen. "Transvaluing Immaturity: Reverse Discourses of Male Homosexuality in E. M. Forster's Posthumously Published Fiction." *Criticism* 50 (1998): 237–272.

DeKoven, Marianne. *Rich and Strange: Gender, History, Modernism.* Princeton: Princeton UP, 1991.

DiBattista, Maria. *Virginia Woolf's Major Novels: The Fables of Anon.* New Haven: Yale UP, 1980.

Doherty, Gerald. "The Art of Appropriation: The Rhetoric of Sexuality in D. H. Lawrence." *Style* 30 (1996): 289–308.

———. "The Chatterley/Bolton Affair: The Freudian Path of Regression in *Lady Chatterley's Lover.*" *Papers on Language and Literature* 34 (1998): 372–387.

Dowling, David. *Bloomsbury Aesthetics and the Novels of Forster and Woolf.* New York: St. Martin's, 1985.

Draper, Ronald. *D. H. Lawrence.* New York: Twayne, 1964.

DuPlessis, Rachel Blau. *Writing Beyond the Ending: Narrative Strategies of Twentieth-Century Writers.* Bloomington: Indiana UP, 1985.

Edwards, Justin D. "At the End of *The Rainbow*: Reading Lesbian Identities in D. H. Lawrence's Fiction." *The International Fiction Review* 27 (2000): 60–67.

Eggert, Paul. "The Biographical Issue: Lives of Lawrence." Fernihough. 157–177.

Ellem, Elizabeth Wood. "E. M. Forster's Greenwood." *Journal of Modern Literature* 5 (1976): 89–98.

Ellis, David. "Lawrence and the Female Body." *Essays in Criticism* 46 (1996): 136–152.

———. "Lawrence and Forster in 1915." *The Cambridge Quarterly* 27 (1998): 1–14.

Farwell, Marilyn R. "Virginia Woolf and Androgyny." *Contemporary Literature* 16 (1975): 433–451.

Fernihough, Anne, ed. *The Cambridge Companion to D. H. Lawrence*. Cambridge: Cambridge UP, 2001.

Finklestein, Bonnie Blumenthal. *Forster's Women: Eternal Differences*. New York: Columbia UP, 1975.

Fitzgerald, Penelope. *Charlotte Mew and Her Friends*. Reading: Addison-Wesley, 1988.

Fletcher, John. "Forster's Self Erasure: *Maurice* and the Scene of Masculine Love." *Sexual Sameness: Textual Differences in Lesbian and Gay Writing*. Ed. Joseph Bristow. London: Routledge, 1992. 64–90.

Forster, E. M. *Abinger Harvest*. San Diego: Harcourt, 1964.

———. "Anonymity: An Inquiry." *Atlantic Monthly* 136 (1925): 588–595.

———. "Aspect of a Novel." *The Bookseller*. 10 Sept. 1960: 1228–1230.

———. *Aspects of the Novel*. New York: Harcourt, 1927.

———. *The Celestial Omnibus and Other Stories*. New York: Vintage, 1976.

———. *Howards End*. New York: Vintage, 1921.

———. "Letters." *The Nation and Atheneum*. 12 April 1930: 888 and 26 April 1930: 109.

———. *The Longest Journey*. New York: Vintage, 1962.

———. *Maurice*. New York: Norton, 1981.

———. "A Moving Document." *Daily Herald*. 30 July 1919: 8.

———. *A Passage to India*. New York: Harcourt, 1924.

———. *A Room with a View*. New York: Vintage, 1986.

———. *Selected Letters*. Ed. Mary Lago and P. N. Furbank. 2 Vols. Cambridge: Belknap, 1983–1985.

———. *Two Cheers for Democracy*. San Diego: Harcourt, 1979.

———. *Where Angels Fear to Tread*. New York: Vintage, 1920.

Freedgood, Elaine. "E. M. Forster's Queer Nation: Taking the Closet to the Colony in *A Passage to India*." *Bodies of Writing, Bodies in Performance*. Ed. Thomas Foster, Carol Siegel, and Ellen E. Berry. New York: NYUP, 1996. 123–143.

Friedman, Ellen G., and Miriam Fuchs. "Contexts and Continuities: An Introduction to Women's Experimental Fiction in English." *Breaking the Sequence: Women's Experimental Fiction*. Ed. Friedman and Fuchs. Princeton: Princeton UP, 1989. 3–51.

Frye, Northrop. *The Secular Scripture: A Study of the Structure of Romance*. Cambridge: Harvard UP, 1976.

Furbank, P. N. *E. M. Forster: A Life*. 2 Vols. London: Cardinal, 1988.

Garnett, David. "Forster and Bloomsbury." *Aspects of E. M. Forster.* Ed. Oliver Stallybrass. London: Arnold, 1969. 29–35.

Gilbert, Sandra M., and Susan Gubar. *No Man's Land: The Place of the Woman Writer, Volume I: The War of the Words.* New Haven: Yale UP, 1988.

Gillespie, Diane F. "May Sinclair and the Stream of Consciousness: Metaphors and Metaphysics." *English Literature in Transition* 21 (1978): 134–143.

———. "'The Muddle of the Middle': May Sinclair on Women." *Tulsa Studies in Women's Literature* 4 (1985): 235–251.

———. "Virginia Woolf's Miss LaTrobe: The Artist's Last Struggle against Masculine Values." *Women and Literature* 5 (1977): 38–46.

Goscilo, Margaret. "Forster's Italian Comedies: Que[e]rying Heterosexuality Abroad." *Seeing Double: Revisioning Edwardian and Modernist Literature.* Ed. Carola M. Kaplan and Anne B. Simpson. New York: St. Martin's, 1996. 193–214.

Grant, Kathleen. "*Maurice* as Fantasy." Herz and Martin. 191–203.

Gray, Cecil. *Peter Warlock: A Memoir of Philip Heseltine.* London: Cape, 1934.

"Green, Thomas Hill." *The Encyclopedia of Philosophy.* 1967 ed.

Hardy, John Edward. *Man in the Modern Novel.* Seattle: U Washington P, 1964.

Harned, Jon. "Becoming Gay in E. M. Forster's *Maurice.*" *Papers on Language and Literature* 29 (1993): 49–66.

Harris, Janice H. "Challenging the Script of the Heterosexual Couple: Three Marriage Novels by May Sinclair." *Papers on Language and Literature* 29 (1993): 436–458.

Heine, Elizabeth. "Editor's Introduction." *The Longest Journey.* By E. M. Forster. London: Penguin, 1984. vii–lxv.

Henley, Ann. "'But We Argued About Novel Writing': Virginia Woolf, E. M. Forster and the Art of Fiction." *Ariel* 20 (1989): 73–83.

Herz, Judith. "The Double Nature of Forster's Fiction: *A Room with a View* and *The Longest Journey.*" *Critical Essays on Forster's Fiction.* Ed. Alan Wilde. Boston: Hall, 1985. 84–94.

———. "The Narrator as Hermes: a Study of the Early Short Fiction." Das and Beer. 17–27.

Herz, Judith and Robert K. Martin, eds. *E. M. Forster: Centenary Revaluations.* Toronto: U of Toronto P, 1982.

Holbrook, David. *Where D. H. Lawrence Was Wrong about Woman.* Lewisburg: Bucknell UP, 1992.

Hynes, Samuel. *Edwardian Occasions: Essays on English Writing in the Early Twentieth Century.* New York: Oxford UP, 1972.

"Idealism." *The Encyclopedia of Philosophy.* 1967 ed.

Ingersoll, Earl G. "Virginia Woolf and D. H. Lawrence: Exploring the Dark." *English Studies* 2 (1990): 125–132.

Jackson, Rosemary. *Fantasy: The Literature of Subversion.* London: Methuen, 1981.

Jagose, Annamarie. *Queer Theory: An Introduction.* New York: NYUP, 1996.

Jeffers, Thomas L. "Forster's *The Longest Journey* and the Idea of Apprenticeship." *Texas Studies in Literature and Language* 30 (1988): 179–197.

Jewinski, Ed. "The Phallus in D. H. Lawrence and Jacques Lacan." *The D. H. Lawrence Review* 21 (1989): 7–24.

Kaplan, Carola. "Absent Father, Passive Son: The Dilemma of Rickie Elliott in *The Longest Journey.*" *Twentieth Century Literature* 33 (1987): 196–210.

Kaplan, Sydney Janet. *Feminine Consciousness in the Modern British Novel.* Urbana: U of Illinois P, 1975.

Kerenyi, Karl. "The Trickster in Relation to Greek Mythology." *The Trickster: A Study in American Indian Mythology.* By Paul Rudin. Westport: Greenwood, 1969. 171–191.

Kermode, Frank. *D. H. Lawrence.* New York: Viking, 1973.

Kinkead-Weekes, Mark. *D. H. Lawrence: Triumph to Exile 1912–1922.* Cambridge: Cambridge UP, 1996.

———. "Eros and Metaphor: Sexual Relationship in the Fiction of Lawrence." *Lawrence and Women.* Ed. Anne Smith. New York: Barnes and Noble, 1978. 101–121.

———. "The Marble and the Statue: The Exploratory Imagination of D. H. Lawrence." *Imagined Worlds: Essays on Some English Novels and Novelists in Honour of John Butt.* Ed. Maynard Mack and Ian Gregor. London: Methuen, 1968. 371–418.

Krutch, J. W. "An Impoverished Art." *Nation* 125 (2 Nov. 1927).

Lacy, G. M. *An Analytic Calendar of the Letters of D. H. Lawrence.* Ann Arbor: U Microfilms, 1971.

Lawrence, D. H. *Aaron's Rod.* Cambridge: Cambridge UP, 1988.

———. *Fantasia of the Unconscious.* New York: Penguin, 1977.

———. "Foreword to *Sons and Lovers.*" *The Letters of D. H. Lawrence.* Ed. Aldous Huxley. London: Heinemann, 1932.

———. *Kangaroo.* Cambridge: Cambridge UP, 1994.

———. *Lady Chatterley's Lover.* Cambridge: Cambridge UP, 1993.

———. *Letters.* Ed. James T. Boulton et al. 7 Vols. Cambridge: Cambridge UP, 1979–1993.

Bibliography

———. *Phoenix: The Posthumous Papers of D. H. Lawrence*. Ed. Edward D. McDonald. New York: Viking, 1936.

———. *Phoenix II: Uncollected, Unpublished, and Other Prose Works by D. H. Lawrence*. Ed. Warren Roberts and Harry T. Moore. New York: Viking, 1968.

———. *The Plumed Serpent*. Cambridge: Cambridge UP, 1987.

———. *The Rainbow*. Cambridge: Cambridge UP, 1989.

———. *Reflections on the Death of a Porcupine*. Ed. Michael Herbert. Cambridge: Cambridge UP, 1988.

———. *St. Mawr & The Man Who Died*. New York: Vintage, 1953.

———. *Sons and Lovers*. Cambridge: Cambridge UP, 1992.

———. *Studies in Classic American Literature*. New York: Penguin, 1977.

———. *Study of Thomas Hardy and Other Essays*. Ed. Bruce Steele. Cambridge: Cambridge UP, 1985.

———. *The Symbolic Meaning: The Uncollected Versions of "Studies in Classic American Literature."* Ed. Armin Arnold. London: Centaur, 1962.

———. *Women in Love*. Cambridge: Cambridge UP, 1987.

Lawrence, Frieda. *The Memoirs and Correspondence*. Ed. E. W. Tedlock, Jr. New York: Knopf, 1964.

Leavis, F. R. *D. H. Lawrence: Novelist*. New York: Knopf, 1968.

———. *The Great Tradition*. London: Chatto, 1948.

Levine, George. *The Realistic Imagination: English Fiction from Frankenstein to Lady Chatterley*. Chicago: U of Chicago P, 1981.

Malik, Charu. "To Express the Subject of Friendship: Masculine Desire and Colonialism in *A Passage to India*." Martin and Piggford. 221–235.

Martin, Robert K. "Edward Carpenter and the Double Structure of *Maurice*." *Journal of Homosexuality* 8 (1983): 35–46.

———. "'It Must Have Been the Umbrella': Forster's Queer Begetting." Martin and Piggford. 255–273.

———. "The Paterian Mode in E. M. Forster's Fiction: *The Longest Journey* to *Pharos and Pharillon*." Herz and Martin. 99–112.

Martin, Robert and George Piggford, eds. *Queer Forster*. Chicago: U of Chicago P, 1997.

Marx, John. "Modernism and the Female Imperial Gaze." *Novel* 32 (1998): 51–75.

McConkey, James. *The Novels of E. M. Forster*. Ithaca: Cornell UP, 1957.

McDowell, Frederick P. W. *E. M. Forster*. New York: Twayne, 1969.

Merivale, Patricia. *Pan the Goat-God: His Myth in Modern Times*. Cambridge: Harvard UP, 1969.

Meyers, Jeffrey. *D. H. Lawrence: A Biography*. New York: Vintage, 1992.

———. *Homosexuality and Literature: 1890–1930*. Montreal: McGill-Queen's UP, 1977.

Miller, Jane Eldridge. *Rebel Women: Feminism, Modernism, and the Edwardian Novel*. London: Virago, 1994.

Millett, Kate. *Sexual Politics*. Garden City: Doubleday, 1970.

Milne, Drew. "Lawrence and the politics of sexual politics." Fernihough. 197–215.

Minow-Pinkney, Makiko. *Virginia Woolf and the Problem of the Subject*. New Brunswick: Rutgers UP, 1987.

Moore, Madeline. *The Short Season Between Two Silences: The Mystical and the Political in the Novels of Virginia Woolf*. Boston: Allen, 1984.

Nadel, Ira Bruce. "Moments in the Greenwood: *Maurice* in Context." Herz and Martin. 177–190.

Nehls, Edward, ed. *D. H. Lawrence: A Composite Biography*. Vol. 2. Madison: U of Wisconsin P, 1958.

Nelson, Scott R. "Narrative Inversion: The Textual Construction of Homosexuality in E. M. Forster's Novels." *Style* 26 (1992): 310–326.

Nin, Anaïs. *D. H. Lawrence: An Unprofessional Study*. Athens: Swallow, 1964.

Nixon, Cornelia. *Lawrence's Leadership Politics and the Turn Against Women*. Berkeley: U California P, 1986.

Peters, Joan. "The Living and the Dead: Lawrence's Theory of the Novel and the Structure of Lady Chatterley's Lover." The D. H. Lawrence Review 20 (1988): 5–20.

Philipson, Morris. "Virginia Woolf's *Orlando*: Biography as Work of Fiction." *From Parnassus: Essays in Honor of Jacques Barzun*. Ed. Doris B. Weiner and William R. Keylor. New York: Harper, 1976. 237–248.

Phillips, Terry. "Battling with the Angel: May Sinclair's powerful mothers." *Image and Power: Women in Fiction in the Twentieth Century*. Ed. Sarah Sceats and Gail Cunningham. London: Longman, 1996. 128–138.

Pinkney, Tony. *D. H. Lawrence and Modernism*. Iowa City: U of Iowa P, 1990.

Poresky, Louise. *The Elusive Self: Psyche and Spirit in Virginia Woolf's Novels*. Newark: U of Delaware P, 1981.

Pykett, Lyn. *Engendering Fictions: The English Novel in the Early Twentieth Century*. London: Arnold, 1995.

———. "Writing Around Modernism: May Sinclair and Rebecca West." *Outside Modernism: In Pursuit of the English Novel, 1900–30.* Ed. Lynne Hapgood & Nancy L. Paxton. New York: St. Martin's, 2000. 103–122.

Rahman, Tariq. "The Under-plot in E. M. Forster's *The Longest Journey.*" *Durham U Journal* 83 (1991): 59–67.

Roe, Sue. *Writing and Gender: Virginia Woolf's Writing Practice.* New York: St. Martin's, 1990.

Rosecrance, Barbara. *Forster's Narrative Vision.* Ithaca: Cornell UP, 1982.

Sanders, Scott. *D. H. Lawrence: The World of the Five Major Novels.* New York: Viking, 1973.

Scheckner, Peter. *Class, Politics, and the Individual.* Rutherford: Fairleigh Dickinson UP, 1985.

Schwarz, Daniel R. "The Importance of E. M. Forster's *Aspects of the Novel.*" *The South Atlantic Quarterly* 82 (1983): 189–205.

———. "The Originality of E. M. Forster." *Modern Fiction Studies* 29 (1983): 623–641.

Scott, Bonnie Kime, ed. *The Gender of Modernism: A Critical Anthology.* Bloomington: Indiana UP, 1990.

Sedgwick, Eve Kosovsky. *Between Men: English Literature and Male Homosocial Desire.* New York: Columbia UP, 1985.

Selig, Robert L. "'God si Love': On an Unpublished Letter and the Ironic Use of Myth in *A Passage to India.*" *Journal of Modern Literature* 7 (1979): 471–487.

Shaw, Marion. "Lawrence and Feminism." *Critical Quarterly* 25 (1983): 23–27.

Showalter, Elaine. *A Literature of Their Own: British Women Novelists from Brontë to Lessing.* Princeton: Princeton UP, 1977.

Siegel, Carol. *Lawrence Among the Women: Wavering Boundaries in Women's Literary Traditions.* Charlottesville: UP of Virginia, 1991.

Simpson, Hilary. *D. H. Lawrence and Feminism.* DeKalb: Northern Illinois UP, 1982.

Sinclair, May. *Arnold Waterlow: A Life.* New York: Macmillan, 1924.

———. *Audrey Craven.* London: Blackwood, 1897.

———. *The Creators.* London: Constable, 1910.

———. *A Defence of Idealism.* New York: Macmillan, 1917.

———. "A Defence of Men." *English Review* 11 (1912): 556–566.

———. *The Divine Fire.* New York: AMS, 1970.

———. *Far End.* New York: Macmillan, 1926.

———. *Feminism*. London: Women Writers Suffrage League, 1912.

———. "The Future of the Novel: An Interview." Scott. 476–478.

———. "George Meredith." *The Outlook* 92 (1909): 413–418.

———. *History of Anthony Waring*. New York: Macmillan, 1927.

———. "Introduction." *A Journal of Impressions in Belgium*. By Sinclair. New York: Macmillan, 1915.

———. "Introduction." *The Judgment of Eve and Other Stories*. By Sinclair. London: Hutchinson, 1914.

———. "Introduction." *The Life of Charlotte Bronte*. By Elizabeth Cleghorn Gaskell. London: Dent, 1908.

———. "Letter." *Votes for Women*. 24 Dec. 1908.

———. *Life and Death of Harriet Frean*. New York: Penguin, 1980.

———. *Mary Olivier: A Life*. New York: Dial, 1980.

———. "The Mormon Prophet." *The Bookman*. Apr. 1899: 373–374.

———. "No. 5 John Street." *The Bookman*. Apr. 1899: 377.

———. "The Novels of Dorothy Richardson." Scott. 442–448.

———. "The Poems of F. S. Flint." *The English Review* 32 (1921): 6–18.

———. "Symbolism and Sublimation II." *Medical Press and Circular* 153 (16 Aug. 1916): 142–145.

———. *The Three Brontës*. Port Washington: Kennikat, 1912.

———. *The Three Sisters*. New York: Doubleday, 1985.

———. "Two Notes." *The Egoist* 2 (1915): 88–89.

Spilka, Mark. *Renewing the Normative D. H. Lawrence: A Personal Progress*. Columbia: U of Missouri P, 1992.

Stallybrass, Oliver, ed. *The Lucy Novels: Early Sketches for "A Room with a View."* London: Edward Arnold, 1977.

Stark, Susanne. "Overcoming Butlerian Obstacles: May Sinclair and the Problem of Biological Determinism." *Women's Studies* 21 (1992): 265–283.

Steell, Willis. "May Sinclair Tells Why She Isn't a Poet." *The Literary Digest International Review* 2 (1924): 513 & 559.

Steiner, George. "Under the Greenwood Tree." *E. M. Forster: The Critical Heritage*. Ed. Philip Gardner. London: Routledge, 1973. 475–482.

Stevens, Hugh. "Sex and the nation: 'The Prussian Officer' and *Women in Love*." Fernihough. 49–65.

Stimpson, Catharine R. "Woolf's Room, Our Project: The Building of Feminist Criticism." *The Future of Literary Theory*. Ed. Ralph Cohen. New York: Routledge, 1989. 129–143.

Stone, Wilfred. *The Cave and the Mountain: A Study of E. M. Forster*. Palo Alto: Stanford UP, 1966.

Summers, Claude J. *E. M. Forster*. New York: Ungar, 1983.

Tanner, Tony. *Adultery in the Novel*. Baltimore: Johns Hopkins UP, 1979.

Taylor, Corrine Yvonne. *A Study of May Sinclair—Woman and Writer, 1863–1946*. Ann Arbor: U Microfilms, 1976.

Thomson, George H. *The Fiction of E. M. Forster*. Detroit: Wayne State UP, 1967.

Touval, Yonatan. "Colonial Queer Something." Martin and Piggford. 237–254.

Transue, Pamela J. *Virginia Woolf and the Politics of Style*. Albany: SUNY P, 1986.

Warner, Michael. "Introduction." *Fear of a Queer Planet: Queer Politics and Social Theory*. Ed. Michael Warner. Minneapolis: U Minnesota P, 1993.

Watt, Donald. "Mohammed el Adl and *A Passage to India*." *Journal of Modern Literature* 10 (1983): 311–326.

Watt, Ian. *The Rise of the Novel: Studies in Defoe, Richardson, and Fielding*. Berkeley: U of California P, 1957.

Weeks, Jeffrey. *Sex, Politics and Society: The regulation of sexuality since 1800*. London: Longman, 1981.

Wexler, Joyce. "Realism and Modernists' Bad Reputation." *Studies in the Novel* 31 (1999): 60–73.

Widmer, Kingsley. *Defiant Desire: Some Dialectical Legacies of D. H. Lawrence*. Carbondale: Southern Illinois UP, 1992.

Wilde, Alan. "Depths and Surfaces: Dimensions of Fosterian Irony." *English Literature in Transition* 16 (1973): 257–274.

———. "Desire and Consciousness: The 'Anironic' Forster." *Novel* 9 (1976): 114–129.

———. "The Naturalisation of Eden." Das and Beer. 196–207.

Williams, Linda Ruth. *D. H. Lawrence*. Plymouth: Northcote House, 1997.

Woolf, Virginia. *Collected Essays*. Ed. Leonard Woolf. Vol. 2. New York: Harcourt, 1967.

———. *Letters*. Ed. Nigel Nicholson. 6 Vols. New York: Harcourt, 1976.

———. *Orlando*. San Diego: Harcourt, 1928.

———. *A Room of One's Own*. San Diego: Harcourt, 1929.

Wright, Almroth. "Suffrage Fallacies." *Times* 28 March 1912: 7–8.

Zegger, Hrisey D. *May Sinclair*. Boston: Twayne, 1976.

Index

Abel, Elizabeth, 3
Addison, Joseph, 12
Adl, Mohammed el, 61, 66
Aldington, Richard, 86
Allen, Walter, 21
Androgyny, 8, 21, 22
  in Forster, 22, 33–4, 52, 53, 62, 112, 152
  in Lawrence, 111–14, 140
  in Sinclair, 67, 112
  in Woolf, 6–7, 9, 13, 16–17, 23, 67, 112, 140, 147
Armstrong, Nancy, xi
Armstrong, Paul B., 151–2
Audoux, Marguerite, 87
Austen, Jane, 15, 110, 123

Bakshi, Parminder Kaur, 51, 148, 150, 151, 152
Balbert, Peter, 140, 142
Balzac, Honoré de, 109–10
  Eugénie Grandet, 109–10
Barron, Janet, 131
Battersby, Christine, 67, 68
Bayley, John, 141
Bazin, Nancy Topping, 147
Becket, Fiona, 156, 157
Beer, Gillian, 11
Beer, John, 148
Bell, Michael, 140
Bennett, Arnold, 11
  Anna of the Five Towns, 110
Bildungsroman, 5, 6, 42, 55, 88, 94
Bisexuality, 21
  in Lawrence, 112–14, 128, 157
  in Woolf, 8, 16, 23, 112
Black, Michael, 111
Blanchard, Lydia, 125, 158
Bloomsbury Group, 18, 22, 152
Boehm, Beth A., 7
Boll, Theophilus E. M., 71, 72, 77, 79–80, 83, 89, 90, 155, 156
Bowlby, Rachel, 14, 17, 147
Bredbeck, Gregory W., 153
Bristow, Joseph, 36, 60, 149
Brönte, Charlotte, 12, 81
  works of:
    Jane Eyre, 81, 110, 111
    Shirley, 110
Brönte, Emily, 15, 31, 81, 84
    Wuthering Heights, 31, 81, 84–5, 111
Brönte sisters, 76, 80–1, 110, 111
Brown, Gillian, xi
Burack, Charles, 158
Burrows, Louisa, 126
Butler, Judith, xi

Cannan, Mary, 125
Carpenter, Edward, 6, 22, 28, 34, 39, 45, 54, 55, 56, 60, 106, 151, 154
Carswell, Catherine, 123
Cavaliero, Glen, 38, 57, 64, 148, 151
Chambers, Jessie, 126
Chevalley, Abel, 83
Cohn, Dorrit, 71–2, 76, 154
Coleridge, Samuel Taylor, 17
Colmer, John, 25, 29, 36, 39, 151

Constructionism, 3
  In Woolf, xii, 17
Cooper, James Fenimore, 124, 126–7
Corke, Helen, 126
Crews, Frederick, 33, 47, 52, 151
Curr, Matthew, 153

Dahl, Liisa, 147
Daleski, H. M., 143–4
DaSilva, Stephen, 152–3
DeKoven, Marianne, 2, 5
DiBattista, Maria, 13
Dickens, Charles, 10
Dickinson, Goldsworthy Lowes, 54
Doherty, Gerald, 156, 158
Doolittle, Hilda (H. D.), 86
Dostoevsky, Fyodor, 31
  The Brothers Karamazov, 31
Dowling, David, 39, 62
Draper, Ronald, 115, 117
Dryden, John, 12
DuPlessis, Rachel Blau, 2, 7, 147

Edwardian Age, 10, 26–8, 32, 57–8
  fiction of, 25–7, 30, 32, 50, 112
  homosexuality in, 27, 66, 150
  novelists of, 10–11, 110, 157
  realism in, 68
Edwards, Justin D., 156
Eggert, Paul, 156
Eliot, George, 110, 111, 123, 137–8
  works of:
    Adam Bede, 110
    Mill on the Floss, 110, 111
Ellem, Elizabeth Wood, 59, 151
Ellis, David, 148, 158
Ellis, Havelock, 3, 34, 77, 106, 151
Essentialism:
  in Lawrence, 112
  in Sinclair, 68–9, 78–9, 99
  in Woolf, xii, 6, 17

Fantasy, 8, 23, 25–8, 30–5, 38–4
  dividings of personality in, 28, 31, 57, 60
  in Forster, xii, 8, 22, 23, 25–8, 29–35, 38–54, 56–64, 66, 149–50
  gods of, 25, 27, 31–4, 42–3, 51–2, 62–3, 66, 150, 152
    Demeter, 32–33, 41, 43, 44, 51, 62, 150
    Dionysius, 33, 44, 153

Hermes, 32–4, 45, 63
Pan, 25, 31–3, 36, 40, 41, 43, 44, 51, 56, 58, 149, 151, 153
  landscapes of, 25, 27, 35, 38, 39–40, 41, 42, 45–7, 49, 52–3, 57–8, 59, 60, 63, 64, 151, 152, 154
  as submode of romance, 26
  in Woolf, 6, 8
Farwell, Marilyn R., 147
Feminism, xii–xiii, 1–2, 12, 22, 29, 104
  in Forster, 29, 54, 65
  in Lawrence, xiii, 22, 104, 109, 123, 131, 140
  in Sinclair, xiii, 22, 68, 76, 77–9, 82, 83
  in Woolf, xii, 1, 8–9, 17
Fernihough, Anne, 156
Finkelstein, Bonnie Blumenthal, 52, 54–5, 62, 152
Fitzgerald, Penelope, 155
Flaubert, Gustav, 109, 110
Fletcher, John, 34, 55, 57, 60
Flint, F. S., 86
Forster, E. M., xi–xiii, 4, 8, 18–23, 25–65, 112, 120, 145, 148–154, 157
  androgyny in, 22, 33–4, 52, 53, 62, 112, 152
  character triangles in, 27, 31, 34–39, 42, 51, 60, 64, 148–50
  class in, 28, 35, 36–7, 53, 57, 58, 59, 60–1
  comradeship in, 54, 61, 151, 152
  double plot in, 27, 35–9, 42, 55, 61, 62, 148
  effeminacy in, 38, 40, 42, 48, 52, 149
  emasculation in, 152
  fantasy in, xii, 8, 22, 23, 25–8, 29–35, 38–54, 56–64, 66, 149–50
  feminism in, 29, 54, 65
  feminization in, 33
  heterosexuality in, 27, 28, 35–9, 41, 42, 47, 48–50, 51, 54, 55, 56, 58, 64, 66, 148, 150, 151, 153, 154
  homophilia in, 42, 46, 50, 57, 61, 66
  homophobia in, 50
  homosexuality in, 22, 23, 25–8, 30–48, 50–51, 54–62, 64–66, 148–54
  misogyny in, 27, 38, 40, 50, 64, 65
  modernism in, 27, 149

Index

mythology in, 31–2, 50
prophecy in, 20, 30–2, 51, 149, 154
queerness in, 25–7, 30–1, 33–5, 38, 41–3, 45–50, 54, 61, 66, 148–9, 151–4
race in, 28, 61–5
realism in, 25, 27, 28, 30, 35, 48, 49, 51, 55–6, 59, 66, 149
romance in, 26–7, 41, 42, 149
sadomasochism in, 36–7, 43, 57, 65, 150
socialism in, 35, 38
theory of the novel in, 29–32
works of:
  "Anonymity: An Inquiry," 34
  Arctic Summer, 55
  "Aspect of a Novel," 41, 151
  Aspects of the Novel, xi, 18, 20, 25, 26, 29–32, 50, 66, 149
  "The Celestial Omnibus," 35
  The Celestial Omnibus and Other Stories, 19–20, 25, 33, 34, 48, 49
  "Cnidus," 43
  "The Curate's Friend," 35
  "The Early Novels of Virginia Woolf," 18
  "The Feminine Note in Literature," 18
  Howards End, 19, 28, 50–5, 62, 151–2, 154
  The Longest Journey, 28, 35, 41–50, 51, 52, 53, 54, 55, 56, 57, 63, 65, 150–1, 152
  The Lucy Novels, 150
  Maurice, 28, 34, 35, 39, 41, 50, 54, 55–61, 66, 151, 152–3, 154
  "Other Kingdom," 48
  A Passage to India, 19, 25, 28, 35, 50, 51, 61–6, 148, 149, 153–4
  A Room with a View, 18, 28, 35, 38–41, 50, 58, 150, 151
  Selected Letters, 18, 19, 37, 59, 66
  "The Story of a Panic," 25, 48
  Where Angels Fear to Tread, 28, 35–8, 39, 41, 43, 53, 150
Foucault, Michel, 4
Freedgood, Elaine, 64–5, 154
Freud, Sigmund, 3, 77, 128, 158
Friedman, Ellen G. and Miriam Fuchs, 2
Frye, Northrop, 26–7
Furbank, P. N., 18, 19, 33, 55, 61, 66, 149, 151, 152

Galsworthy, John, 11
Garnett, David, 120, 149
Garnett, Edward, 32, 149
Gaskell, Elizabeth, 137–8
Gender:
  "crisis," xii–xiii, 3–4, 18, 21, 22, 69
  and genre, xi–xiii, 1–4, 5–6, 9, 18, 21–3, 27, 66, 68–9, 84, 101, 105, 145
  and literary criticism, xii, 1–2, 4, 5, 8, 10–12, 14–15, 109, 119, 123, 157
  and literary history, 8, 21, 104, 143, 157
  roles, xii, 13, 22, 23, 73, 79, 91, 98–9, 104, 105, 129–30, 145
  and sexuality, xii, 2, 3–4, 8, 18, 21, 23, 26, 28, 37, 45, 104, 105, 129–30, 145
Gilbert, Sandra M. and Susan Gubar, 2, 6, 126
Gillespie, Diane F., 5, 68, 155
Goncourt, Edmond and Jules de, 87
Goscilo, Margaret, 35, 37, 38, 39, 150
Grant, Kathleen, 57, 60
Gray, Cecil, 157
Green, T. H., 70, 154
Grey, Zane, 129

Hardy, John Edward, 152
Hardy, Thomas, 80, 111, 113–15
  works of:
    Jude the Obscure, 114
    Tess of the d'Urbervilles, 114
Harned, Jon, 153
Harris, Janice H., 73, 155
Hawthorne, Nathaniel, 124, 126
  The Scarlet Letter, 125
Heine, Elizabeth, 149, 150, 151
Henley, Ann, 19
Herbert, Michael, 119
Herz, Judith, 27, 32, 33–4, 35, 39, 40, 152, 153
Hocking, William Henry, 120, 121
Holbrook, David, 158
Homosexuality, xii, 2, 3–4, 6, 7, 22
  as comradeship, 38, 54, 61

in Forster, 22, 23, 25–8, 30–48, 50–1, 54–62, 64–66, 148–54
in Lawrence, 103–8, 111, 112, 115, 119–23, 126–28, 130, 157, 158
theory of, 34
in Woolf, 6
Houseman, A. E.:
A Shropshire Lad, 152
Hull, E. M.:
The Sheik, 129, 158
Hynes, Samuel, 32, 39

Imagism, 68, 86–7
Ingersoll, Earl, 20

Jackson, Rosemary, 7
Jagose, Annamarie, 26
Jakobson, Roman, 156
James, Henry, 149
James, William, 87
Jeffers, Thomas L., 148
Jewinski, Ed, 144
Jones, Ernest, 3
Joyce, James, 1, 17, 27, 89–90, 129
works of:
A Portrait of the Artist as a Young Man, 87, 89, 155
Ulysses, 31
Jung, Carl, 77
Psychology of the Unconscious, 77

Kaplan, Carola, 150
Kaplan, Sydney Janet, 69, 89, 90, 94, 147
Keats, John, 17
Kerenyi, Karl, 34
Kermode, Frank, 111
Keynes, J. M., 120
Kinkead-Weekes, Mark, 108, 115, 120, 121, 157
Kipling, Rudyard, 11
Klein, Melanie, 3
Krutch, J. W., 100

Lacan, Jacques, 144
Lawrence, D. H., xi–xiii, 4, 10, 12, 18–23, 28, 31, 32, 33, 78, 101, 102, 103–145, 148, 154, 156–8
androgyny in, 111–14, 140

anti-feminism in, xiii, 116–17, 125, 130
bisexuality in, 112–14, 128, 157
"blood-consciousness" in, 124, 143–4
"Book of Life" or "Truth" in, 23, 104, 105, 106, 113, 145
Christian theology in, 108, 111–112, 115–16, 132, 144
comradeship in, 126–8
effeminacy in, 104, 107, 134, 136
emasculation in, 22, 104, 118, 124, 129, 133, 136–7, 139, 143, 155, 157
essentialism in, 112
feminism in, xiii, 22, 104, 109, 123, 131, 140
feminization in, 104, 109, 112, 118, 129–30, 133–4, 136–8, 139, 143, 157
gendering of literary history in, 104, 143, 157
heterosexual union in, 19, 22, 23, 104, 105, 106, 107–9, 111–17, 118–19, 121–3, 127, 130–3, 139–45, 156–8
homophobia in, 23, 119, 125, 128, 157
homosexuality in, 103, 104, 105, 106, 107–8, 111, 112, 115, 119–23, 126–8, 130, 157, 158
lesbianism in, 116–17, 125, 142, 156
literary criticism by, 109, 119, 123
"Magna Mater" in, 108, 115, 122, 125
"mind-consciousness" in, 124, 125
misogyny in, 23, 103, 105, 106, 108, 111, 116, 122, 124–5, 127, 131, 140, 142, 157
modernism in, 126, 157
"phallic consciousness" in, xiii, 22, 103, 104, 106, 126, 129, 130–2, 134–6, 141–2, 143–5
"phallic" novel in, 22, 23, 109, 110, 134–6
realism in, xiii, 21, 109, 123, 136, 138, 143, 155, 157
romance in, 125, 127
stream of consciousness in, 137
works of:
"A Propos of *Lady Chatterley*," 104, 143–4, 157
Aaron's Rod, 127–8

Index

"Art and the Individual," 107
"Art and Morality," 134
The Boy in the Bush, 126
"The Crown," 108, 117–19, 121
"Daughters of the Vicar," 21
David, 138–9
"Do Women Change?," 142
"Education of the People," 127
Fantasia of the Unconscious, 105–6, 128–9, 157
The First Lady Chatterley, 138–9
"Foreword to *Sons and Lovers*," 108–9
"German Books: Thomas Mann," 109
"Give Her a Pattern," 143
"Is England Still a Man's Country?," 142
John Thomas and Lady Jane, 138
Kangaroo, 106, 128
Lady Chatterley's Lover, 10, 12, 104, 106, 111, 131, 136–44, 157–8
Letters, 19, 20, 110, 111, 115, 120, 123, 125, 133, 139, 144, 157
The Man Who Died, 144
"Matriarchy," 142–3
"Morality and the Novel," xi, 23, 104–5, 133
"The Novel," 104, 133, 135–6
"The Novel and the Feelings," 134
"On Being a Man," 132
"On Human Destiny," 132
The Plumed Serpent, 106, 130–2, 133, 142
"Pornography and Obscenity," 143
"Prologue to *Women in Love*," 121, 122
"The Proper Study," 132
"Psychoanalysis and the Unconscious," 128
The Rainbow, 21, 106, 107, 111, 115–17, 124, 126, 128, 144
Reflections on the Death of a Porcupine, 117, 119
Sons and Lovers, 107–8, 111, 126
Studies in Classic American Literature, 123–7
Study of Thomas Hardy, 78, 103, 104, 108, 111–15, 118, 128
"Surgery for the Novel – or a Bomb," 129–30, 134
The Symbolic Meaning, 124
The White Peacock, 111
"Why the Novel Matters," 104, 135
"Women Are So Cocksure," 142
Women in Love, 20, 21, 31, 103, 106, 108, 115, 117, 120–3, 124, 125, 126, 128, 142, 158
Lawrence, Frieda, 120–1, 126, 157
Lawrence, Lydia, 126
Leavis, F. R., 110–11
Lesbianism:
  in Lawrence, 116–17, 125, 142, 156
  in Sinclair, 75, 155
  in Woolf, 7, 8, 22
Levine, George, xii, 136–7, 157
Lewis, Sinclair:
  Babbitt, 129
Lewis, Wyndham, 124
Literary History, 5, 9, 12, 21, 23, 29
  gendering of, 8, 21, 104, 143, 157
Luhan, Mabel, 126
Lukács, Georg, xi

Malik, Charu, 54, 61, 153
Mann, Thomas, 109
Mansfield, Katherine, 123
Martin, Robert, 33, 44, 45, 54, 60, 148
  and Piggford, George, xiii, 148
Marx, John, 154
Masood, Syed Ross, 48, 150, 152
McConkey, James, 30–2, 50–1, 52, 54
McDowell, Frederick P. W., 46, 53, 65, 152
McKeon, Michael, xi
Melville, Herman, 31, 124
  Moby Dick, 30, 31, 124
Meredith, George, 80, 81
Meredith, Hugh, 42, 149–50, 152

Merivale, Patricia, 32
Merrill, George, 34, 60
Mew, Charlotte, 155
Meyers, Jeffrey, 39–40, 120, 123, 148, 151, 152, 157
Michelangelo, 112
Miller, Janet Eldridge, 68, 69, 74, 82, 154, 155
Millett, Kate, 131–2
Milne, Drew, 156
Minow–Pinkney, Makiko, 8, 11, 147
Mitford, Mary Russell, 137–8
Modernism, 1–3, 21, 23, 26, 77, 126
  in Forster, 27, 149
  in Lawrence, 126, 157
  and the novel, xii, 4, 18, 22, 68
  in Sinclair, 22, 68, 77, 84
  in Woolf, 17, 26
Moore, Madeline, 7, 14
Morrell, Lady Ottoline, 120
Murry, Kathleen, 120
Murry, Middleton, 120, 121, 157

Nadel, Ira Bruce, 55
Nehls, Edward, 20
Nelson, Scott R., 27, 47
New Woman, 3–4
  movement, 2, 117
  novel, 82, 115, 117
  writers, 33, 154
Nin, Anaïs, 140
Nixon, Cornelia, 106, 120, 127, 141, 156, 157, 158
Nordau, Max, 104

Pater, Walter, 33, 45
Peters, Joan D., 158
Philipson, Morris, 147
Phillips, Terry, 155–6
Pinkney, Tony, 157
Pope, Alexander, 12
Poresky, Louise, 147
Pound, Ezra, 86
Proust, Marcel, 1, 17, 27
Psychoanalysis, 3
Pykett, Lyn, 3, 4, 6, 29, 33, 51, 52, 76, 79, 82, 104, 112, 115, 117, 118, 121, 124, 127, 128, 137, 154, 155

Queer Theory, xiii, 25–26,
Queerness:

  in Forster, 25–7, 30–1, 33–5, 38, 41–3, 45–50, 54, 61, 66, 148–9, 151–4

Rahman, Tariq, 45
Realism, xii, 5, 8, 10, 21, 26, 28, 68, 86, 138
  in Forster, 25, 27, 28, 30, 35, 48, 49, 51, 55–6, 59, 66, 149
  in Lawrence, xiii, 21, 109, 123, 136, 138, 143, 155, 157
  in the novel, xiii, 22, 25–7, 30, 109, 143
  in Sinclair, 22, 68, 69, 72–6, 80, 81, 86, 87, 90, 100, 101, 154, 155
  in Woolf, 5–6, 10–11
Richardson, Dorothy, 21, 22, 68, 87–8, 89, 90, 129
Pilgrimage, 87
Roe, Sue, 7
Romance, xi, 26–7
  in Forster, 26–7, 41, 42, 149
  in Lawrence, 125, 127
  in Sinclair, 22, 72, 81, 96, 99
Rosecrance, Barbara, 54
Russell, Bertrand, 120, 148

Sackville–West, Vita, 7
Sanders, Scott, 139
Schwarz, Daniel, 149, 153
Scott, Bonnie Kime, 1–2, 147
Sedgwick, Eve Kosovsky, 37, 51, 121, 150
Selig, Robert K., 64
Sentimentalism, 80, 81, 109, 119, 124, 134, 138, 143, 155
Shakespeare, William, 17
Shaw, Marion, 144
Shelley, Percy Bysshe, 47
Showalter, Elaine, 2, 147
Siegel, Carol, 10, 12, 111, 126
Simpson, Hilary, 141, 158
Sinclair, May, xii–xiii, 4, 18, 20–23, 66, 67–101, 112, 115, 145, 154–6
  androgyny in, 67, 112
  essentialism in, 68–9, 78–9, 99
  feminine consciousness in, 69
  feminism in, xiii, 22, 68, 76, 77–9, 82, 83
  genius in, xiii, 22, 67–9, 73–6, 78, 92, 154–5
  heredity in, 69, 71, 77, 95

and imagism, 68, 86–7
lesbianism in, 75, 155
"Life–Force" in, 69, 77–9, 85, 92–3, 99
literary criticism by, 79, 86–8
modernism in, 22, 68, 77, 84
mysticism in, 81, 85, 87, 88, 92–4, 95–6, 97, 98
philosophical idealism in, 68, 69, 70–3, 77, 78, 81, 83, 86, 87, 88, 93, 100, 154, 155
pointillism in, 82–4, 88
psychological novels of, 68, 69–70, 86, 155
psychology and, 68, 76–7, 79, 82–3, 155
psycho–narration in, 71–2, 73, 83–4, 89–90, 94–6
realism in, 22, 68, 69, 72–6, 80, 81, 86, 87, 90, 100, 101, 154, 155
repression in, 70, 78, 81, 82–3, 89, 94–6, 98, 156
romance in, 22, 72, 81, 96, 99
stream of consciousness in, xiii, 22, 23, 69, 70, 84–5, 86–7, 88–101, 154, 155
sublimation in, 69, 77, 78, 93, 94–6, 98, 101
works of:
　Arnold Waterlow: A Life, 70, 96–9, 101, 156
　Audrey Craven, 67, 71
　The Creators: A Comedy, 67, 73–6, 81, 123, 155
　A Defence of Idealism, 77, 86–7
　"A Defence of Men," 79, 99
　The Divine Fire, 71–3, 75
　Far End, 100–1, 155
　Feminism, 78, 85
　"The Future of the Novel: An Interview," 155
　The Helpmate, 73
　The History of Anthony Waring, 70, 99–100
　"Introduction" to Mrs. Gaskell's Life of Charlotte Brönte, 80–1
　A Journal of Impressions in Belgium, 86
　The Judgement of Eve and Other Stories, 73, 155
　"Letter," 77–8
　The Life and Death of Harriet Frean, 70, 94–6, 99, 155–6
　Mary Olivier: A Life, 20, 70, 77, 88–94, 95, 96, 97, 101, 155–6
　"The Mormon Prophet," 80
　"The Novels of Dorothy Richardson," 87, 100
　"No. 5 John Street," 80
　"On Imagism," 86, 100
　"The Poems of F. S. Flint," 86
　The Romantic, 86
　"Symbolism and Sublimation II," 77
　The Three Bröntes, 80–1, 98
　The Three Sisters, 21, 69, 76–7, 81–5, 86, 92, 101
　"Two Notes," 86
Skinner, Mollie, 126
Socialism, 2–3
　in Forster, 35, 38
Spilka, Mark, 141, 142, 158
Stallybrass, Oliver, 150
Stark, Suzanne, 71
Steell, Willis, 73, 94, 96
Steiner, George, 61
Sterne, Laurence, 17
　Tristram Shandy, 30–1
Stevens, Hugh, 157
Stimpson, Catharine, 7
Stone, Wilfred, 53–4, 61, 66, 150
Stream of Consciousness:
　in Lawrence, 137
　in Sinclair, xiii, 22, 23, 69, 70, 84–5, 86–7, 88–101, 154, 155
　in Woolf, 16
Summers, Claude J., 53, 54, 62
Symonds, John Aldington, 34, 60

Tanner, Tony, xi
Taylor, Corinne Yvonne, 98
Thackeray, William Makepeace, 10
Thomson, George H., 44, 52
Thornton, Marianne, 33
Tolstoy, Leo, 135
Touval, Yonatan, 153
Transue, Pamela J., 17
Trilling, Lionel, 152
Turgenev, Ivan, 123

Victorian Age, 5, 9–10, 13, 77, 81–2, 88, 94, 97, 109, 110
  and femininity, 2, 82, 96, 112
  novelists of, 70, 80, 136–8, 157
  realism in, 9–10, 68

Warner, Michael, 26
Watt, Ian, xi
Weeks, Jeffrey, 2–3
Wells, H. G., 11, 68, 73, 110
Wexler, Joyce, 131, 157
Whitman, Walt, 39, 60, 126
Widmer, Kingsley, 157, 158
Wilde, Alan, 38, 59, 149
Wilde, Oscar, 26–7
Williams, Linda Ruth, 139, 141, 142
Woolf, Leonard, 18
Woolf, Virginia, xii, 1–23, 27, 28, 34, 68, 87, 104, 112, 140, 143, 145, 147, 153, 157
  androgyny in, 6–7, 9, 13, 16–17, 23, 67, 112, 140, 147
  "Angel in the House" in, 15, 17
  bisexuality in, 8, 16, 23, 112
  constructionism in, xii, 17
  essentialism in, xii, 6, 17
  fantasy in, 6, 8
  feminine consciousness in, 6, 147
  feminism in, xii, 1, 8–9, 17
  gendering of literary history in, 8, 104, 143
  homosexuality in, 6
  lesbianism in, 7, 8, 22
  literary criticism by, 4, 5, 8, 10–12, 14–15
  modernism in, 17, 26
  poetry in, 5, 6, 14, 155
  realism in, 5–6, 10–11
  "woman's sentence" in, 1, 6, 16–17, 147
  works of:
    "The Art of Fiction," 19
    Between the Acts, 5
    "The Leaning Tower," 10–11, 12, 147
    Letters, 12, 18, 20
    Mrs. Dalloway, 6
    "Mr. Bennett and Mrs. Brown," 11
    "Modern Fiction," 3, 11, 14–15, 21, 87
    "The Narrow Bridge of Art," 147
    Night and Day, 6
    Orlando, 4, 5, 6–10, 11, 12–14, 15–17, 26, 93, 147, 156
    "Professions for Women," 15, 17
    A Room of One's Own, 4, 5, 6–9, 11, 14–15, 16, 17, 28, 78
    To the Lighthouse, 6
    The Voyage Out, 5, 6, 18
    "Women and Fiction," 1, 11, 15, 17
Wright, Sir Almroth, 78

Zegger, Hrisey S., 21, 68, 70, 71, 73, 75, 77, 82, 88, 94, 154